Handful
of Rogues

Handful
of Rogues

Thomas Muir's Enemies of the People

Hector MacMillan

ARGYLL ✠ PUBLISHING

First published by
Argyll Publishing
Glendaruel
Argyll PA22 3AE
Scotland
www.argyllpublishing.com

The author has asserted his moral rights.

British Library Cataloguing-in-Publication Data.
A catalogue record for this book in available from the British Library.

ISBN 1902831896

Origination: Cordfall Ltd, Glasgow

Printing: St Edmundsbury Press

To the memory of my parents

Christina Paterson MacNeill
Robert Galbraith MacMillan

Who knew the importance of the history
they and their kind had lived
and who valued the songs.

JOHN KAY

A self portrait of the caricaturist John Kay whose etchings of many of the leading characters in the trial of Thomas Muir lend a satirical eye to events that had serious political and historical significance. In the company of his cat he contemplates a bust of Homer.

Contents

Thomas Muir of Huntershill as depicted at the time of his trial in 1793

CAVEAT

Thomas Muir, younger, of Huntershill

Throughout the two hundred years since his death Thomas Muir's patronymic has remained, for some, a talismanic political mantra. Others, judging the man victim to his own personal failings, have subscribed to the equally longstanding 'diseased in body and mind' dismissals. So much unweighed baggage heaped on the head of one individual serves only to delay understanding of a vital period in Scottish history.

The last decade of the eighteenth century witnessed the unprecedented growth of a movement aimed at the social, political and cultural regeneration of Scotland. It was a vigorous movement, rooted in democratic principle, greatly influenced by the recent revolution in France and driven on by many of the best minds of the day. This development was opposed by a powerful minority in the country who, enjoying virtual *carte blanche* from Westminster, were prepared to use any and all means to resist a threat to their privilege. Recognising the danger of the situation developing into something like civil war, the radical leaders put their trust in a rapid political education and organisation of the people, not least among the ranks of the already quite disaffected armed forces.

Muir's contribution to all this can not be assessed in isolation from that of his many associates, nor can it be understood divorced from a background of popular demand, both nationally and internationally, for a radical renegotiation of the contract between Governors and Governed.

Liberté! Égalité! Fraternité!

The roots of the democratic spirit in Scotland that responded so enthusiastically to those early aims of the French Revolution are varied and complex. The combined opus of the nation's previous generation of philosophers, now becoming as influential at home as it had long been in France, is the most immediate and obvious factor but there were more ancient traditions at work. In the Lowlands, the movement was informed by the popular government basis of Presbyterianism and in the Highlands by the notion exemplified in the centuries-old MacGriogair slogan – *s'rioghal mo dhream!* – when all blood is considered royal, no single mortal need consider himself divine.

Despite the oft-repeated insistence that eighteenth century protest in Scotland pre-dates concepts of nationalism, there was, after three generations since the Union without a national Parliament in Edinburgh, growing awareness that an ancient culture was coming under potentially terminal threat. In any case, if the evidence of Scotland's oldest known epic poem can be relied upon, some embryonic sense of unifying purpose existed among the Celtic tribes more than 700 years before even Wallace's *War of Independence*. Research into that poem, *The Gododdin*, has suggested that a warrior aristocracy, drawn from southwest Ayrshire across to the East Neuk of Fife, gathered in alliance at Dun Eideann [Edinburgh] prior to moving south to confront a massive Anglo-Saxon invasion force then heading north intent on conquest and the imposition of an alien culture.

In Muir's time, communities bordering a line linking Drymen, Doune, Crieff and Dunkeld continued in daily contact with the western *Gaidhealtachd* and *mì-rùn mór na Gall* [the great ill-will of the lowlander] was still understood as far south as Galloway. To some extent, then, rooted in renewal as well as innovation, that eighteenth century sense of democratic nationhood in Scotland grew in opposition to a concept of power increasingly imposed on it by fellow Scots intent on serving Hanoverian notions of rule.

Under what even apologists describe as a Dundas Despotism, Scotland was subject to a forerunner of twentieth century McCarthyism and faced with 'a written test of political orthodoxy' many of the country's finest talents had no option but to emigrate. In his wide-ranging *The Age of Revolution* E.J. Hobsbawm refers to the stream of 'brilliant, hard-working, career-seeking, and rationalist' young Scots who then settled in England, naming James Watt, Thomas Telford, Loudon McAdam and James Mill as examples. Most if not all of those named were supporters of reform, at least, and many more radical talents were forced to find refuge further afield. Allied with the Ulster-Scots of similar temperament and education, their combined potential to effect historical change in these islands – and therefore in Europe – seems indisputable. Far from being the panic over-reaction usually presented, the behaviour of government at that time stemmed from an alarmed awareness of a very real threat to its continued existence.

The recent renewal of serious research into Scotland's connection with this pivotal period in European history has been explained as due to changes in 'institutional historical orthodoxy', perhaps a necessary polite nod towards release from past political pressures, but it appears there is still no final release from a concept referred to as 'historical objectivity'. This is the more surprising since, in the discipline commonly supposed to set standards for all others – science – it has long been recognised that any assumptions of objectivity are at best extremely doubtful.

In any case, though not all history is recorded by the victor, not all history is recorded. The officially-sanctioned record of public events in Muir's time were very heavily censored and even privately published versions acknowledged the need for ommissions if prosecution and imprisonment was to be avoided. In these circumstances, reliance on such evidence alone can produce no rounded account.

> Strange whim of the people! They demand their history from
> the hand of the poet and not from the hand of the historian.
> They demand not a faithful report of bare facts, but those facts
> dissolved back into the original poetry whence they came.
> *Heinrich Heine*

Any attempt at an accurate estimate of the general mood in Scotland at that time necessitates a lengthy search through a great variety of sources. Much can be gleaned from popular poetry and song of the time, from local traditions, even from fiction, and if the information drawn from such is honestly tested alongside what is known about the basic character of the people – not I think greatly changed over the intervening couple of centuries – then the resulting conclusions have the potential to be as valid as any singularly official version of events. Any who doubt this might consider how true a guide to recent Chilean history would be General Pinochet's public pronouncements were they not tested alongside the songs that led to the murder of Victor Jara and many others in that Santiago football stadium.

Though some element of dramatic if not poetic licence has thus been necessary in this work, in these excursions a consensus from the various records has been supplemented and informed by additional material that could only be safely recorded more than a generation later. Otherwise, quotations are taken *verbatim* from the official correspondence of the time and from the writings and memoirs of some of the principal characters involved. Where there has been no previous publication, or only an inaccurate or misleadingly out-of-context selection available, these quotations are given in some detail.

Scotland's radical voice, across the gap of two centuries, still has a startlingly modern sound to it and it is a voice that should have been heard more clearly and in much greater detail long ere this.

Hector MacMillan
Auchterarder
20th July, 2005

CHAPTER 1
Revolutionary Ideas

Tom Muir began his university education at 12 years of age, not exceptionally young for the times, when he enrolled as a student in the Humanity class of Glasgow College, then situated in the High Street just up from his father's shop. Though the family business was successful, his father acquiring some property in other parts of the town and eventually the small mansion and forty-acre estate of Huntershill, on the rising ground to the north of the city, the Muirs' status as general grocers placed them well down-scale from the opulent Tobacco Merchants they served.

> JAMES MUIR – Has brought from Kent, a large parcel of Kentish Hops, which he sells as low as any merchant in London.
> Also – Kentish apples – Golden pippens, Nonpareils, Golden Remets, Lemon pippens, Long Lasters, Grey Rustins, Polonia Peermains & etc.
> Also – Sun-raisins, currants, Jordan & Valencia Almonds, Carvey-seed, Orange Peel, Poland starch. (4th door above the Cross-well)
> ADVERT *Glasgow Mercury*, 18th October, 1781

There seems an air of douce but hard-working respectability about Muir's parents, religiously-inclined folk of old Presbyterian stock, and they must have been well-pleased with the prospect of their only son graduating from College with a degree in divinity, eventually to answer the call from some bien Scots kirk of their own faith.

There was a similar orderly aspect to Muir's birthplace, 'one of the cleanliest, most beautiful, and best built cities in Great Britain' according to Daniel Defoe, and in other visitors' praises the fine expanse of the communally-owned Green is usually prominent. Here, families like the Muirs would take their Sabbath promenades by the banks of the Clyde and here, in high-summer, lovers would row up-stream into the country early in the day prior to drifting romantically back to town on the clear, wide and slow-moving waters at sunset.

But the adult is moulded by all aspects of childhood and even in pre-College days Muir would have been made graphically aware of another very different aspect to his birthplace, the one affected by political upheavals. Though the final Jacobite rebellion had been crushed nineteen years before he was born, there was still a vivid local memory of how the Young Pretender, at the head of the small army that had been with him all the way to Derby and back, had marched into Glasgow to establish a Christmas and New Year court at Shawfield House in the Trongate. To the dismay of the Merchant-Magistrates, the city was forced to supply 6000 of everything required by the rebel army which then, to the delight of others, went on to parade their new finery on that same Glasgow Green – flags flying and pipers playing – before leaving to rout the forces of King George II at the Battle of Falkirk.

ADVERT *Glasgow Courant*, 29th September, 1746

That there is to be sold by James Duncan, printer in Glasgow, in the Salt-Mercat, the second shop below Gibson's Wynd, a book entitled A FULL, PARTICULAR, AND TRUE ACCOUNT OF THE LATE REBELLION IN THE YEARS 1745 AND 1746.

Beginning with the Pretender's embarking for Scotland, and then an account of every battle, siege, and skirmish that has happened in either Scotland or England: to which is added, several addresses and epistles to the pope, pagans, poets and Pretender, all in metre, price fourpence.

The like has not been done in Scotland since the days of Sir David Lindsay!

The author, Dougal Graham, had been eye-witness to most of the movements of the armies, from the rebels first crossing the ford of Frew to their final defeat at Culloden and his account in rustic rhyme proved a multi-editioned bestseller. During Muir's childhood, Graham was officially appointed Glasgow's Bellman and as a humorous and charismatic figure crying out the day's news on the streets it would be surprising if his personal reminiscence did not attract a trail of fascinated youngsters. A little later, just about the time he was settling to his studies at the College, Muir had opportunity to witness for himself some manifestations of a new rebellion.

Glasgow Mercury, 17th January, 1778
Reported from *London Gazette*
Most Gracious Sovereign,
As your ancient City of Glasgow has in all ages been distinguished for an attachment to constitutional liberty and the rights of mankind; and as these are still trampled upon by your rebellious subjects in America, we beg leave in the most humble manner to represent to your Majesty that we think vigorous and speedy efforts ought to be made in order to restore the peace to your American colonies; and that for this end we are ready to raise a regiment of men to be employed in

such manner as your Majesty shall be pleased to direct. This offer we make as a small proof of our loyalty and attachment to your Majesty's government, which has been distinguished by excellent laws and by the support of your glorious constitution.

We pray God, that he will be pleased to put a speedy end to the delusion of the rebels who, under the sacred name of Liberty, are exercising every act of tyranny; and we are confident that your Majesty will extend your known and declared clemency towards them as soon as they shall return to a proper sense of their duty. We pray for the best blessings on your Majesty's family; and that the King of Kings will be pleased to make your Majesty's reign long and prosperous over a happy empire.

Signed in presence and by appointment of the Council of Glasgow, the ninth day of January, one thousand seven hundred and seventy-eight.

Robert Donald, Provost.

So important a document had to be delivered personally, and after being ushered to the royal presence by the Lord of his Majesty's bed-chamber-in-waiting, Provost Donald was permitted to kiss the King's hand. There were, of course, other prominent Glaswegians who took a quite contrary view to that of the Lord Provost. John Glassford, now owner of the fine Trongate mansion in which Prince Charlie had held court and acknowledged to be the city's 'most extensive foreign merchant' ordered most of his fleet of 25 ships to be laid up in Port Glasgow rather than see them used against the American rebels. However, for the Lord Provost's now regally-sanctioned recruiting drives, the other Magistrates and Merchants dusted off bagpipes, fifes and drums to form makeshift bands and lead parades from Bell o' the Brae to Saltmarket, Gallowgate to Trongate, in quest of men who might fight to save their commerce across the Atlantic. Grand musket volleys marked the completion of these processions, after which free beer was freely available and good gold guineas were pressed into eager and needy palms. As always, though, *all that glisters . . .* and . . . *it's an ill wind*, remained true. Shortly after these patriotic exhibitions further notices began to appear in the *Glasgow Mercury*.

DESERTED. From a party of recruits, enlisted 15th January. WILLIAM BROWN, 20, 5'6", grey eyes, brown tied hair. Black coat, black silk breeches, cocked hat.
ROBERT STEWART. 5'8", marked with smallpox, brown tied hair, grey eyes. Grey great coat, with red collar, slouched hat. Whoever gives information will be genteely rewarded.

DESERTED. From a Recruiting party of the Duke of Hamilton's Regt lying at Ruglen,
JOHN ROSS, by trade a shoemaker, aged about 20 years, 5'8" high, of a fair complexion, fair hair, light blue eyes, pock-pitted; he had on, when he left Ruglen, a brown great coat, black coat, a striped red-and-white silk vest, black breeches and white thread-ribbed stockings. He says he was born in the parish of Logie, and County of Clackmannanshire. Whoever will take him up, and give information so as to get him confined, that he may be returned to the party will receive ONE GUINEA of reward over and above what is allowed by His Majesty.

Editors were also forced to acknowledge that these detailed descriptions might prove of little value as, immediately after the recruiting drives ended, local entrepreneurs were doing brisk business in their clothing-exchange boutiques.

A third and often neglected aspect of Glasgow at the time is that, post-Culloden, one of the last communities to uphold the old Celtic traditions survived only thirty miles from the city boundary. Up to the time of the 1745 Rebellion, Tom Muir's grandfather, like all other farmers in Campsie Parish, would have had to pay the MacGriogair blackmail for cattle protection, and though the MacGriogair name was to remain proscribed for nearly another forty years, Rob Roy's widow is said to have continued to receive the traditional clan tribute of *càin* despite the fact rents had now also to be paid to the feudal landlord.

Professor Richardson, tutor in Latin classics at the College, no doubt regaled his young charges with tales of his own upbringing in the Aberfoyle area; this one-time diplomat-attendant at the Russian Court of Empress Catherine had, as a child, been present in the house when Rob Roy's son, Robin Og, committed the offence for which he was later hanged. These factors, plus contact with the smugglers of illicit whisky who continued to stream over the Campsie Hills and down the *Rathad Crodh* past his kinfolk's farms would have left young Muir with an awareness of the Gaeltachd that was later to prove of importance.

Such were some of the influences on Muir's early development and by the time he graduated MA, at the age of 17, he had responded enthusiastically to the most significant of all, those of John *Cockie* Millar and John *Jolly Jack Phosphorous* Anderson, two of the most advanced educationalists of the era. In addition to being of high academic ability both professors, much in tune with the *zeitgeist*, had set out to revolutionise education itself and in so doing had lasting influence on many students who went on to take leading roles throughout Great Britain and its Empire abroad.

Millar, a student of Adam Smith and David Hume, was for financial reasons forced in 1761 to accept the 'obscure post' of Civil Law at Glasgow University but quickly went on to make it the best of its kind in Britain. He replaced the traditional prepared Latin lectures with *extempore*, free-ranging and unrestricted discourse and discussion in Scots and English, discussions which frequently continued into the evening at his home. On such occasions he would also oblige any student who fancied his chances over a round or two of boxing, wrestling or fencing, in which popular university sports he is said to have been more than competent. Professor Anderson, who occupied the chair of Oriental Languages before moving four years later to head the Department of Natural Philosophy, was a great enthusiast for *applied* science, and liaison with local manufactories led to the subsequent institution of what he called his *anti-toga* classes, free lessons for artisans at times to suit their needs, with much use of models and demonstrations to aid their understanding of scientific principles.

Muir's career after graduating MA in 1782 is also connected to other important events in Glasgow College at that time. The Rector from 1781 to 1783 was Henry Dundas, later Home Secretary. For more than a decade Professor Anderson had alleged serious mismanagement of the College funds and affairs, but the forces of reaction, under Principal Leechman, finally got Rector Dundas's ruling that they did not have to minute anything 'indecent or extraneous' and Professor Anderson's no doubt passionate protests were thereafter censored. Not long afterwards, when he was suspended from the *Juris-dictio Ordinaria*, most of the students – Muir prominent among them – organised protests against this action, demanding investigation and reform of College practices. Anderson drew up a petition in 1784 for a Royal Visitation to investigate his complaints, but though a majority of students and a great many townspeople signed in support, when sent to King George III the petition found its way down to an appropriate level for the reply that His Majesty remained well pleased with Principal Leechman.

By another strange coincidence, one of the team of two who formulated this rejection of the demand for increased openness and democracy in College affairs was the new Rector, Edmund Burke. According to MacKenzie's *Old Reminiscences of Glasgow*, Muir was one of the leaders of the subsequent student protests directed at Burke, and when a pamphlet ridiculing Principal Leechman's behaviour was published he was one of a number of students instructed to apologise to the Faculty or be expelled. Some apologised, one had his MA degree withdrawn and some were expelled. Muir, refusing to apologise or be expelled, chose to walk away.

That same year, 1785, Principal Leechman died and Factor Morthland resigned, receiving a pension and presentation of valuable silver plate for his sterling services. It was discovered too late that Leechman had been covering for the fact that Morthland, who died bankrupt, owed the College thousands of pounds.[1] This minor local swindle is typical of nationwide corrupt practices, the financial scale of which seemed to increase exponentially the higher up the chain of government they operated.

Professor Millar, a son of the manse, had initially studied for the ministry before deciding to switch to Law and there is little doubt he influenced Muir's similar decision. After the Leechman affair, Muir continued his studies of Law in Edinburgh and was admitted to the capital's Faculty of Advocates in 1787. Thereafter he gained experience in his profession by defending the penniless – a common practice for any young lawyer not enjoying the patronage and privilege of the ruling families – and as an elder of the kirk he had opportunity to hone his debating skills in Edinburgh's St Giles during the General Assembly of the Church of Scotland. He was soon involved with the losing side of the *McGill Controversy*, a prolonged locking of theological horns between progressives in the kirk and four *Auld Licht* conservatives for whom he acted as counsel. It may be that the progressive young man in politics was reactionary in his faith, but in the time-honoured manner of his profession he may simply have accepted the brief with a view to his own personal advancement. If so, it was a bad career move; after two years of grim wrangling, the 1791 General Assembly finally rejected the plea his clients should be heard by a vote of 93 to 7.

Muir's increasing interest in politics about this time is typical of many who had enjoyed a similar education, one which made them aware that, both at home and abroad, the divide between the labouring masses and an increasingly insolent and insensitive minority of the priveleged was rapidly deepening. That Adam Smith, now a close friend of Professor Millar, had been appointed the new Rector of Glasgow College would have pleased the students greatly, but in that same year, 1787, there was warning that other much-needed changes would be firmly resisted.

---

1. Coutts *History of the University of Glasgow*

Despite reasonably buoyant markets, Magistrates in Glasgow – many of whom were employers themselves – attempted to reduce weavers' wages. A strike resulted, in the course of which webs were cut from *Blackleg* looms and returned to employers, but when the Magistrates offered rewards for the names of web-cutters, the offending material was simply burned in the streets. This was the excuse for the magistrates to read the Riot Act, after which three weavers were shot dead by the military and several others fatally wounded.

Two years later, the long-fermenting anger against even more hopelessly corrupt government reached a climax in Paris when the hungry dispossessed armed themselves and, reinforced by mass desertions from the army, went on to take the Bastille and make the 14th day of July an international date. The following year, 1790, while men like Professor Anderson and Professor Millar organised popular celebrations all over Scotland to comemorate the anniversary of France's historic day – seen as a landmark advance in a world still fatally ill-divided – the one-time Rector of Glasgow University, Edmund Burke, published his *Reflections on the Revolution in France* and in doing so set light to a smouldering reactionary fear that was later to blaze up in that very peculiarly North British hysteria.

Whilst seeing no need for this country to emulate the French experience of revolution, many now did all they could to lend support across the Channel. Professor Anderson was on the *Altar of Liberty* with the Bishop of Paris, 14th July, 1791, adding his voice to that of the half-million congregation as it sang *Te Deum* in celebration of a great human advance, and a recoil-less cannon he invented – 'The gift of Science to Liberty' – was sucessfully tested and used in France. The professor then went on to devise a small varnished-paper balloon, gas-filled, that could be used in vast numbers to carry French newspapers and manifestoes over encircling enemy troops, each balloon despatched having a small flag with the message in German:

> O'er hills and dales and lines of hostile troops, I float majestic,
> Bearing the laws of God and Nature to oppressed men,
> And bidding them with arms their rights maintain.[2]

Following events in America and France, the nature and value of monarchy was everywhere increasingly in question, and though quite modest reform of Parliament would have answered for many, future

---

2. *Biographical Dictionary of Eminent Scotsmen*

research into this much-neglected period is likely to produce evidence that by now a large number of leading Scots were at heart Republican Nationalists.

> *The injured Stuart line is gone,*
> *A race outlandish fills the throne;*
> *An idiot race, to honour lost;*
> *Who know them best despise them most.*

Robert Burns was probably expressing majority Scots opinion when, in 1787, he scratched those lines on the window in Stirling, though some insist he was drunk at the time, obviously believing there never can be *veritas* in *vino*. It is true that the failed Jacobite rebellions had put paid to all notion of restoring the Stuarts, and the behaviour of most of the clan chiefs thereafter had put an end also to the ancient clan loyalties, but that North British minority apart, there is little evidence of much interest in Scotland for any royal family at all, least of all imported Hanoverians.

> George the First and Second were sensible of a rival in the remains of the Stuarts; and as they could not but consider themselves as standing on their good behaviour, they had prudence to keep their German principles of government to themselves; but as the Stuart family wore away, the prudence became less necessary.
> Thomas Paine *Rights of Man* Part 1

Towards the end of the eighteenth century only some 3000 land-owning voters elected 30 of Scotland's MPs, the remaining 15 being chosen by the self-elected and mainly corrupt councils of town and burgh. Estates forfeited after 1745 were now in the hands either of *ci-devant* clan chiefs sworn to servility or re-distributed among a *cosa nostra* of government supporters. The political destiny of the country was thus nominally in the hands of an unrepresentative 0.3% of the population; nominally, because in reality most of this number were subservient North Britons when called upon by Home Secretary Dundas to vote at Westminster or to pronounce – in the name of the Scottish nation – his and Prime Minister Pitt's version of political truth. Most of what such placemen and their hangers-on recorded as public opinion in the last decade of the eighteenth century is little more than the bleatings of a tiny minority alarmed at the threats, very real and more numerous by the day, to their own *arriviste* privileges. Little genuine assessment of the mood of the country can be had from such sources. The threat to privilege was coming from an increasingly educated and democratically-inclined section of the main population, but one which had little access to public forms of communication. When any of their number did achieve access in this field, it was seldom long before they found themselves in court facing stiff fines or jail sentences.

> Go on, Sir! Lay bare with undaunted heart and steady hand
> that horrid mass of corruption called politics and state-craft.

So wrote Robert Burns in November 1792 to Captain Johnston, ex-army, who had founded the radical *Edinburgh Gazetteer*. Within months, Johnston was in prison and Burns all but silenced.

* * *

> Hey for the New Jerusalem!
> The millennium!
> And peace and eternal beatitude
> be unto the soul of Thomas Paine.[3]

When the first part of *Rights of Man* was published at the end of 1791, Thomas Paine responded to praise for his work by proposing the toast – *The Revolution of the World!* – and the London gathering made the rafters ring with its response. Despite official endorsement and promotion of the views expressed by Edmund Burke the previous year, reform of government remained a popular cause in Britain and Paine's answer to Burke's attack on the French Revolution went on to make it even more so. His reply to Burke's insistence that aristocracy must remain the sole guardian of good government is typical of the direct and vigorous style of writing which could express enlightened ideas in language readily appreciated by literate artisans.

> There never did, there never will, and there never can exist a parliament, or any description of men, or any generation of men, in any country, possessed of the right or the power of binding and controulling posterity to the 'end of time,' or of commanding forever how the world shall be governed, or who shall govern it.
> Every age and generation must be as free to act for itself in all cases as the ages and generations which preceded it. The vanity and presumption of governing beyond the grave is the most ridiculous and insolent of all tyrannies.

3. Aldridge *Man of Reason* p135

In lines set to an old Jacobite air, Burns gave both lead to and expression of this reform mood in his country.

> *May Liberty meet wi success!*
> *May Prudence protect her frae evil!*
> *May Tyrants and tyranny tine i' the mist,*
> *And wander their way to the devil!*

Only a *junta* intent on ruthless censorship could have jibed at the heartfelt;

> *Here's freedom to them that wad read,*
> *Here's freedom to them that would write,*
> *There's nane ever feared that the truth should be heard,*
> *But they whom the truth would indite.*

The song ends on a call for co-operation, not confrontation;

> *Here's friends on baith sides o the firth*
> *And friends on baith sides o the Tweed;*
> *And wha wad betray old Albion's right,*
> *May he never eat of her bread!*

The subsequent behaviour of the ruling *junta* – the Tory Party in embryo – ensured that the year of the poem's publication, 1792, was the last one for more than a generation when there could be realistic hope of co-operation bringing about any type of reform through the Westminster parliament.

During that summer there seemed to be unrest or riot in just about every town and village of Scotland, the most serious of all commencing in the High Street of Edinburgh, on the King's Birthday, with posters advertising the event in advance.

> FELLOW CITIZENS AND COUNTRYMEN
> The Return of the King's Birthday brings in mind the Stigma
> shewn an enemy of our Country, John Wilkes – But that Lash of
> this country, Dundas, under the Cloak of Patriotism secretly at
> least seeks her ruin. Think of his opposition to the abolishing
> of the Test Act by which our Church is drained, the reform
> from the illegal and selfish views of our present Magistracy
> who act contrary to the bulk of the people in every matter –
> These, and other circumstances of his conduct make him
> merit the Lantern more than any of the French Aristocrats.

Provocative use of dragoons and footsoldiers eventually contained minor disturbances on the day itself, 4th June, but the following night riot increased in George Square, where both Lord Braxfield and the

Dundas family had town houses. Lord Advocate Dundas, his brother Lt-Col Francis Dundas and their brother-in-law Admiral Duncan were all present in the family home when the mob appeared. Colonel Dundas paused only long enough to arm himself with his great-aunt's crutch – presumably Lady Arniston was seated when he snatched it – then dashed from the house resolved on teaching democracy a lesson. The rioters, many of whom were women and children, then proceeded to deal the colonel such chastisement with his own chosen implement that he retreated back inside with 'a ghastly and formidable countenance'.

After being decoyed on a false alarm to St Andrew Square, the troops returned to find the mob putting in the windows of the Lord Advocate's house, the rioters dispersing only after one of their number had been killed and several wounded. On the third night, Admiral Duncan, who was later to play a crucial international role, added his considerable weight behind the dragoons and foot soldiers facing the estimated 2000-strong crowd which re-appeared in the Square. Armed with a cudgel and having a loaded blunderbuss to hand, Duncan was resolved to defend the house 'to the last extremity'. This time the crowds did disperse without violence but only to re-appear shortly afterwards in St Andrew Square, where they put in the windows of Lord Provost Elder's house.[4]

It is true there was little political organisation behind much of this nationwide unrest, the immediate causes being hunger and deprivation of rights, but these two are preconditions of most revolutions. It is significant that the rallying symbol on almost every occasion of riot was the effigy of Home Secretary Henry Dundas, in flames. Penny's description of this happening in Perth is representative of such events, if more humorous than most.

> . . . fire was set to the effigy; the belly of which being filled with combustibles, and the head with gunpowder, poor Harry, in the face of his enemies, ended his career in a luminous manner, and with good report.

Writing to the Home Office, the commander-in-chief in Scotland, Lord Adam Gordon, warned that Perth was 'a very dangerous place'; a sentiment no doubt shared by the Duke of Athole, who about this time was forced to make public salute to *Liberty and Equality!* by what should have been a forelock-tugging peasantry. With the largest

---

4. Meikle *King's Birthday Riot*

population of any in Scotland, Perthshire was still very much the heartland of the *Gaidhealtachd*, and though it now contributed significantly to the 12,000 Scots in King George's armed forces, several recent mutinies had demonstrated the power these might wield if actions were ever to be co-ordinated. Private initiatives were now having radical literature translated into *Gàidhlig*, and in any case, many ex-soldiers with direct experience of European and American politics had for some time been returning to talk about this even in the remotest of glens.

Robert Dundas, Scotland's Lord Advocate at the time, had been left virtually governor of the country by decree of his uncle, the Home Secretary at Westminster. All the evidence is that this nephew, professionally no more than mediocre and morally rather challenged, was about as unfitted to the task as could be imagined. It is true the Lord Advocate in his governorship had the close co-operation of Lord Braxfield, the Lord Justice Clerk; John Pringle, the Sheriff Principal of Midlothian; and Thomas Elder, the Lord Provost of Edinburgh, but from what is known of two of these three collaborators they may simply have added greatly to the resultant *bùrach*. It is probable that Sheriff Inglis was a man of some professional skill but Lord Provost Elder, though highly successful as the capital's leading wine-merchant, does not come across as any kind of political thinker. Little need be said about Braxfield. 'Hing a thief when he's young and he'll no steal when he's auld!' Such reactionary growls of his have been well documented.

There was growing belief that with the removal of only a handful of such people from power, an educated artisan class – led by enlightened members of the professions – could begin to lay the foundations of a genuine democracy. Few had seen the need for this to involve widespread upheaval and bloodshed since, by the establishment of universal suffrage, the necessary great changes could be brought about through the ballot-box. Before that could begin to happen, however, there was one very serious problem that was only now beginning to be confronted.

What the majority of ordinary people in Britain shared was an obvious, basic, everyday requirement for the means to support life in tolerable discomfort; but this they shared with the whole of the known world. In discussing specifically British parliamentary reform, too many continued to ignore the fact that not all the peoples of these islands were starting out from the same point in history. In short, the Scots and Irish radicals did not have nearly as much in common with their English colleagues as the majority supposed they ought, and within the shores of the Kingdom that majority could not be other than English.

Muir, who had already been mixing with leading reformers in London, came into some greater prominence himself as direct result of that King's Birthday riot in Edinburgh. Despite the offer of quite large rewards, the Crown could find only two men to accuse and Muir defended one of them, Alexander Lockie, against Lord Braxfield. Despite his best efforts, Lockie was found guilty of throwing one stone towards the military and sentenced to fourteen years in Botany Bay. After that, Muir would need to have been more than an innocent abroad to have expected justice for himself in the event of arrest, and his continued public support for reform through Parliament is therefore not at all surprising. Hope for such reform, though in reality coming close to a lost cause in Scotland and Ireland, was not yet entirely dissipated in England. Muir continued to follow this constitutional line partly because there still was some possibility of that change in government but mainly because such reform campaigning was the only cover available when, during the latter half of 1792, he addressed numerous artisans' political meetings. In this he was probably responding to the dictum of Tom Paine.

> The danger to which the success of revolutions is most
> exposed is in attempting them before the principles on which
> they proceed, and the advantages to result from them, are
> sufficiently seen and understood.

Whether reformation or revolution was the ultimate aim, it is clear that at this time Muir and his closest associates had two immediate priorities; political education of the Scottish working class and the closest possible political alliance with Ireland. There had been moves for greater contact between Scotland and Ireland at least since August 1792 [the first edition of Captain Johnston's *Gazetteer* carried an article pointing out that Ireland was also now in danger of losing its Parliament and being driven into an incorporating Union with London][5] and on 19th December an intelligence report from Ireland to the Home Office in London warned that Muir was shortly expected in Belfast and Dublin for talks with the United Irishmen.[6] In a founding Declaration [1791] the United Irishmen of Belfast, mainly Ulster-Scots, did not mince their words.

---

5. McFarland. p90, n52.

6. Meikle. p131, n2.

> WE HAVE NO NATIONAL GOVERNMENT; we are ruled by
> Englishmen, and the servants of Englishmen, whose object is
> the interest of another country, whose instrument is
> corruption, and whose strength is the weakness of Ireland; and
> these men have the whole of the power and patronage of the
> country, as means to seduce and to subdue the honesty and
> the spirit of her representatives in the legislature.

That was written less than ten years after Westminster had been forced to recognise the Declaration of Independence in America, in the achievement of which many Scots and Ulster-Scots had been active and influential. An effective alliance between Ireland and Scotland now threatened the King's authority at home and Muir appears to have been the principal activist in Scotland for that alliance.

> Look now, we pray you, upon Ireland. . . . The rights, or rather
> duties of conquest were dreadfully abused, and the Catholic
> religion was made the perpetual pretext for subjugating the
> state by annihilating the citizen. . .

This was the message from Ireland to reformers in Scotland;

> It was not till very lately that the part of the nation which is
> truly colonial reflected that though their ancestors had been
> victorious they themselves were now included in the general
> subjection; subduing only to be subdued.

Many Plantation Protestants, at the end of their one hundred year leases, had found themselves priced off the land into common cause, politically, with Catholics.

> We will not buy or borrow liberty from America or France, but
> manufacture it ourselves, and work it up with those materials
> that the hearts of Irishmen furnish them with at home.

In the spirit of the times, with the reference to three individual nations, the address ends with a clear call for separate but co-operating democracies

> Let all unite for all, or each man suffer for all. In each country
> let the people assemble in peaceful and Constitutional
> Convention. Let delegates from each country digest a plan of
> reform best adapted to the situation and circumstances of
> their respective nations, and let the Legislature be petitioned
> at once by the urgent and unanimous voice of Scotland,
> England, and Ireland.[7]

---

7. *State Trials*

Muir was arrested two weeks after taking full personal responsibility for presenting this Address to the national Friends of the People
Convention, held in Lawrie's Large Room in James's Court, at the head
of Edinburgh's Royal Mile.

There is yet no record of Muir arriving in Ireland at the end of
1792 as had been expected but his membership of the society dates
from this period. On the margin of his membership certificate, with
the emblem of the Irish harp, was the motto – 'It is new strung, and
shall be heard' – another example of breathing life into every *auld*
sang that still had contemporary relevance. It seems possible Muir
made direct contact just before the end of 1792 and for that reason
Authority acted when it did. He was arrested on 2nd January, 1793, at
Holytown, in Lanarkshire, when on his way to Edinburgh to defend
James Tytler against a charge of Sedition in the High Court there.

Tytler had not been charged with being part of any riotous mob.
His offence was much more serious. He had composed and printed a
pamphlet drawing the public's attention to the ancient principles of
Magna Charta Liberatum.

> Let not money, or land, or houses be thought to make a man fit
> for being an elector or representative; an honest and upright
> behaviour is the only qualification. Wealth has too long
> usurped the place and rights of virtue; let virtue now resume
> its own power and dignity, to the exclusion of everything else.[8]

The trial had been fixed for the seventh day of January, 1793, but
radical colleagues more worldly than himself urged him not to appear.
Self exile to America was a healthier alternative to the short life-
expectancy resulting from banishment to Botany Bay. After some time
hiding in a friendly shepherd's cottage on the north slopes of Salisbury
Crags, Tytler was smuggled out of the country via a boat over to Ireland,
where he completed his *System of Surgery* before setting off across
the Atlantic. The Friends of the People, Canongate Lodge, undertook
to care for his wife and children until they could eventually join him
in America but for whatever reason, Tytler never did see his family
again. Recent research into Irish National Archives lists a spy report
that Tytler had learnt *Gàidhlig* in preparation for returning to Scotland
disguised as an itinerant Highland piper.[9] The plan that he could then
act as an undercover agent for the radicals was aborted at the last
moment, apparently much to Tytler's disgust, though almost certainly

---

8. *State Trials*

9. McFarland. p136

because *inconspicuous* was the one thing this multi-talented individual did not do. In that same first week of the new year when Muir was arrested and Tytler fled from Scotland, Robert Burns, himself now the victim of an informer, was so concerned he might also see 'faithful wife and prattling innocents, turned over to beggary and ruin' that he made the firm vow 'I have set, henceforth, a seal on my lips as to these unlucky politics'.

Following his arrest at Holytown, Muir was conveyed to Edinburgh for examination by Sheriff Pringle, in the presence of William Honyman, the Sheriff of Lanarkshire. He was questioned about meetings he had addressed in the weaving towns and villages adjacent to Glasgow, and about books and pamphlets he was alleged to have circulated. Refusing to answer any of the individual charges, Muir confined himself to a legalistic and formulaic repetition of his stance.

> I decline answering any questions in this place. I consider a declaration of this kind, obtained in these circumstances, to be utterly inconsistent with the constitutional rights of a British subject. I have solemnly maintained this principle in pleading for others in a criminal court. When it comes to be applied to my own particular case I will not deviate from it. I have neither composed, published nor circulated books or pamphlets, inflammatory or seditious. In public and in private I have always advised and earnestly entreated those who might be engaged in the prosecution of a constitutional reform in the representation of the people in the House of Commons, to adopt measures mild but firm, moderate but constitutional. I have always inculcated upon all whom I may have addressed upon any occasion that there is no mode of accomplishing a constitutional reform in the representation of the people in the House of Commons but by the mode of respectful and constitutional petition to the House for that purpose. I do not doubt but the wisdom of that House will listen to the voice of the people when thus constitutionally presented.[10]

It seems likely there was an element of tongue-in-cheek in this rehearsal. The resolve of the Friends was now for a *radical* reform of the representation of the people in Parliament and at public meetings Muir had already made clear his opinion as to how that Parliament would treat petitions on the subject. *Authority* decided it could not arrange bail at such a late hour and took the opportunity to have this principal democratic offender spend the night in the Old Tolbooth, recently described from the Bench by Lord Henderland.

---

10. *State Trials*

That unhallowed place, which is the sink of corruption; and where all things that are vicious, base and criminal, are huddled together.

By decision of an English court the week previously, Tom Paine, now in France, had become an outlaw and *Rights of Man* an unlawful publication.

PENSION HUNTER

Revd James Lapslie was the author of an Essay on the Management of Bees. The Bible in this John Kay portrait lies open at the Book of Revelations showing the words: 'And the World Wondered after the Beast'. He was a friend of Muir's parents but this did not prevent him from assisting the authorities in the search for incriminating evidence against Thomas Muir

CHAPTER 2
Justified Sinners

Throughout the second half of 1792 the Lord Advocate had been making increasing use of informers and the three most noteworthy of these were men who had been trained to serve religion. The Reverend James Lapslie, minister at Campsie Parish and a frequent guest of Muir's parents at Huntershill House 'for weeks at a time', proved unusually diligent in assisting Sheriff Honyman in the search for incriminating evidence. It is said he professed an interest in liberal political principles to ingratiate himself with the parents. The other two informants, Patrick Moir and Robert Watt, appear to have studied for the ministry at St Andrews University without taking the final *Tryals*. It is probable all three subscribed to the motivation recorded by Watt, August 1792, in his initial letter to Home Secretary Henry Dundas.

> Although I have not the honour of being known to you, yet
> from my attachment to the constitution of this country, and of
> which I have the happiness of being a native, and the fears I
> entertain of its constitution being subverted, have hereby
> taken the liberty of laying before you facts which merit your
> most serious attention.

After explaining that he had been educated at Perth and was now a resident of Edinburgh, with his own small business, wine merchant, which allowed him to travel the country freely and legitimately, Watt offered to put his wide knowledge of reform societies in places like Dundee, Perth and Glasgow at the disposal of the Home Office.

> I cannot, as a friend to my country, but inform you of their
> proceedings and intentions; the leaders of these factious clubs
> have the audacity to go from house to house, endeavouring to
> enamour the weak in understanding, and to inflame factions
> in minds by representing to them certain supposed
> grievances, and enforcing, by suspicious arguments, the evil
> consequences that will unavoidably result to the nation if they
> are not speedily redrest.

Having listed the meetings he had attended, the numbers present and names of the leaders, he then went on to offer the Home Secretary some personal advice.

> Be pleased to advise Lady Arniston {your mother} not to go to Mr Elder the bookseller's shop, to look after seditious books; suffice it to say that that fellow has at one of these seditious committees where I was present irritated the risibility of the company at the expense of your's and her ladyship's character.[1]

Home Secretary Dundas replied immediately, encouraging this patriot's efforts and promising confidentiality of all future correspondence. He was in Scotland from October to assess the political situation for himself and during this visit advised his nephew and Sheriff Pringle to make enquiries into Watt's background, which checks proved satisfactory. At the beginning of December, when Henry Dundas returned south again to deal with related problems in England, he left behind a temporary political advisor and the stern instruction to his rather disconcerted nephew that, henceforth, he must make up his mind to act upon his own discretion.[2]

Henry Dundas wrote a warning from Edinburgh to his secretary in London, 25th November, about 'enclosures that must not be left in the office'; then on the 15th December, after the Home Secretary had returned to London, the nephew felt it necessary to write the uncle a needless reminder. 'You need not be reminded, of the necessity of keeping the Information we now regularly receive, secret'.[3]

---

1. *State Trials*

2. In the subsequent official records there are letters signed by the Revd James Lapslie, reports bearing the signature of Patrick Moir, and a couple of letters direct to the Lord Advocate signed by Robert Watt. There are also a very large number of transcribed documents which, instead of a signature, bear only the initials *JB* by way of indentification. A casual note in G.W.T. Omond's *The Lord Advocates of Scotland* [1883] suggested that Watt and *JB* might be the same person, and a study of the relevant Home Office Correspondence [1792 to 1794] leads to the conclusion that before the year was out Robert Watt had become the Lord Advocate's principal informant. Not long afterwards, the Procurator Fiscal [William Scott, Solicitor-at-Law, Merchant Street, Edinburgh] was responsible for setting up an arrangement whereby all future Watt reports he received would be transcribed before being passed up to loftier departments and there can be no doubt at all that both uncle and nephew were from the outset aware they were venturing into rather murky waters.

3. All official quotations – Home Office [Scotland] Correspondence – unless otherwise stated.

It was at first arranged that the new man would make his reports via the other ex-divinity student [Patrick Moir, 17 Thistle Street, Edinburgh] who for some time had been employed in daily contact with Procurator Fiscal Scott. Almost at once Watt objected to this arrangement. He had already visited the Lord Advocate at his George Square home and had no desire to work through an intermediary; he desired to correspond with the Procurator Fiscal direct – 'or even with the Right Honourable Henry Dundas'. Watt also took the opportunity to record in this letter the first criticism of what was being demanded of him.

> To point out individuals as objects of ministerial or sub-ministerial vengeance is {as I have already told you repeatedly} an invidious task unworthy of a man or a christian – much more of a friend to freedom as I must own I always was and ever will be. This task however, which I have uniformly declined, you may probably find others ready and willing to perform.

On the same morning Watt wrote that letter from his home in North Grey's Close, the prime object of such ministerial vengeance had been released on bail from the Tolbooth just a step or two away up the High Street. Money for Muir's bail had been presented by the lawyer William Moffat, a leading member of the Canongate Friends of the People in whose home Muir had become as part of the family, but though both men presided over an open meeting in Blackfriar's Wynd the following night, Muir as Chair and Moffat as Secretary, their private discussions are likely to have been very private indeed. Muir must have left Scotland almost immediately after that public meeting, probably about the same time that Watt, who had also been present, was writing-up his report on it for the Procurator Fiscal.

Having travelled rapidly south, possibly surreptituously at first to avoid obstruction, Muir met up with many reform colleagues in London; Scots such as Thomas Hardy, the ex-Falkirk shoemaker who had founded the London Corresponding Society; the Earl of Lauderdale; Major Thomas Maitland; and Colonel Macleod of Macleod, MP for Inverness. Macleod, 20th chief of the clan, was Lt Colonel of the 73rd Highland Regiment and already there had been reports to the Lord Advocate that some of his soldiers, returning home after fighting Hyder Ali in India, were spreading sedition everywhere as they marched back through Scotland to their headquarters in Perth. In London, Muir would certainly be in discussion with James MacKintosh, from the shores of Inverness, whose growing reputation as campaigning journalist had recently soared on publication of a major new work of political philosophy.

Vindiciæ Gallicæ
by
James MacKintosh
A Defence of the French Revolution and its English admirers
against the accusations of the right honourable Edmund Burke.

It was arranged that Muir would address The Friends of the Liberty of the Press in London's Freemasons' Tavern, Friday 11th January,[4] and it is unlikely to be coincidence his certificate of having taken the United Irishmen oath dates from this same day; someone from Ireland, authorised to conduct the *tests*, probably used the occasion to further existing matters with Muir. Many leading London reformers were present on the day, men such as the Irish politician-playwright Richard Brinsley Sheridan, the politicians Charles James Fox and Charles Grey, and the young Scots Lord whom Burns had already immortalised.

Nae honest, worthy man need care
To meet wi' NOBLE, youthfu' Daer
For he but meets a BROTHER.

At the meeting, Muir delivered a plea for assistance to deal with an *Authority* in Scotland that was now exercising corrupt power far in excess of anything that would be tolerated in England.

> Liberty of the Press and Speech in Scotland are almost at an end. Spies intrude into all meetings. Treasury agents are in every tavern offering bribes to informers.

His speech was reported with great enthusiasm in the *Morning Post*, the London Whig newspaper, but this may have had much to do with the newspaper's editors being the Stewarts of 52 Frith Street, Soho, brothers-in-law to James MacKintosh.[5]

> With regard to Loyalty, if affection for the Constitution is intended, I am exceeded by no one. But if the word means, as I fear is the case at present, an inclination to rivet more tightly the yoke of oppression about the necks of my countrymen, I have none of that loyalty! Though a man love his sovereign he should not on that account forget the People. Thank God even the Scots are beginning to realise they have rights.

4. Bewley *Muir of Huntershill*

5. *Biographical Dictionary of Eminent Scots*

Though the meeting had in general been very supportive of Muir's stance, his tone seems to have proved rather too plebeian for Charles [later Earl] Grey's elegant lugs, and in an effort to eliminate obvious non-understanding Lord Daer was driven to deliver something of a reprimand. If national divisions were to be avoided, he insisted in a subsequent letter to Grey from Scotland, men such as Muir 'whose manner even disgusts, and whose conduct cannot be approved of as wise or prudent' must be regarded in London as envoys from brethren in distress. In trying to explain to Grey that his very Anglo-centric views could be questioned, Daer made it clear that Scots saw their present unacceptable situation as arising out of the 1603 Union of the Crowns and the 1707 Union of Parliaments. To the argument that these Unions had been of commercial benefit to Scotland, he pointed out that they had done little but remove part of the obstacles that England's greater power had previously thrown around the country.

> But, if it did more, what would that amount to but the common saying that we bartered our liberty and with it our morals for a little wealth?
> . . . You say we have gained emancipation from feudal tyranny. I believe that had no union ever taken place we should have been more emancipated than we are.

To point out obvious benefits resulting from Union, the letter went on, in no way negated the possibility that Scotland might have achieved much more without it, the problem arising from the fact that the Governing powers were united, while the nations were not. Daer's letter finishes with the dangling carrot that English support for national democracy in Scotland would result in important changes at Westminster too. It would 'relieve you of that vermin from this country who infect your court, parliament and every establishment'.[6]

The inescapable fact was that the differences within the Reform movement, evident from the outset, were increasing by the hour. The London organisation of Friends of the People, seeking very limited and quite inadequate electoral reform, had maintained exclusivity by demanding high subscription fees and as result of recent events in France was now losing that exclusive membership at an increasing rate. In contrast, the versions of the same Society in Scotland continued to promote rather than repudiate the works of Thomas Paine and from the outset had encouraged the widest possible membership by limiting subscription charges to a few copper coins.

6. Bewley *Muir of Huntershill*

In the meantime, in Edinburgh, Lord Advocate Dundas was having a prolonged run of bad days at the office. *Authority* was having difficulty dealing with widespread protest against the threatened outbreak of war with France, typified by the resolution passed at a public meeting on the South Inch of Perth, despite a magistrates' proclamation designed to prevent it.

> The Friends of the People in Perth, and in its neighbourhood, solemnly declare to the world, that a sense of duty alone prevented them from joining in the late rage, of resolving and anathematising republicans and levellers; because we are convinced, that no seditious spirit prevailed in the country, and that the whole furore was the effect of a gross political delusion, cruelly and artfully played off by designing men, with a view to throe the public mind into that state of confusion and incapacity, in which it is best prepared to receive the idea of war with the least possible hazard of its revolting against it.
> ... The Country is about to be plunged into a War, so wholly unprecedented in our history, that even with success itself, no man can say it will be productive to the British nation.
> ... Is it to defend us against invasion? – none is threatened. Is it to vindicate our National honour? – that is not called in question. Is it to defend our Trade? – there is at present no dread of it being injured. Is it to preserve the faith of treaties? – none which are founded on the unalterable laws of justice have been invaded.[7]

Dundas must have been further dismayed at this time to find his own actions under attack from within. The temporary political advisor left behind by his uncle had advocated the formation of Loyal Associations to counter the Friends movement, but now his own spy, Watt, was filing reports highly critical of these new organisations.

> I have only to add that the numerous counter associations, whose Declarations daily appear in the papers, would almost tempt me to become an Enemy of those whose servility leads them to proclaim as infallibly perfect a most defective and faulty Constitution. That nation, that people, surely deserve everlasting bondage who can seriously and solemnly subscribe what not one of them I'm sure believes. They all must be conscious that the Constitution has faults which require amendment and this is all that I and the great majority wish. Although there may be a few amongst us who wish a total overthrow of the whole Constitution, if anarchy, blood

---

7. *Traditions of Perth* and *Gazetteer of Scotland*

and murder should ensue, yet believe me when I assure you
that the great majority agree in wishing peace and truth, as old
Hezekiah did, conjoined with liberty in our days.

But while the Lord Advocate recorded his feelings of shock and
hurt at critical letters received from men like Captain Inglis of the
King's Navy, whose North British loyalty he felt should have been
unquestioning[8] he seems to have accepted Robert Watt's criticisms
as a price that had to be paid for genuine intelligence.

> Watt was with me last night. He was in Perth about a week ago.
> James Wylie, merchant there, whom I know to be the most
> intemperate Revolutioner in Scotland, is he informs me
> engaged in a foreign correspondence with France – he
> suggested & very earnestly the propriety of opening his letters
> at the Post Office. Any coming from abroad, addressed to Mr
> James Wylie, merchant in Perth, may be attended to in London
> if you think that measure proper. All letters from Perth which
> of course have the Perth mark on them, addressed to France
> can easily be stopped here.

It was indeed a very easy matter to stop letters in Edinburgh; as
well as being the country's leading wine merchant, Lord Provost Elder
was also the Postmaster-General. On this same subject, though, the
contribution of the Procurator Fiscal's original informer, Patrick Moir,
might have seemed more worrying than useful.

> To the Perth account I should have added a circumstance
> which I heard of Wylie, merchant, Perth. It is said he furnished
> the Westcoat and Breeches for Mr Dundas's Ephegy at his own
> private expense & which was Sattin!

Of more serious concern would be a letter received about this time
from Lord Provost Dunlop of Glasgow, advising against the idea that
a national armed militia should be formed.

> I am fully convinced it would be highly improper to trust arms
> in the hands of the lower classes of people here and in Paisley.
> The Friends of the People are I know very fond of the idea
> which is at least a presumption against the propriety of the
> measure.

This warning, typical of the fears of many self-elected councils in
other Scots towns and cities, drove the Lord Advocate to rely ever more

8. Inglis had objected to Westminster's continued use of *England* to
   describe the kingdom.

heavily on Robert Watt, and the new spy responded with an increased stream of accurate and up-to-date information. He reported that, though the actions against Tytler and Muir had given rise to some alarm and despondency amongst Scots reformers, there had also been a quick recovery. After that London meeting, Lord Daer and Col Macleod had hurried north to deal with the situation in Edinburgh and were, with William Skirving the farmer and innovative agriculturist from Kinross-shire, 'labouring hard to keep up the spirits'. Further evidence that the battle was not in any way regarded as over is provided by Burns. When North Britons in Dumfries formed the True Loyal Natives club during that eventful January, the poet immediately abandoned the vow of political abstinence made three weeks earlier.

> Ye true 'Loyal Natives', attend to my song,
> In uproar and riot rejoice the night long!
> From Envy and Hatred your corps is exempt,
> But where is your shield from the darts of Contempt?

Having heard the contents of a letter from Muir read out at a Canongate meeting, Watt reported this and the fact that Muir was off to France 'to circulate it as the opinion of the people in Britain that the death of the King would disgrace the Cause of Freedom forever'. It continues to be repeated that Muir's enormous ego took him to France to try a personal intervention to save the French King's life, but the Lord Advocate, who conjured up that charge at the subsequent trial in the attempt to paint Muir's conduct treasonous, knew the truth from this informer's report.

Many thousands of French sympathisers, from just about every nation in Europe and others from America, were in Paris at that time; Tom Paine's *Revolution of the World* was a common objective and most were agreed that the execution of the ineffectual, bumbling but conniving Louis Seize would have very damaging consequences for that cause. In choosing to join this international plea for clemency, Muir was giving himself a valid excuse for leaving Britain while at the same time keeping options open till the nature of the charge against him be declared. If it proved to be Sedition, he could return and attempt to make political gain for Reform out of an intelligent and high-profile defence; if High Treason, he could set sail for America, where many friends within conversational distance of George Washington were ready to assist.

Regicide will achieve two things. It will divide all our friends.
It will unite all our enemies.

Had the trial of the king accused of plotting against his own people
not dragged on beyond the day appointed for a final vote, Muir would
have been too late even to witness events, let alone have influence on
them. It is unlikely he arrived in Paris until two or three days after the
guilty verdict was pronounced, Tuesday 15th January, but it is almost
certain he would have been present as the final scenes of this great
European drama drew to a close. With few abstentions, Tuesday's
verdict had been a unanimous Guilty! but the debate on punishment
dragged on till Thursday. Tom Paine, now the Deputy for Pas de Calais,
had been one of the strongest advocates of the king's life being spared,
pointing to the success of measures used to deal with the Stuarts and
suggesting exile to America as a reliable solution to the problem of
Louis Capet. Others were vehement that so long as the ex-king
remained alive so long would he remain the excuse for continued
foreign attacks on France, and with the country long surrounded and
threatened by the massed armies of foreign royalty, this was the
powerful argument that succeeded. But when the result of the voting
was announced on Friday morning, it was found that though a
majority of 53 out of thirteen times that number had voted for death,
26 of those had recommended some element of mercy. Subtract the
26 and the actual call for regicide was still a majority, but a majority
of just one. There was then bad-tempered agreement that a new
question be allowed. Sursis? This meant there would be a final debate
on the question of whether the sentence should be carried out
immediately, or delayed for an indeterminate period, and though
Friday and Saturday would be used up in argument for and against
such delay, only one of two words would be allowed in the final vote.

Oui, ou Non

The disputes dragged on through Friday, Saturday and till well
into the wee small hours of Sunday morning when sprawling Deputies,
mouth agape, snored loudly till rudely awakened to pronounce their
one word. The jeering, cheering tricoteuses kept score from the Gods,
the baying Jacobins continued to hold the high ground while the
Girondins strove to remain jesuitically grounded; alcohol was on sale
as in any tavern and wagers on the outcome deftly changed hands as
colourful mistresses circulated, high-rouged and flushed anyway in
the excitement of it all. That last scene in the Salle de Manège must
have been rather a sudden education for the young man trained to

debate in the Church of Scotland's General Assembly.

By a majority of 70, Louis Capet was sentenced to die without delay and Muir would certainly have been present in Place de la Révolution on the morning of Monday, 21st January, to hear the command 'Tambours!' trigger a crescendo drumroll that drowned out sound of the scything blade.

Vive la République! Vive la République!!
VIVE LA RÈPUBLIQUE!!!

He would have seen the head fetched from the basket and held up as proof that Louis Capet had paid the demanded price, less for his own folly, perhaps, as for the very many and very real sins of his fathers.

* * *

A report is circulated but not credited that Thos Muir Esq has got a commission in the National Guard of France!!!

Although Robert Watt's information to the Procurator Fiscal's office was once again accurate, it would not have taken official hysteria for the rumour to have been believed. It was known to the authorities that a number of Scots had been active in France, more or less officially, for some time.

One of them, Dr William Maxwell of Kirkconnel, in Dumfries-shire, *was* a member of the French National Guard. He had been on duty in Place de la Revolution that Monday morning and so close to the guillotine he later returned to Scotland with a souvenir of the occasion, remaining quite proud of that handkerchief of his, stained as it was said to be by the blood of Louis Capet. John Oswald, his father an Edinburgh goldsmith, was another Scot in French service. More than a little eccentric, it seems, he was released from duty as Adjutant to Colonel McLeod's 73rd Perthshire regiment in India, where he is said to have converted to Hinduism. After arrival in France, he was appointed Colonel of a Battalion of Pikemen, in which he enrolled his two sons with him as drummers; sometime after Muir's arrival in Paris the Battalion left for the war in La Vendee, on the French west coast, where Oswald and both his sons were killed.[9]

9. Oswald Appendix D

Thomas Christie, son of the banker Provost of Montrose, was likely to have been the man Muir spent most time with in the French capital. It is possible they had known each other from Edinburgh University days and Muir is likely to have had contact with Christie's family through Friends of the People work in Dundee and Montrose. Now married and resident in Paris, Christie had previously been a frequent visitor to France and witness to many important events there. Described by one admirer as 'a young prodigy in science and literature' he had already gained the respect and friendship of many eminent men, among whom was England's Dr Johnson. In France, he was on closest terms with leaders such as Condorcet and Mirabeau, and the National Assembly had entrusted him with the work of translating their new Constitution into English; which meant, of course, he too would now be regarded as as High Treason material.

As with Muir in Glasgow and Edinburgh, Christie would be held personally responsible for the recent vigorous outbreaks of democracy all around Fife and Forfarshire. Some two years previously, as a response to Burke's *Reflections*, he had published his *Letters on the French Revolution* and from the detailed knowledge he had of the French Constitution after the translation work was able to refute many of Burke's statements. Though respectful of the other man's abilities, he did not hesitate to label Burke's work an attempt to conduct the reader 'to the Temple of Superstition', drawing' on his own experiences in Paris to present an alternative view to that being widely propagated in Great Britain.

> I went over to Paris immediately after the king's arrival there, and I lived in that city six months in the middle of the great events then accomplishing in the most perfect harmony and security. I walked about everywhere, mixed with all classes of society, spoke my opinion publicly of every public measure, and was abroad at all hours, and never met with injury, nor even experienced alarm.

Christie, together with his friend Tom Paine, had been out in the streets amongst what was described as 'a mob of principle' on the night the French king attempted to betray the revolution by joining the ranks of the invading forces. 'You see the absurdity of monarchical governments' was Paine's comment to the young man from Montrose, 'here will be a whole nation disturbed by the folly of one man'.[10]

Paine, like many others, had found Tom Christie to be congenial

---

10. Aldridge *Man of Reason* p146

and intellectually stimulating company and so the young Scot's home had become one of the many salons of political debate in Paris. Now partner in a London mercantile house, Christie, who had decided to follow his father's profession from a French base, was in a position to afford Muir a very rapid *entrée* to the heart of republican France and Muir responded with enthusiasm.

> When you and my friends judge it expedient or proper, I will immediately return, but I cannot leave Paris without regret. I am honoured by the notice and friendship of an amiable and distinguished circle, and to a friend of humanity it affords much consolation to find according feelings in a foreign land.

So Muir wrote to his Edinburgh agent just two days after Louis Capet was guillotined. Although expressing eagerness for news of events at home, this letter also contained the caution 'but tell my friends, it is only through the channel of Newspapers I can receive that intelligence'. Written communications at the time had to be very guarded. Before leaving the southern coast of the English Channel letters were scrutinised by the *Comité de Surveillance* for anti-French sentiments, whilst on the northern shores information useful to the Home Office was routinely sought. Despite which, this frequently quoted letter seems generally to be accepted at face value. Perhaps it should be; but given a dangerous political situation growing more dangerous by the day in that first month of 1793, it is likely Muir was writing between the lines, a common practice at the time, even in correspondence between a Lord Advocate and his avuncular Home Secretary.

The first sentence might suggest Muir was still waiting to learn what charge he faced and what changes there might have been in the political climate following his self-imposed exile. After that, he might simply be recording his reactions to Paris, or he might equally be reporting useful contacts. The phrase 'a friend of humanity' could easily mean a supporter of the Friends of the People and 'according feelings' could indicate to political colleagues that there was already the potential for assistance from France. This is far from being unlikely.

Back in Edinburgh, in his last report of January 1793, Robert Watt warned the despots that increasing official pressure on him for results might cause him to give himself away. He suggested in this letter to the Procurator Fiscal that sufficient money to clear his debts would avoid this, as it would almost certainly at the same time clear his head. He also took the opportunity to seek appointment to a minor permanent post. 'If the office vacant by Mr Cumming's death is not filled up or promised away, let me know and oblige'. Then in what was becoming a familiar pattern of this religious man's epistles, there was added a rather tongue-in-cheek postscript. In this he expressed wonder at the French hurry to execute Louis Seize, suggesting they should have delayed the business nine days to make it coincide with this date, 30th January, the anniversary of the date on which Charles I had been executed in London. If Procurator Fiscal Scott took the trouble to check that historical note he would have found Robert Watt's information to be, as ever, accurate; but at a time when official propaganda was striving desperately to portray the French as uniquely savage regicides, he might have wondered at his spy echoing the counter-arguments of the French.

What right had the English to preach to another nation?
Could they say, hand on heart, that this thing of Charles 1
was now a matter of deep regret ?
Do the majority in England now even remember?
Had not the execution of Charles 1 proved to be the salvation of the
English people?

Payment for such critical information was proving a constant drain on the Secret Service Fund. By mid-January, £400 had already been paid out through the Lord Advocate's office and although the remainder received from London was thought 'to take care of future needs' it proved not so. Before the end of the month there was another *JB* postscript – 'A little cash would be very acceptable'. So the Lord Advocate then sent instructions to Nepean, the Home Office Secretary – 'Tell Mr D that we are in want of a little pecuniary assistance'. Into February and the cry had to be repeated twice more, the first bleat from the Procurator Fiscal – 'Money is much wanted'. This was dutifully relayed to the Home Office by the Lord Advocate – 'Sheriff Pringle in need of the promised money'. Despite all of which, and this time by-passing the Procurator Fiscal, Robert Watt wrote of his desire to exchange his rewarding sideline for something more permanent.

North Grey's Close, Edinburgh. 9th February 1793.
My Lord Advocate,
After having had the honour of your lordship's command I embraced every opportunity of informing myself of the true state of the Friends of the People, & which I take the liberty of doing myself the pleasure of hereby laying before your Lordship.
It is with pleasure I can say that owing to the rigorous measures adopted & pursued by your Lordship & which merit the approbation & thanks of every friend to his country, the

most of the Societies in & around Edinburgh are not so well attended, nor is the language of the members so full of invective as before. Still, it is requisite that Government keep a watchful eye over them.

After advising that leaders such as William Skirving were now urging moderation of speech on their meetings as the most efficacious way of deceiving the agents and government into a false sense of security, Watt reveals the real reason for this direct letter.

As Mr Calder, Clerk in the Exchequers is seemingly dying – if not already dead – may I solicit your Lordship's interest to procure me his place; if agreeable to the rules of that Court? I hope your Lordship will excuse this freedom. I have the honour to be, my Lord, your Lordship's most obedient and most humble servant, Robert Watt.

On the 26th January, five days after Louis Capet was executed, the Lord Advocate's office served the indictment papers on Muir's agent in Edinburgh. The charge was to be Sedition, not High Treason, and the trial was due to commence on 11th February. Muir did not receive notice of this till 8th February but his letter to the Friends, published in Edinburgh newspapers on 1st March, makes clear his intention. The distinction made between England and Scotland in this letter may be no more than subconscious acceptance of political realities.

War is declared between England and France and the formalities requisite to be gone through, before I could procure my passport, would at least have consumed three days. I will return to Scotland without delay. To shrink from danger would be unbecoming my own character and your confidence. I dare challenge the most minute investigation of my public and private conduct. Armed with innocence I appeal to justice, and I disdain to supplicate favours.

A new arrival from Scotland met Muir in Paris at this time and on 15th February wrote of it to the Glasgow branch of the Friends of the People, confirming Muir's declared intention.

Mr Muir makes a great sacrifice in coming so soon back as he has already made a very great proficiency in the language, has made valuable and dear connections, and is enchanted with the climate.

When this letter was opened by the authorities at Glasgow Post Office they might have taken its contents at face value. In the spirit of the times, however, 'valuable and dear connections' and 'enchantment with the climate' might well have been judged to be political comments. The writer, James Smith, was a Glasgow gunsmith who had himself been cited for Sedition after composing the founding resolutions for the Sons of Liberty and Friends of Man in Partick.

Preferring to leave himself some freedom of operation Smith had, like Muir before him, departed Glasgow for Paris. He too seemed to like the city.

> I had the honour to dine with Mr Maxwell and Mr Muir. We met by mere accident in a coffee house in the Palais Royal. We had all the fashionable dishes, with variety of wines – Burgundy etc – for 3/6d. All perfectly quiet here since the death of the King . . . much safer than Glasgow, no robberies or pickpockets . . . women very well-dressed.

Though the prosecution at the subsequent trial made much of Muir's failure to appear at this time, there is every reason to believe he had now decided to return and use Edinburgh's High Court as a political platform. He would be well aware that many in Paris were openly critical of his friend, Tom Paine, for not having remained in London to defend *Rights of Man* personally instead of leaving it in the hands of Thomas Erskine, brother of Edinburgh's Henry Erskine, and by many accounts a very egotistical and self-serving lawyer. Many believed Paine's appearance in the London court could have been just the *cause célèbre* the English reform movement so desperately needed.

On appeal by his Edinburgh agent, Muir's trial was postponed for fourteen days but in the circumstances it is difficult to see this as much more than a cosmetic ploy; from such a gesture the Lord Advocate could claim a measure of official magnanimity, whilst giving himself more time to find or fabricate better prosecution evidence. In any case, if Muir failed to appear for this postponed trial, sentence of outlawry would be automatic and he could then be exposed and treated as a common criminal. Muir did fail to appear in Edinburgh on 25th February and, as protocol demanded, his name was called *oft times* within the High Court and *three times* at the public door. It is not difficult to imagine Braxfield's delivery of the subsequent verdict.

> Thomas Muir is judged t'be an ootlaw and fugitive frae His Majesty's Laws. It is ordainit that he be pit t'His Highness's horn, and aw his moveable goods and gear be escheat and inbrocht t'His Majesty's use, for his coantempt and disobedience in no appearin this day and place, t'hae underlyen the Law for the crimes o Sedition and ithers

specified in the said criminal letters raised against him thereanent. It is ordainit, forbye, that the bond o caution granted by William Moffat and ithers for the appearance o the said Thomas Muir be forfeit and the penalty therein contained be recovered by the clerk o this Coort. T'be disposed o as the Coort shall direct.

The Lord Justice Clerk could speak English and Latin perfectly well but in common with a number of prominent Scots, including Home Secretary Dundas, he refused to abandon his native tongue. The offence for which Captain Johnston of the *Gazetteer* had been found guilty arose directly from this fact, his newspaper being judged to have imputed partiality and injustice to the High Court by publishing a verbatim account of Braxfield's interlocutor at a trial for sedition. It seems the Lord Justice Clerk's dismissal of the French as a nation of Atheists had been couched in the earthiest of language.

They deny their dependance oan the great Goad o Providence, in whaes sicht we are mere mushrooms. Oor blasphemies can dae nae herm tae him wha is all powerful; he looks oan us as beneath him. But, t'blaspheme against his maist gracious majesty, whit impiety! . . . The reformers talk o liberty and equality, this they hae in everything consistent wi their happiness, and equality also. . . . But that they hae richt t'representation in parliament, I deny! . . . In Goad's name, let them gang. I wish them not to stey; . . . I also maintain that the landed interest pey aw the taxes. The shoon, I alloo, are dearer by almaist a hauf than I remember them, owing t'the additional taxes oan leather, which the exigencies o the state requires, but it was not the mechanic nor the labourer that peyed the tax, but the proprietor o the land; for I remember when I could pey a labourer wi hauf the sum which I now doe.[11]

Verbatim or otherwise, this was sufficient to send Captain Johnston away for a three month stay in the Tolbooth. The capital's radical newspaper was not immediately silenced, however, as Johnston offered easy financial terms to allow others to continue the business.

At Muir's subsequent trial scepticism was expressed over the length of time it took him to obtain a passport and the considerable delay after that before he actually left France. The suggestion that the delays suited his purpose is feasible but ignores the fact that France was now engaged in a life or death struggle. The people's army had suffered serious reverses in the Low Countries and Deputies in Paris suspected treachery among its Generals, while the Generals, short of

11. *State Trials*

supplies, suspected treachery among the Deputies. Factions all over the country were becoming ever more entrenched in their frustrations. The people, still short of food, blamed the government and the government, suspecting foreign agents behind the ensuing riots, began to suspect all foreigners. Paine became quite despondent over this growing trend.

> If every individual is to indulge his private malignancy or his private ambition, to denounce at random and without any kind of proof, all confidence will be undermined and all authority destroyed. Calumny is a species of treachery that ought to be punished as well as any other kind of treachery. It is a private vice productive of public evils.[12]

And all around this cauldron which they had created, the allied royalist forces increased the threat on every border, ever more firmly united against change in feudal Europe. To the armies of Austria and Prussia massed in the east was added the threat of those of the Netherlands in the north-east, Britain's in the north and west, and Spain's in the south. It counted for nothing that feuding between the royal houses of these nations had defaced Europe with generation after generation of blood-soaked battlefields, now that the *institution* of monarchy was under threat, its maintenance had become a common cause that now threatened France with the bloodiest war of all time. Given that situation, it is perhaps surprising it took only a little over eight weeks for officials to deal with Muir's personal difficulties.

From the passport document it seems that Muir was about 5' 3" tall, auburn-haired, blue-eyed, with an aquiline nose, medium mouth, round-chin, and with a high forehead above a longish, full face. From a copy of the passport then in his possession, MacKenzie gives the height as 5' 9", so it is possible an ill-written 3 was taken for a 9, or vice versa.

* * *

---

12. Aldridge *Man of Reason* p201

Mr Muir is not yet come to town nor have any letters arrived from him. His friends here suspect that their letters to him have been held up, in order that he may not appear and of consequence be outlawed. Some alledge his first visit to his native country will be like that of Coriolanus, with an army of the enemy at his back!!!

Robert Watt was in business again. An official rebuke from the Procurator Fiscal for his temerity in writing a soliciting letter direct to the Lord Advocate seems to have been accompanied by the wherewithal to settle a few more dunning creditors. On the 1st March, however, a little over a week later, that Christian conscience was again bothering the Lord Advocate's main man; to the extent he now hoped the business would soon be over.

I will be happy to have done with it. Only you must allow you are considerably in my debt. Send me five guineas and let us discharge one another and oblige. Yours respectfully, JB.
    PS. Return my MSS {which you say were all transcribed} that they may not rise up in Judgement against me.

Watt may have been genuinely worried and anxious to get out from under Procurator Fiscal Scott, or he may have hoped to up his earnings by playing hard to get. Perhaps both. Whatever the truth, it seems *Authority* was very disinclined to lose his services; within the week there was another letter to the Procurator Fiscal, this time grateful, if once more tongue-in-cheek.

Sir, if the old Scots proverb holds good that 'nae news is guid news' I certainly have good news to give you, in return for your favour last night.

There was every reason for this renewed buoyancy on the fifth day of March. The previous night's 'favour' had been delivered personally by Procurator Fiscal Scott, as is revealed in the explanatory letter Scott had to write at the end of the month to the Lord Advocate, by then in London. The enclosed *JB* report, dated 28th March, had listed some of those attending a Friends meeting in Mather's Tavern as Skirving, Moffat, Palmer and a 'Mr Watt'. After drawing cautious but particular attention to this 'son of Mr Watt of Bowlin' by expressing surprise that 'one so well brought up' should be present, the Fiscal continued:

... What occurred to me was to propose half a guinea per week certain so long as it should be thought requisite to apply to him and that his Services merit it. But that if any occasion he furnished information of material consequence or was put to extra expense or trouble he should be considered for it.

The Procurator Fiscal then went on to make sure his own dowp was suitably covered.

> Accordingly, with the approbation of the Sheriff, I met & closed with him on those terms. At the meeting he said the money he wanted was to enable him to take a share in Government Tontines & from a scheme he showed me finding these to be something more than 2 guineas I gave him 5 guineas to enable him to take out one for himself and another for his wife with a view to make him the more attentive.

Personal life-pensions having been arranged for Watt and his wife, Scott then explained there might be additional payments for what would be termed *Extras*.

> He is no doubt needy. He is also given to excuses which increase his wants. Having them in view Extras must be given with caution. At the same time I presume for a few pounds yr Lordship would not wish to be deprived of his information or that he should be allowed to run rusty.

Recording his own presence at Friends meetings would seem to be the spy's way of providing proof he was due some of those *Extra* payments. Having got Watt where he wanted him and possibly where Watt at least half-wanted to be, the Procurator Fiscal suggested how his other justified sinner should now be dealt with. Patrick Moir had been 'very serviceable' but was now redundant. Moir had expressed a desire to pass his *Tryals* and enter the church, but preferably somewhere out of Scotland. The Fiscal explained that Moir's public service efforts had rendered him 'very obnoxious' in Edinburgh, the country in general, and his home town of Perth in particular. Scott's advice to the Lord Advocate was that a post for Patrick Moir, out of Scotland, would now be a good thing as it would 'keep him out of view' and at the same time avoid possibly troublesome ill-feeling over replacement by a man who had been hired, initially, as his acolyte.

In the months following Muir's sentence of outlawry, the authorities in Edinburgh were tormented by letters of alarm arriving with increasing frequency. Robert Watt reported that discussions at Friends of the People meetings now centred on the widespread poverty, disease and starvation in the country; Sinclair's new *Statistical Account of Scotland* having recorded that some parishes were now existing for nine months of the year on little more than potatoes. Provosts of several towns and burghs wrote of the need for increased armed protection. Henry Dundas wrote from London that he wanted more Fencible units raised. The Provosts in West Central Scotland warned that armed Fencibles were a bad idea as they would almost all be unemployed and very disaffected weavers. Robert Dundas responded to all this by writing a request to his uncle for a warship to patrol and protect Scotland's east coast against invasion, then hurried off to London for urgent talks with Westminster's Secret Committee.

Only Procurator Fiscal Scott seemed able to maintain a positive outlook at this time. Robert Watt, responding to the new financial inducements, had become much more active just at the time the second Convention of the Scottish Friends of the People was taking place in Edinburgh, with delegates attending from all over the country, and Watt's reports continued to provide him with consistently accurate intelligence.

Throughout April, May, June and July specific tasks were assigned to Watt, targeting leaders such as Skirving and the Revd Fyshe Palmer for evidence that might lead to effective prosecutions, and in these commissions he was accorded greater and greater latitude. The Procurator Fiscal wrote the Lord Advocate that these exertions, if successful, 'would be considered Extra and rewarded accordingly', stressing that Watt must be allowed to 'take his own way'.

By the end of July, the Fiscal was able to record Watt's success in the case against Fyshe Palmer, but not even Watt's intelligence could find anything of substance concerning Muir's whereabouts. At his trial, Muir claimed that from France he had only two choices of destination, the freeport of Hamburg, or America. This is probably true. In an attempt to deal with the dangers arising from the great internal turmoil, *Comités Revolutionaires* had been set up in every town and village of France, and in ports at a distance from the capital the members of such local committees were unlikely to know anything at all about Muir. As far as such people were concerned, if the passport issued in Paris gave his destination as America, then America was where he must be going – if not to a provincial jail. But even American ships were not totally free of troubles at this time, particularly if it was suspected they may have unloaded supplies in England, and after Muir bought his ticket for New York the local committee embargoed the ship he had booked to sail in. There was nothing he could do but wait, impatiently, for another neutral vessel.

Sailing from Le Havre just after mid-July, bound for Philadelphia, the ship *Hope* would pass Caen, home of Charlotte Corday, who was at that moment in Paris with important information for a Jacobin leader. She also had the large sheath knife she had purchased in the Palais Royal. About the same time Muir left Le Havre, the Jacobin leader Jean-Paul Marat finally agreed to see Charlotte Corday and, as history records, she pushed the knife into his chest. *Killed one man to save a thousand!* And that great sacrificing and self-sacrificing intention quickened the internal strife in France, fuelled the wars that thundered on every border and had no good effect at all for any still travelling the world in search of the dawn of that New Millennium.

CHAPTER 3
Another Auld Alliance

Though Ireland and Scotland did have much shared language and history, and as result a great many shared attitudes, there had arisen one major difference between them. The sectarian divide in Ireland, caused when Plantation Protestants had been used to drive Catholics from their own lands, had proved such an obstacle to radical unity that Friends of the People societies could have little meaning there.

By 1790, with universal emancipation in the air, formation of the United Irishmen movement had become just possible. Free Market Forces had played a part. The 100 year leases of many plantation Protestants having recently ended, the land was rented over their heads at prices they could not afford, thus driving them further into common cause with Catholics. One of the Belfast radicals, James Hope, put the United mood of the time into his song.

> *Och, Paddies, me hearties, have done wid your Parties,*
> *Let min of all creeds and professions agree,*
> *If Orange and Green, min, no longer were seen, min,*
> *Ahh, naboclis, how aisy ould Ireland we'd free!*

But vitally important as songs may be in any people's political struggles, politicians tend to be more influenced by vested interests and for once it was the Lord Advocate's least justified sinner who provided just what was needed by way of supportive facts. In almost his last communication, Patrick Moir included an extract from a letter that had just been received from Portaferry, near Belfast, by one of Edinburgh's Canongate reformers.

> I can give you no particulars of these meetings, only that Ulster is united in the Cause of Catholic Emancipation and Parliamentary reform. In a few days I shall take care to send you the Belfast papers, in which you will see our Provincial Resolutions & a sketch of the debates at Dungannon.
> You may judge of the respectability of the meeting when I tell you that nearly £40,000 per annum landed property was personally represented there from this County alone. Every inch of Ground was disputed in the Committee, and several places in public, with a warmth and force to which I never

experienced anything equal, yet in the end every Resolution was carried with perfect unanimity.

If Westminster had apprehension over joint Catholic-Protestant action for self-government in Ireland, the thought of Scotland and Ireland then effectively joining forces raised very much greater fears.

It has often been stated that Thomas Muir's actions at this time caused former colleagues to distance themselves, and it is true that after the sentence of outlawry his name had been struck from the Roll of the Faculty of Advocates, Dean Henry Erskine having raised the matter himself. But such professional colleagues were indulging in no more than a shitten-faced sidestep to the old tune – *Please, m'Lord, it Wisnae Me!* Though it remains difficult to assess its strength with any accuracy, official correspondence makes clear that elsewhere in the capital, as in growing industrial Scotland and in the armed forces, support for radical reform was very far from diminishing. As in all such situations, the underdogs would have their own network of informants working within the establishment, in many cases inside officials' homes, history's great problem being that records of such activities are not usually folio-bound for benefit of future researchers.

Official records alone, however, suggest the radicals in Ireland and Scotland – impelled by history as much as contemporary politics – were now presenting the potential for rapid growth towards majority popular power in both countries; and following initiation of cross-North Channel co-operation the previous year, Muir was now seen as the Scot most likely to further that greatly feared political development. It was for that reason he was targetted with such singularly vindictive focus.

It was not unusual for a ship leaving a French channel port, bound for America, to call in at one of the Irish ports before continuing across the Atlantic and this is probably what Muir had in mind from the outset. Despite, perhaps because of the state of war between France and Britain, it is unlikely Muir's departure from Le Havre and his destination would remain long unknown, and it is possible the information would have reached Westminster before *Hope* docked at Belfast on 17th July. In any case, informants in the Irish port would have been able to get word across from Donaghadee to Portpatrick that same day and on to Edinburgh in another two days at most. The network of Excise Offices round the coast was a fairly reliable instrument of government at the time and during this disturbed period they had long been on alert for Scots-Irish radical activity.

The first Society of United Irishmen had been formed in Belfast in the autumn of 1791 and before that year was out the second was started in Dublin. Other areas responded and a dozen and more new groups were formed in the following year, their declared aim being to provide a forum for debate and action on Parliamentary Reform, with means for the rapid exchange of information throughout the country. In this aim they were similar to the Friends organisations developed in England and Scotland.

Muir already had a number of contacts in Belfast, some of which were possibly of long standing. Samuel Neilson, son of a local Presbyterian minister and said by some to be the father of the United Irish movement, was one and Dr William Drennan another. Drennan had studied medicine at Glasgow and Edinburgh Universities and was popular in his profession of *accoucheur* to Belfast society ladies, though now gaining a new popularity in his role as pamphleteer and spokesman for reformers. After renewing such contacts, Muir posted on to Dublin for week-long discussions with leading United Irishmen there, men such as John P Curran and Hamilton Rowan. Given what he had learnt in Paris from their mutual friend Paine, it seems certain Muir would also have been very keen to meet Edward Fitzgerald, though Fitzgerald, judging their resolutions too wishy-washy, was not then a member of the United Irishmen. Wolfe Tone, who had helped draw up their constitution, was not then a member either and some suggest his reasons were quite the opposite of Citizen Eddie's. It is not known if Muir and Tone had met by this time, but the bitter animosity that later developed between them might have its origins in this period. Tone, with rather gentrified tendencies, is said not to have had much sympathy with the Irish *Gaidhealtachd*, while men like Edward Fitzgerald and the Ulster-Scots acknowledged that emancipation and political education of this majority population was essential.

There has been a deal of speculation concerning the motivation behind Muir's actions over this period of Spring and early Summer 1793, the conclusions usually being critical.

He was unwise not to continue to America.
It was folly to make any contact at all with the United Irishmen.
The outlawry sentence was still in force against him!
He must have been utterly naïve not to realise that the moment he
set foot in Scotland again he would be recognised and imprisoned.

As a lawyer, Muir fully understood what a sentence of outlawry entailed, and would be aware his movements must be spied upon from the hour *Hope* arrived in Belfast Lough. Any speculation on reasons for his decisions at that time must also speculate on many factors that, if they are recorded at all, are likely to be found only between the lines; even of songs.

> Fareweel to a' our Scottish fame,
> Fareweel our ancient glory;
> Fareweel even to the Scottish name,
> Sae fam'd in martial story!
> Now Sark rins o'er the Solway sands,
> And Tweed rins to the ocean,
> To mark where England's province stands
> Such a parcel of rogues in a nation.

Written by Robert Burns in 1792 from an older work dating from the 1707 Union of Parliaments, it seems likely this reworking was at very least informed by current efforts being made to turn Scotland, politically and linguistically, into North Britain.

> What force or guile could not subdue,
> Thro' many warlike ages,
> Is wrought now by a coward few,
> For hireling traitors' wages.
> The English steel we could disdain,
> Secure in valour's station;
> But English gold has been our bane –
> Such a parcel of rogues in a nation!

It can not be coincidental that Scots radicals were now using the phrase 'a handful of rogues' to identify the unelected minority in the country who continued to derive ever greater personal benefits from piecemeal sale of the nation's heritage. This, and the related situation in Ireland, marks the fundamental difference between these two countries and England. No matter how long it took to regain Westminster from despotic control, the English people would remain English; they could endure a lengthy *status quo* and, having ridden out the storm, expect to emerge if anything a stronger nation from the experience.

Many in Ireland and Scotland were now viewing that same situation quite differently, decades of bitter experience having shaped the conviction that to acquiesce in the Westminster *status quo* was to acquiesce in an accelerated erosion of civil liberties, languages and cultural development – in effect, a complete surrender of nationhood. In these circumstances, having been cut off from uncensored news of events at home for six months, it seems most likely Muir was using his time in Ireland to re-assess the political moment for himself.

On return to Scotland, he carried a letter from Hamilton Rowan to Col Macleod, in which the Irish leader wrote of increasing political repressions leaving them only one of two alternatives – 'unconditional surrender, or defiance' – the letter also expressing hope that 'ceremonial may be thrown aside and a frank and ingenious correspondence take place between the Friends of the People in our Nations'.[1]

From a letter written by Muir's father to the master of *Hope*, at Belfast, it is clear he believed Muir to be in Philadelphia, apparently not knowing of the embargo placed on that first ship. Muir senior had forwarded 'letters to General Washington; and there are many letters wrote for him to the first people of America'. Muir received this letter when he rejoined the ship at Belfast on 30th July, and so knew beyond doubt he had one very safe option for his own personal future across the Atlantic. That he chose instead to cross the North Channel and land at Portpatrick indicates his acceptance of the United Irish analysis.

There are varying accounts about what happened next, the only certainty being that a report from Stranraer informed Edinburgh that Muir was now detained in the town jail. The riders despatched by Mr Ross, the magistrate, must have had several changes of worn-out mounts for the news to have reached the Lord Advocate on 2nd August, the day he wrote of it to his uncle in London.

> I have little doubt, though he avow his intention of coming home to have been with a view to stand trial, that he is an emissary from France or the disaffected in Ireland.

It is possible Muir did not intend to surrender himself on arrival, planning rather to stay quietly with friends till ready to make his own dramatic and rather triumphant reappearance in the capital. So perhaps it was just one of those bizarre coincidences that the first man he met on stepping ashore was an ex-Edinburgh lawyer's clerk, now apparently with the Excise service in Solway and able to recognise him instantly. One nineteenth century account [MacKenzie] claims that Muir wrote from Dublin requesting his agent in Edinburgh to apprise the Crown lawyers that he had arrived there and would appear in Edinburgh in a few days to wipe out the sentence of outlawry. On receipt of this information, it is said, the Lord Advocate employed spies at Portpatrick and elsewhere on that coast ready to seize Muir the instant he landed.

1. McFarland p94

If such a letter was sent from Dublin to Edinburgh, it would explain the open manner of his arrival at Portpatrick and his recorded indignation over arrest, but it would leave him open to accusations of naïvety – he already had ample evidence that honour was not the strongest suit of the Dundas regime. However events came about as they did, Muir was detained at Stranraer till 4th August when the King's Messenger, George Williamson, arrived to convey him to Edinburgh. This was the same man who had arrested him at Holytown, at the beginning of the year, but this time the circumstances were different and Williamson had his orders. He was dealing with an outlaw. There is no record of Robert Dundas expressing regret at seeing his brother advocate return to the capital in manacles and leg-irons.

Hey, tuttie taitie

There is a tradition, which I have met with in many places in Scotland, that it was Robert the Bruce's March at the Battle of Bannockburn. This thought, in my yesternight's evening walk, warmed me to a pitch of enthusiasm on the theme of Liberty and Independence which I threw into a kind of Scots Ode, fitted to the air, that one might suppose to be the gallant ROYAL SCOT'S address to his heroic followers on that eventful morning . . . associated with the glowing ideas of some other struggles of the same nature, not quite so ancient.

So Burns wrote to George Thomson, enclosing his new anthem.

Scots, wha hae wi Wallace bled,
Scots, wham Bruce has aften led,
Welcome to your gory bed, –
Or to victorie.
Now's the day, and now's the hour;
See the front o battle lour;
See approach proud EDWARD's power,
Chains and Slaverie.

It seems the basic form was thought out and a first draft put together when the poet and his fellow Dumfries radical, John Syme, made a journey to New Galloway and along the Solway coast. Their tour began on 27th July. Can it simply be coincidence that Robert Burns had taken a week's leave from his work as a Government Excise Officer to tour this area at exactly the same time Muir was in Ireland and expected to make a landing on that coast? The Excise service, an arm of government, had been alerted to look out for Muir landing in that area and that Burns was ignorant of this is scarcely credible. The possibility that these two Ayrshire radicals had ventured out on something more than a simple summer break might repay further investigation. It is known that for three days the pair were guests at Kenmure Castle, the original seat of the Lords of Galloway and little over thirty miles from Stranraer. Their host, John Gordon, would have been 14th Viscount Kenmure but for the attainder that deprived his family of lands and title after their support of the Jacobite Rebellion, Gordon's grandfather being executed at the Tower of London. Exploring the relics, portraits and secret passages of the castle, long a stronghold of the Stuart royal family, would be like walking back through five hundred years and more of Scottish history.

On the day Muir was arrested at Portpatrick, Burns and Syme were only some thirty miles away on the coast at Gatehouse; and the next day they were closer even than that as guests of the Earl of Selkirk, father of Muir's colleague, Lord Daer. The Earl's Isle of Whithorn estate had itself ancient connections going back to the very beginnings of the Scottish nation, and before a week of such renewals was over the new song was forming in the poet's head. On return to Dumfries and news of Muir's arrest and conveyence to Edinburgh, it seems the poet had his latest allegorical work well enough completed to provide copies for friends.[2]

> *Wha will be a traitor knave?*
> *Wha can fill a coward's grave?*
> *Wha sae base as be a slave?*
> *Let him turn and flee!'*
> *Wha for Scotland's King and Law,*
> *Freedom's sword will strongly draw,*
> *FREE-MAN stand, or FREE-MAN fa'*
> *Let him follow me!*

The Lord Advocate was in a difficult position. The People had writers able to provide rousing material for which they refused to accept payment, while he had to fund the establishment of loyalist newspapers and pay recompense to some university professors for anti-radical propaganda that was proving rather ineffective. With his great powers constrained by Law, at least in public, the Lord Advocate had no alternative but to make full use of the opportunity now presenting itself; the Law, with all its constraints, would be used to reveal Muir's true character. After leaving his prisoner to stew in the

2. Gilfillan *The National Burns*

fetid conditions of Edinburgh's Tolbooth overnight, the Lord Advocate confronted the morning's posse of Muir supporters. There was no possibility of bail. Indeed, bail could not even be discussed. Certainly not. Not while the sentence of outlawry and fugitation remained in force.

But what if that sentence of outlawry were to be reviewed? And found to be unjust?

Ahhhh, that would make a difference!

Sufficient of a one that the Lord Advocate's Office would then agree to bail?

Why, certainly. All according to law!

May we now then apply to have Mister Muir's sentence of outlawry reviewed?

Why certainly. All according to Law!

May we then have it reviewed this afternoon?

Ahhhh. There's the rub. All according to Law.

Friday, then?

Friday it shall be. You have our word on it.

All according to Law.

But *Authority* was dealing with a dangerous criminal, associate of such desperadoes as might even within the capital city of Scotland attempt to enforce a release, so Muir was once more in chains that Friday as he was taken to Court from the Tolbooth; and since most things can be improved upon with a little practice, for this venture into the public eye the prisoner was surrounded by an escort of troops, bristling all with fixèd bayonets.

May we now apply to have the sentence of outlawry reviewed?

Why certainly! All according to Law!

But, like the millstones of God, the molars of Law can grind both long and sure. Long, particularly, when teeth are also being sucked.

One must have misgivings. Mister Muir went to France when his trial was pending.

Mister Muir had no way to foresee that the outbreak of war would impede his return!

Perhaps not, but we did re-schedule the date to allow him additional time.

An insufficient postponement.

We have only Mister Muir's word for that!

Mister Muir, Sir, has returned of his own free will!

We have only Mister Muir's word for that!

Will the sentence of outlawry be removed?

We must continue to have misgivings.

But prevarication had served its purpose. The Lord Advocate now chose his moment to be decisive, and his words to provide editors with their copy.

Mister Muir's motives in leaving his country at such a critical period are best known to himself. That said, if Mister Muir should ultimately meet the full severity of justice, after trial by jury, he shall not have occasion to complain that unfair advantage has been taken of him.

The sentence of outlawry and fugitation is hereby reversed. It is, gentlemen.

The dapper little Lord Advocate beamed good-naturedly a time over this scene of happy congratulations, then with a gesture checked the Turnkey who was about to unlock Muir's manacles. Turning to the bench he petitioned for a warrant from the Court to re-arrest the accused. Granted immediately. Just as immediately the infuriated defence team insisted their client must at once be admitted to bail. He could not possibly prepare his defence in a crowded jail.

But who will stand surety for such bail as will guarantee Mister Muir does not flee the country again?

Mister Muir's father is willing to pledge everything he owns, wealth, land and property!

Mister Muir's father put up bail in January and still the accused fled from justice!

Then other guarantors will be found.

Unrelated by blood or marriage to the accused?

Certainly.

Bring legal proof of such and the matter will be considered.

It will be done this very afternoon!

Ahhh. There's that rub again.

Saturday morning?

Impossible. And since we are all good Christians, no one can possibly suggest the Sabbath.

Monday, then?

Not Monday either, unfortunately.

Tuesday, then?

Tuesday it shall be. You have our word on it.

Another four times twenty-four hours in the stench of Edinburgh's Tolbooth before reappearance below the Bench on Tuesday, the thirteenth day of August; when bail was granted, with a smirk, in the sum of two-thousand merks Scots.

All according to Law.

> *By Oppression's woes and pains!*
> *By your sons in servile chains!*
> *We will drain our dearest veins,*
> *But they shall be free!*
> *Lay the proud Usurpers low!*
> *Tyrants fall in every foe!*
> *LIBERTY's in every blow!*
> *Let us Do – or Die!!!*

At the close of the first Friends of the People Convention, held in December the previous year, the delegates had stood to take the oath *Live Free – or Die!* In the last days of August, 1793, Burns sealed the final draft of his anthem and despatched it to his publisher in Edinburgh. It had been decreed that Muir's trial would commence on the thirtieth day of that month.

Lord Advocate Robert Dundas prosecuting counsel in the Muir trial.
Robert was the brother of Home Secretary Henry Dundas – hence the
term, the Dundas Duo

CHAPTER 4

Trial

There was but one topic and interest. Muir and the trial.
All had gone to witness it.

On that morning of Friday, 30th August, 1793, interest was not confined to the citizens of Edinburgh. For days, delegates of the Friends societies had been arriving in the capital by every possible means of transport; some from Paisley, Glasgow and Kirkintilloch in the west using the new Union Canal; others by trading-boat from the east coast of Fife and Forfar; from lowland villages such as Stewarton and Strathaven they came on foot, or horseback, and there were even a few wealthier gentlemen who had arrived from England by coach.

The trial was of such wide importance because many believed events about to unfold were directly related to imminent changes in how Great Britain and Ireland might in future be governed. Through its writers and philosophers, Scotland had already made its contribution to the theory of such development and now a growing body of the nation's increasingly organised and educated artisan class was enthusiastically supporting the drive to turn theory into practice. On Friday, promise of warm, early-autumn weather had seen this crowd begin to assemble in the High Street round the ancient Heart of Midlothian from shortly after dawn, and in such numbers that late-comers arriving breathless up the Canongate or out the West Bow found it impossible to get anywhere near the most recent news or rumour. The barefoot bairns who had emerged from the dark closes of the Royal Mile to scamper the fringes of this unprecedented excitement then turned it to advantage, finding themselves profitably commissioned for the remainder of the day as nimble messengers.

When the doors to Old Parliament House finally did open, those assembled outside surged forward through the Great Hall, hoping to gain a place for themselves in the surprisingly small and gloomy Courtroom just off the Hall's south-east corner. The ante-room at the back of the Court's gallery was reserved for use by the prosecutors and it was from here, after the last stroke of ten from the steeple of St Giles died away, that they emerged. First the black-clad functionaries filed to their places, then the five Law Lords – Abercromby, Dunsinnan, Henderland, Swinton, with Braxfield presiding – assumed their crimson and ermine-tipped prominence on the gallery that was to overlook and dominate the day's proceedings.

But almost immediately the structured solemnity of the occasion appeared to be threatened; Muir was not in court, and his failure to appear at the Bar after his name was called caused immediate confusion and much excited speculation. Whether due to unavoidable circumstance, last minute wrangling over conduct of the defence, or the desire to enhance his entrance is not known, but he did not appear until quite a number of increasingly conjecture-filled minutes had elapsed. He had certainly taken some special care over his appearance. Instead of the more common blue or brown, he wore a suit of dark green velvet, cambric lace trimmed, his auburn hair drawn back with a ribbon at the nape of the neck in the French fashion that had become the uniform of Reformers. It is said the five judges maintained a stony-faced hostility when he recognised the Bench with the customary formal bow, and the attempt at apology for being late was brushed aside by Braxfield with the instruction he should give attention to the indictment about to be read out.

> Whereas it is humbly meant and complained to us by our right trusty Robert Dundas, esquire, of Arniston, our advocate for our interest, upon Thomas Muir, younger of Huntershill.
>
> That by the laws of this and every other well-governed realm, the wickedly and feloniously exciting, by means of seditious speeches and harangues, a spirit of disloyalty and disaffection to the King and the established goverment; more especially, when such speeches and harangues are addressed to meetings or convocations of persons, brought together by no lawful authority, and uttered by one who is the chief instrument of calling together such meetings.

There followed a great lengthy bluster, very little of which was to prove of any value whatsoever to the prosecution, but it was best the Lord Advocate had been able to cobble together.

> . . . as also, the wickedly and feloniously advising and exhorting persons to purchase and peruse seditious and wicked publications and writings, calculated to produce a spirit of disloyalty and disaffection to the King and government. . .

A few present would be horrified at such a catalogue of crimes, but it is probable most would be appalled they should be considered crimes at all.

... as also, the wickedly and feloniously distributing or
circulating any seditious writing or publication, of the
tendency aforesaid ...

... as also, the wickedly and feloniously producing and
reading aloud, in a public meeting or convocation of persons,
a seditious and inflammatory writing, tending to produce in
the minds of the people a spirit of insurrection and of
opposition to the established government ...

Yet true it is, and of verity, that the said Thomas Muir is guilty,
actor, art and part, of all and each, or one or other, of the said
crimes, aggravated, as aforesaid.[1]

The Lord Advocate's indictment then went on to provide a long
list of Muir's activities throughout September, October, November and
December of the previous year, in which he was charged with not only
addressing Reform meetings but actually being the 'chief instrument'
in calling such meetings together. The alleged offences took place at
Glasgow, Kirkintilloch, Lennoxtown, Campsie or 'at some other place
to the prosecutor unknown'. Sedition was indeed a one-size-fits-all
charge.

The two men who had shadowed Muir's activities in the west of
the country were William Honyman, Sheriff of Lanarkshire, and James
Lapslie, the Campsie parish minister, and the presence of both in that
small Courtroom must have been cause of some strong feelings as
the charges resulting from their known activities were read out. In
one sense, Honyman had only been carrying out official duties but
his zeal in pursuing Muir would not be unconnected to the desire to
please his father-in-law, Lord Braxfield.

There was another personal factor that might have fuelled the
Sheriff's open animosity. Two years earlier, Muir had acted for the
defence of a youth, George Davidson, a junior clerk in the Sheriff's
Glasgow office. Davidson was charged with forging Honyman's
signature on two monetary documents which netted him the sums
of £10 16s., and £68 15s., respectively, for which offence he was
sentenced to be hanged. As Davidson lay in the Tolbooth he was
allowed daily visits from a friend for the purpose of 'exhorting him to
prayer' but almost on the eve of execution the visitor discarded the
bible for a brace of pistols. Davidson and his accomplice escaped and
made their way to America, leaving behind nothing but an unexplain-
ed failure of security. It was widely believed at the time that George

1. *State Trials*

Davidson was a natural son of Sheriff Honyman.[2] In a small country, it is possible to make mortal enemies not by what you do, but by simply having knowledge of what the other party has done.

The behaviour of the Campsie parish minister is difficult to explain other than in terms of overwhelming greed and ambition. Born on a small farm in that parish, Lapslie studied for the ministry at Glasgow University before touring the continent as tutor to a titled family. While a student, his step-mother was not at all sanguine he was the right material for religion, letting it be known as her opinion that 'the craws will never drite on oor Jamack's kirk' – a phrase that went into local history to describe any utterly doomed venture. In a sense, the stepmother proved correct. The congregation objected when the Crown appointed Lapslie as parish minister at Campsie. In the spirit of the times, they were told they would accept the official choice and like it. Good democrats that they were, they did neither. They deserted en masse, elders and all, thereafter labouring to build, by their own hands, an alternative place of worship. It was a very simple structure they completed, with an earthen-floor and backless wooden forms for pews, but the first minister to address them in their new House of God was a man of their own choosing.[3]

* * *

Of more worth is one honest man to society, and in the sight of God, than all the crowned ruffians that ever lived.

Tom Paine's *Rights of Man* might now be banned, to circulate copies might be judged seditious, even to praise the work publicly could result in imprisonment but here were some of Paine's most seditious thoughts resounding from the most public platform in the land – and not even Robert Dundas could raise a prosecution against publication of an official indictment.

What are the present governments in Europe but a scene of iniquity and oppression? What is that of England? Do not its own inhabitants say it is a market where every man has a price, and where corruption is common traffic, at the expense of a deluded people? No wonder then that the French Revolution is traduced.

2. MacKenzie *Old Reminiscences of Glasgow*

3. Cameron *Parish of Campsie*

Though interjections are absent from the official record, it is known that the crowd jammed into that small courtroom and the vast Hall beyond were not there to witness proceedings in silence. When the Clerk quoted from *The Patriot*, one of the publications Muir was accused of distributing, doubtless the glowering Law Lords would have been more than a little put out at enthusiastic but anonymous foot-stamping.

> Rouse, then, ye Britons! Awake from the slumbering state of apathy in which you have so long suffered yourselves ingloriously to remain! Open your eyes to the injuries which have been heaped upon you; and assert your rights to have them redressed!

After a lot more similar quotation, the Clerk came closer to home when he read from a declaration Muir had received from reformers in Paisley, a resumé of how they saw the existing situation under George III.

> A government where the executive and legislative power meet in a single person, has no more pretence to freedom; it is perfect despotism; and the people who submit to it are in a state of slavery. . . . If those men who are said to represent us are only registers of the Royal edicts, the government is degenerated into an absolute monarchy.

Without a doubt, Muir's greatest pleasure would have been the recital of *The Address from the Society of United Irishmen in Dublin to the Delegates for promoting a Reform in Scotland*, the paper which had come close to making the charge against him one of High Treason. In the face of some opposition, he had taken upon himself 'the whole responsibility and the whole danger of the measure' of reading it out to the 1792 General Convention of the Friends, in James's Court, Edinburgh, and now its rallying cry could be heard ringing through the nation's Old Parliament Hall.

> We greatly rejoice that the spirit of freedom moves over the face of Scotland; that light seems to break from the chaos of her internal government; and that a country so respectable for her attainments in science, in arts, and in arms; for men of literary eminence; for the intelligence and morality of her people, now acts from a conviction of the union between virtue, letters, and liberty; and now rises to distinction, not by a calm, contented and secret wish for a reform in Parliament, but by openly, actively, and urgently willing it, with the unity and energy of an embodied nation. We rejoice that you do not

consider yourselves as merged and melted down into another country, but that in this great national question you are still – Scotland – the land where Buchanan wrote, and Fletcher spoke, and Wallace fought.

That Irish echo of poet Burns's newly-composed anthem must surely have raised a self-congratulatory cheer in the small, gloomy courtroom as the spirit of Scots settlers in Ireland, prior to the enforced plantations, now manifested itself.

Universal Emancipation, with Representative Legislation, is the polar principle which guides our society, and shall guide it, through all the tumult of factions and fluctuations of parties.

It is a pity development of the camera was still some fifty-years in the future. Braxfield's reaction to the concluding confrontation with his own great prejudices would now be a historical document in itself.

We do not worship the British, far less the Irish Constitution, as sent down from heaven, but we consider it as human workmanship, which man has made, and man can mend. An unalterable Constitution, whatever be its nature, must be despotism. It is not the Constitution, but the People which ought to be inviolable, and it is time to recognise and renovate the rights of the English, the Scotch, and the Irish nations.

Words that are sufficient answer to those who still insist that early radicalism predates the concept of nationalism.

Let us unite for all, or each man suffer for all. In each country let the people assemble in peaceful and Constitutional Convention. Let delegates from each country digest a plan of reform best adapted to the situation and circumstances of their respective nations, and let the legislature be petitioned at once by the urgent and unanimous voice of Scotland, England, and Ireland.

Such was the visionary song from kinsmen in Ireland that was increasingly to drive and direct Muir's every future decision.

An initial list of 135 potential jurymen, carefully selected by the three Sheriffs of the Lothians, was sifted down to the 45 names required to be present in Court. From this select band the presiding judge picked the necessary fifteen men 'of proper principles' to serve. By such means, any desired verdict could be assured in advance, the only challenge possible against a juryman being on the grounds of convicted infamy, special malice, insanity, deafness, dumbness and minority. Muir's objections, though politely phrased, were on the grounds of special malice.

> *My Lords, I demand Justice. Let me be tried fairly, not by a Jury of the Association of Goldsmiths' Hall, not by a Jury of the Association of the Friends of the People, but by men unconnected with either, and whose minds are not warped with prejudices.*

Only one of the chosen fifteen, Captain John Inglis of the King's navy, thought it unfair such a case should be tried by servants of the Crown. 'My mind feels scrupulous and I labour under much anxiety'. Braxfield instructed Inglis to serve. Perhaps Captain Inglis was now being made to suffer for his protest at the continuing description of the kingdom as England. If so, it would be a safe indulgence; a guilty verdict required no more than a majority of one, and by the choice of the other fourteen jurymen the verdict was already declared.

THE FINAL JURY:

Gilbert Innes of Stow. Foreman of Jury.

Sir James Foulis of Collington.

Captain John Inglis of Auchindinny.

John Wauchope of Edmonstone

Andrew Wauchope of Niddrie-Marishal

John Trotter of Morton Hall

James Rocheid of Inverleith

John Alves of Dalkeith, portioner

William Dalrymple, merchant, Edinburgh

Donald Smith, banker, Edinburgh

James Dickson, bookseller, Edinburgh

George Kinnear, banker, Edinburgh

Andrew Forbes, merchant, Edinburgh

John Horner, merchant, Edinburgh

John Balfour, younger, of Pilrig. Clerk to Jury.

With possibly one exception, all were members of the Goldsmiths' Hall Association, which the previous year had offered 5 guineas reward for evidence against anyone who had sold or distributed gratis Paine's

Rights of Man, or any other person who had 'circulated among the working people of Scotland copies of that libel on the Constitution'. Just before they were sworn-in, Muir made one final appeal against the injustice of such obvious prejudication.

> *Gentlemen, I believe you all to be men of truth and integrity, but I must call your attention to the peculiarity of your situation. You have already determined my fate. As you value your own reputation and eternal peace, I entreat . . .*

Braxfield had cut short the appeal; the bench was unanimous the objection had already been repelled and it was judged 'very improper' for Muir to take up their time in this way. The Courtroom was then left in no doubt as to the severity of sentence to be expected. If the charges were proven, said Lord Henderland, he was in favour of 'everything short of capital punishment'. Lord Swinton thought it all amounted to Treason and so, if proven, must 'infer the highest punishment the law can inflict'. Lords Dunsinnan and Abercromby felt they had no option but to 'coincide' with the latter opinion.

In accordance with Law, the substance of the defence had been conveyed to the Prosecutor the evening before the Trial, and after the indictment Braxfield warned Muir this was his last opportunity to add anything to that defence, as he would henceforth be precluded from adding anything extraneous. Muir replied by referring only to what had previously been submitted in writing.

> *The truth of every word in that defence I shall strongly prove before I leave this bar. I admit that I exerted every effort to procure a more equal representation of the people in the House of Commons. If that be a crime, I plead guilty to the charge. I acknowledge that I considered the cause of Parliamentary reform to be essential to the salvation of my country; but I deny that I ever advised the people to attempt to accomplish that great object by any means which the Constitution did not sanction.*

Fifty-five potential witnesses had been listed for the defence, twenty of whom came from the Glasgow area, seven from Paisley and district, thirteen from the countryside around Kirkintilloch and twelve from Edinburgh. Some could be described as artisans but by far the majority were either merchants or men with their own manufactories. One was David Dale junior, nephew of the mill owner. John Tennant, the brewer, was another. Robert Boak, unfortunately named, was a surgeon. The Revd William Dunn, who had already been in jail for supporting reform, was included. The list ended with four reform leaders – Colonel William Dalrymple; William Skirving, the radical farmer from Fife; Captain William Johnston, who had been jailed for those articles in the *Gazette*; and the Right Honourable Lord Daer, son of the Earl of Selkirk.

The prosecution listed forty witnesses, over half of whom were friends of Muir and some even relations. The James Campbell listed was Muir's own legal agent and a David Blair was probably his rather suspect new brother-in-law. The remainder were largely employees and agents of the Crown, among them Sir James Colquhoun of Luss; William Honyman, the Sheriff-depute of Lanarkshire; Sheriff Pringle; Procurator Fiscal Scott; Henry Davidson, the Sheriff substitute of Edinburgh; George Williamson, the King's Messenger; James Carmichael, who was alleged to have recognised Muir at Portpatrick and William Ross, the magistrate at Stranraer.

In terms of law, the prosecution case was almost non-existent and the Lord Advocate's incompetence all but turned it into a debacle. After the evidence of his first witness proved of more value to the defence than the prosecution, Dundas tried to unsettle the second by ridiculing his behaviour and Scots speech. Robert Weddel, vice-president of the Kirkintilloch branch of the Friends, comes across as a countryman rather out of his depth in Edinburgh's High Court, yet he too had to be abandoned after his testimony proved unhelpful to the prosecution.

Despite these early setbacks, the Lord Advocate was probably quite confident his third witness, the Revd James Lapslie, would be able to pull all the chestnuts out of the fire for him. He could not have been more wrong. When Lapslie was called, Muir was immediately on his feet. 'Let this witness be removed. I have many objections to state against him'. After Lapslie was so removed, Muir explained that his objections were on the grounds of admissability and credibility. It was widely known the minister had used bribery as inducement to gather evidence for the Crown, in addition to which he had presented himself at Court that day as a volunteer witness, not one officially cited. Without revealing details of the charges, Muir intimated that he would shortly bring a criminal prosecution against the man. Braxfield tried to bluster through the objection but the first three witnesses called by Muir fully supported his claims, and when a fourth was called, the Lord Advocate informed the Bench he would give up on James Lapslie.

The next prosecution witness was Henry Freeland, Muir's distant cousin and another of the Kirkintilloch weavers Lapslie had tried to bribe. While Freeland was under pressure to agree that Muir had lent him a copy of *Rights of Man*, a disturbance occurred in the Courtroom; someone had emerged from the crowded spectators and crossed to thrust a scrap of paper into Muir's hands. Consternation and horror – 'Seize that man!' – and the macers wrestled the culprit's nose into the stour. When he was allowed to rise again he told the Bench 'in a manly manner' that his note was simply to let Muir know that, in a similar situation, he would have lent a copy of Paine's book to anyone. The man who had finished up face-down on the courtroom floor was John Wylde, later Professor of Civil Law at Edinburgh University and so vehemently opposed to the French Revolution he was known as The Scottish Burke.

Though he had been denied the Revd Lapslie's direct witness, Lord Advocate Dundas knew he might still benefit from the fruits of some of the reverend gentleman's labours. Anne Fisher, the only woman involved in the trial, had been a kitchen servant for Muir's parents; but while he was still in France she had left that employment and it was now widely believed that during her subsequent stay in the home of a Glasgow city official she had been regularly catechised by Lapslie. Fisher was no better educated than any other young woman of her humble occupation but by all accounts she had a bold and gallous quality about her, and far from being overawed by the High Court pomp she seems to have revelled in all the be-robed male attention. The evidence she provided, detailed and remarkably exact, was indeed helpful to the prosecution case but her memory for the titles of publications she had seen Muir handling was too precise and her knowledge of his extensive library at Huntershill House just too detailed for anyone present to believe it her own. The fact that a scullery maid could name a book she had seen lying open on the table – Volney's *Ruins. A Survey of the Evolution of Empires* – almost certainly owed much to Lapslie's previous visits to Huntershill or just possibly to that suspect brother-in-law who was listed as a prosecution witness but never called. She even remembered Muir reading an extract from Volney – *A Dialogue between the Governors and the Governed* – to his mother and sister.

Civil Governors: The Law enacts that ye be submissive.

People: The law is the general will, a new order.

CG: Ye will be a rebellious people.

People: Nations cannot revolt; tyrants are the only rebels.

CG: The King is with us, and he commands you to submit.

People: The Kingly office originates in the people, who elect one of themselves to execute it for the general good. Kings, therefore, are essentially indivisible from their nations. The King of ours, then, cannot be with you; you only possess his phantom.

Anne Fisher's detailed recollections of Muir's comments to others on such works was, for most in court, just too unhesitatingly glib to be true but when asked if he wished to cross-examine, Muir's reply was 'I disdain to put any questions, m'Lord, to a witness of this description'. Anne Fisher immediately asked the Bench if she could question Muir, but Braxfield refused and briskly rolled the business up by thanking her and putting it on record that he had 'never heard a mair distinct and accurate witness in his life'. The troubled juryman, Captain Inglis, then risked the wrath of the Bench by rising and crossing to ask Anne Fisher if he might question *her*. He wanted to know if, when she left her last employment, there had been any quarrel between her and Mister Muir's family. She said no, quite the contrary. 'Auld Mistress Muir gied me five shillin abune ma wages, and young Miss Muir hanselled me wi a petticoat and some ither claes'. Which reply probably left the scrupulous seadog considerably more troubled.

With the departure of Anne Fisher went the prosecution's last real hope. Dundas had cited fifteen witnesses, but most of those were friends, relatives or supporters of Muir and if the threat of imprisonment made it impossible for them not to appear for the prosecution, it was clear their testimony had not been affected by Lapslie's offers of reward. The next seven to be questioned, like two of the first three, could well have been witnesses for the defence and the Lord Advocate decided to cut his losses by informing the Bench he would not be calling the thirteenth witness. Again Muir rose in protest.

> The testimony of this witness will reveal inaccuracies in the testimony of a previous witness. Justice demands that he be called and that I be allowed to cross-examine.

The witness not called was Alexander Muir, Tom Muir's uncle, and the Lord Advocate sought to make a virtue out of this necessary retreat by explaining to the Bench that humanity would not allow him to force an uncle to give damning evidence against his own nephew. The extent of the prosecution's deviousness was then revealed when Dundas informed the Bench that, in the interests of economising the Court's time, it would not now be necessary to call any further prosecution witnesses at all. Muir was on his feet again, this time stung to anger.

> *The two witnesses remaining on the original citation are*
> *Carmichael and Ross, employees of the government at Stranraer.*
> *The testimony of both these men will refute the charge that I re-*
> *entered this country in a private and clandestine manner!*

Braxfield took no pains to conceal his opinion of such repeated objections, but Muir persisted.

> *M'Lord; the testimony of these men will not only refute the*
> *charge of a clandestine return, but will show that, far from*
> *being arrested like any criminal, I made no secret of my arrival*
> *and announced my name immediately!*
>
> *Objection repelled.*
>
> *But m'Lord! Had the prosecution not already cited these two*
> *men, I would have named them as witnesses for the defence!*
>
> *Objection repelled.*

Braxfield then asked the Lord Advocate if he was firm that no further witness need be cried-up against Muir. Robert Dundas was very firm indeed.

* * *

The man who is his own lawyer has a fool for a client

This is a recurring criticism of Muir, arising from his rejection of offers by others to undertake his defence, but the behaviour of the authorities prior to and during the trial does not support the implication that advocates such as Henry Erskine could have obtained a not guilty verdict, or at worst, a light prison sentence.

The French *Encyclopédistes* had not been wrong when they held Scotland up as proof of Voltaire's dictum that a small state neighbouring a large wealthy one will inevitably become venal. England's smaller and materially less wealthy neighbour, regarded by the French as formidable when independent, had become so venal after Union that some of the best minds in the country were now prepared to run great personal risk in the struggle to reverse the condition. They had no alternative. Just three months earlier, the British Reform petition to Parliament – almost half of which originated in Scotland – was not even given the casual consideration of a committee prior to the House voting, by a majority of 282 votes to 41, for its outright rejection. With the exception of Colonel Macleod, every MP from Scotland had voted rejection, once again pointing-up the bitter joke that the leader of the North British MPs must never be less than six-foot-three-inches tall, in order that his followers could always see his head and know which way they were required to vote. Such a situation confronted Scots reformers with the same stark choice Hamilton Rowan had outlined for those in Ireland – abandon the fight – or raise the stakes.

Further evidence of what they were up against was provided when William Muir was forced to appear as a prosecution witness in Muir's trial. On taking the stand he promised to tell the truth but refused to swear the formal oath. 'Yon gangs coantrar t'ma religious principles' he explained to the Bench. Muir had spoken up for his kinsman, who was 'of the mountain',[4] saying that although this witness was appearing for the prosecution, he was quite prepared to accept his promise to tell the truth and would, in advance, admit every word the witness might choose to utter. The judges would have none of it, the witness would swear the oath or go behind bars. 'Perpetual imprisonment!' Lord Henderland promised. 'I know of no legal device whereby you might ever be released!' The witness, refusing to be cowed, replied that he knew the Lord would be present in a prison cell as everywhere else, and was immediately hauled below to put that belief to the test. Such behaviour was proof where none was now needed that civil liberties in Scotland had been eroded to the point of non-existence.

A trimming defence with a guilty verdict at the end of it is the best that Henry Erskine could have achieved for Muir, and that would have left the cause of Scottish Reform, like Paine's *Rights of Man*, still undefended. The result would have been similar had Muir decided not to return to Scotland from Belfast and had opted instead for self-imposed exile in America.

He either fears his fate too much,
Or his deserts are small,
That puts it not unto the touch,
To win or lose it all.

These lines by the Marquis of Montrose, sentenced in this same Parliament House to be hanged and quartered, would be as much warning as inspiration to Muir and there is no reason to believe he

---

4. A Cameronian. A contemporary note suggests the objection may have been as much political as religious, none of the ruling Authority having sworn the Solemn League and Covenant.

would have chosen to conduct his own defence in that Court if subsequent political developments had been as predictable as many have suggested. English towns such as Sheffield, Birmingham and Manchester were home to vigorous radical movements whose potential to effect change at Westminster would have been greatly strengthened by militant action in Ireland and Scotland. Already there had been outbreaks of serious violence in parts of Ireland and the threat of insurrection caused urgent demands for military barracks to be built in Scotland, the practice of billeting the military on the civilian population being increasingly seen as the cause of them picking up 'dangerous principles'. This was the period when discipline in both navy and army was maintained by utter brutality of officers against men who, if they had not been press-ganged into service, were frequently forced into it by social circumstance. An occurrence on Perth Inch, just a few years before Muir's trial, speaks volumes on the relationship that had developed between officers, men and the general population. A soldier, driven by absolute want, pulled a couple of potato shaws from a field to feed his wife and four children. He was caught, court-martialled and sentenced to five hundred lashes. Despite the wife's pleadings after the first twenty-five lashes were completed, a left-handed drummer was then employed to ensure the next twenty-five would tear the flesh most effectively. The forcible prevention of the wife's attempted intervention was then the signal for the local washerwomen, who:

> . . . with their laps full of stones and backed by the willing multitude, broke through the line, drove the officers from the circle and liberated the prisoners. The soldiers had only their side arms with them, except the guard on the prisoners, and appeared more willing to assist than to resist the people. The moment the prisoner was untied from the halberts a general attack was made upon the officers. The adjutant was less fortunate than some of the others in escaping. He got a terrible mauling from the women; who laid him down on his belly, in which position he was held by some score of vigorous hands, till he got a handsome flogging on the bare posteriors, in the presence of thousands – inflicted with an energy that would remain imprinted on his memory till the day of his death.

This mob, it was pointed out, was not indiscriminate in its fury. When roused shortly afterwards by another act of military brutality, one officer known to be opposed to it was allowed to go about unmolested while the others had to flee for safety.[5]

5. Penny *Traditions of Perth*

In the aftermath of Culloden, the men of the *Gaidhealtachd* were regarded by officers such as General Wolfe as no more than a source of cannon-fodder – 'They are hardy, intrepid, accustomed to a rough country, and no great mischief if they fall' – but forced to serve under a military discipline quite foreign to their ancient traditions, many of these were ready recruits to the new discipline of political democracy. The powerful tool of Empire abroad was increasingly a potential weapon against corruption at home. As recently as fifteen years previously there had been a mutiny in a Highland regiment temporarily in Edinburgh, when six hundred of the men, a piper at their head, marched in good order to the summit of Arthur's Seat, where they posted sentries against all but the citizens of the capital who brought supplies up to them. They would make a stand, they declared 'until their demands were met or the last man was dead'. Their demands were met. A year later, Lord MacDonald's Highlanders [76th Regiment] mutinied at Burntisland, and four years after that, only ten years before Muir's trial, the new regiment formed by the Duke of Athole mutinied at Portsmouth. These *volunteers* of the Duke's 77th regiment insisted they had not been recruited to fight a war in India, refused to embark for one, chased their officers and held the town in their control for a week. They were proved legally correct and the only vengeance open to authority was to march them in small companies back to the Scottish border at Berwick, where they were turned loose and left to find their own way back to reinforce the radical cause in Perthshire.[6]

If political awakening among the ranks could be increased and brought to national focus, there were experienced officers such as Major [Lord] Maitland, Captain Johnston, Colonel Macleod and Lord Sempill ready and well able to give it the kind of leadership that could achieve political change with little or no bloodshed. Despite the growing hysteria among the privileged classes, Scotland was not starting from the same situation as France and was therefore unlikely to need the services of *Madame Guillotine* in the numerous George Squares of the country.

* * *

In opening his defence, Muir confirmed he would be calling twenty-one witnesses in total, and the Lord Advocate rose immediately to seek Braxfield's condemnation of this unnecessary imposition on an already overburdened and over-running Court schedule.

6. Prebble *Mutiny*

M'Lord, the Court knows that I cited twenty-one on my deposition. I am accused of committing the crime of sedition in many places. Kirkintilloch, Miltoun of Campsie, Lennoxtoun, Paisley, Glasgow, Kilmarnock, Edinburgh and, in the Courts own indictment, elsewhere.

Yes, but I cannot see, m'Lord, that justice is in any way served by us hearing the same thing repeated twenty-times over!

I hope they will say the same thing, m'Lord; for I believe their testimony will prove that I nowhere preached sedition.

Cry-in your witnesses, sir, Braxfield growled. *But dinna think t'delay this Coort's decision.*

It would be late-afternoon by now and a long-threatened thunderstorm still had not broken. In the gloomy and oppressive atmosphere of the small courtroom off the Great Hall, the clammy heat must have greatly irritated grizzled scalps under heavy legal wigs as witness after witness told exactly the same story.

Mister Muir had, everywhere and elsewhere, cautioned against violence.
Always he had warned of the dangers in certain writings
that were circulating.
Indeed, he had advised that both sides of every argument
must be thoroughly examined.
Knowledge!
That was what Mister Muir had continually stressed to them.
Knowledge!
That was the key he said could safely open the door to Reform.

Many of those appearing for Muir's defence were professional men and not at all intimidated by the occasion. One such was John Russell, a manufacturer with his own business, known in his native Glasgow as *Sturdy* Russell.

It is quite singular, is it not Mister Russell, that the testimony you have just given differs only in degree from that of all the other defence witnesses who have preceded you? Did any person instruct you what to say?

No one. Except t'tell the truth.

Who instructed you in that way?

Ohh, the instruction t'speak the truth is sae general, Ah cannae remember at the moment the particular person concerned.

The Lord Advocate immediately moved that this witness be committed to prison for prevarication under oath. Muir protested that

Russell was guilty of quite the opposite of prevarication.

Ye hae nae business t'interfere for a witness! Sit doon!

When Muir resumed his seat, Braxfield beckoned the Macers, who gripped the collar of this 'middling class' Glasgow man and shoved him on his way to three weeks stay in the Tolbooth. That proved about the only success, if success it was given the Court-room reaction, that Braxfield and Dundas managed to achieve in the course of a long afternoon and early-evening session. Attempts to belittle and ridicule later defence witnesses proved so obvious and so wide of the mark they consistently backfired on the prosecution, but there were twenty-one such witnesses to be introduced, questioned, and sometimes cross-questioned, leaving tempers frayed on all sides. When it came, Muir must have been as ready as any for the evening break.

The thunderstorm that finally did erupt over the Capital sent rivers of water brawling down the narrow wynds on either side of the Royal Mile, but though this and the setting sun helped disperse the clinging heat of the Courtroom, it in no way guaranteed a cooling of tempers. When the Court reconvened the main participants would have dined well-enough to sustain them right to the end and it is certain that by now a considerable quantity of wine had been consumed by most, if not all, involved. This was an era of heavy drinking, when some lawyers were said to 'quaff three bottles of claret in the course of one sederunt, and look nothing perplexed'.

Sometimes they *were* perplexed, as on one occasion the hard-headed Braxfield sent two such packing. 'Ye may just pack up yir papers and gang hame. The tane o ye's riftin punch and t'ither belchin claret and there'll be nae guid got oot o ye the day'.[7] It was in this atmosphere, well past eight-o'-clock in the evening, that the Lord Advocate emerged into the light of the many candelabra to present his summing-up for the prosecution.

Gentlemen of the Jury! This is the moment which I have long, and anxiously, looked for, and I now require your most serious consideration of what has passed. The pannel at the bar is a man that has been sowing the seeds of discontent and sedition under the pretext of Reform. He has appeared here before you after having been fugitated in this country. By your verdict, from which there is no appeal, by your verdict, his guilt must either be fixèd, . . . or extinguished.

7. Cuthbertson *Quaint Scots*

I declare that in the range of my official capacity, if there has been any one whose actions particularly pointed him out for prosecution, whose conduct appeared the most criminal, who has betrayed the greatest appearance of guilt, Gentlemen, this is that man!

We all know the pernicious effects of the many instances of seditious writings and practices which have lately appeared in this country. All those persons who have had the courage to come and stand trial at this bar have met with the same fate. They have all been found guilty. I trust, that as the evidence has clearly unfolded the diabolical and mischievous conduct of this person, that he will receive a similar verdict. I could not have conceived that a man who has received a liberal education, who has practised as an advocate at this bar, should be found, on any occasion, among ignorant villagers and low manufacturers, purposely to sow sedition among them.

Politics aside, there seems a virulent personal vendetta behind the Lord Advocate's attitude to Muir and it is difficult not to see this as having its roots in their different family backgrounds and greatly differing professional abilities. Scion of a family long used to serving power, son of one Lord President of the Court of Session and grandson of another, Robert Dundas is likely to have believed from childhood in his own inherited right to highest honours and position. In fact, he was a small man in every sense of the word and even his apologists acknowledge that his professional talents were at best mediocre. It probably rankled severely that a young man of Muir's lowly origins had personal and professional qualities that, in public, made his own appear even more impoverished.

Gentlemen, we all remember the transactions of last winter, when sedition raised its hydra head. There, in that Convention, I shall call it by no other name, there he, and he almost alone, was found the supporter and defender of a paper penned by some infamous wretches who have, like himself, fled from the punishment that awaited them. That paper came from a society styling themselves United Irishmen! Even in such a Convention the paper was considered dangerous! Yet this person was the ringleader who advised, who insisted, the paper be welcomed. He, and he alone, said it should be received and answered!

This time the Lord Advocate's information was at least partially accurate. In their reports on that first Friends Convention in Edinburgh, the spies made clear that Muir had indeed played a leading part among more than one-hundred-and-fifty delegates, but they also reported that when there were some objections to his reading the

Address from the United Irishmen there was majority demand the meeting be allowed to hear these fraternal greetings from Dublin.

> *Gentlemen, in one thing only do I agree with the person at the bar. This trial is of consequence to posterity. Yes; I grant that it is; but whether in the sense it strikes him, you are this day to judge.*

The Lord Advocate then went on to direct the Jury's attention to the examples of circulating Seditious writings.

> *The witness Freeland is again an evidence here. I must observe to you that it appears extremely doubtful whether he told all that he knew. You might have seen by his face that he prevaricated. When closely questioned the sweat broke upon him. He says he got Paine's book out of the accused's overcoat pocket. This is a mode of circulating a book which a man of his disposition would very naturally adopt!*

A conspiracy was being constructed out of the fact that, in response to Freeland's request to read Paine's book, Muir had invited him to take the copy from the pocket of his overcoat lying over a chair in the same room.

> *Indeed, every evidence goes to prove that this wretch . . . this wretch is tainted with Sedition from head to foot and more unworthy the protection of the Law than the meanest villain!*

Such display of passion was best complemented by appeal to reason.

> *The next witness I shall speak of is Anne Fisher. Though the pannel, by an expression he made use of, has endeavoured to prejudice you against her, I dare say, Gentlemen, you will agree with me that her evidence is correct, well-founded, stands on the basis of truth, and is corroborated by the evidence of others. Anne Fisher was repeatedly sent to purchase Paine's book!*

The Crown prosecutor continued to ignore the protest that Paine's book had been perfectly legal at the time of the alleged offence.

> *There, in his father's shop, did he harangue all the poor and ignorant country people. He persuaded them to lay out their miserable sixpence to purchase* The Rights of Man. *There was he always found, in the backshop, reading Seditious publications. In that den of Sedition he sat like a spider, spinning his filthy web to entrap the unwary! The witness names the persons for whom she purchased Paine's book. One of these persons she condescends upon is the uncle of that*

unfortunate wretch at the bar! But I decline bringing the uncle as an evidence against the nephew.

Gentlemen, you have only to read the passages quoted from Paine's book in the indictment. In this particular, his reference to the King.

'The time is not very distant when England will laugh at itself for sending to Holland, Hanover, Zel, or Brunswick, for men, at the expense of a million a year, who understand neither her laws, her language, nor her interest, and whose capacities would scarcely have fitted them for the office of a parish constable.'

Gentlemen, if you are loyal to your rightful monarch, . . . if you love your country, . . . if you are desirous to preserve it, . . . then you will return a verdict against this man who has dared to recommend that wretched outcast, Paine, and his even more wretched writings!

Paine's wretched writings had by this time sold over 200,000 copies world-wide. The Earl of Charlemont considered *Rights of Man* a work of genius but one which should be read with caution – 'He does, indeed, tear away the bandage from the public eye, but, in tearing it off, there may be some danger of injuring the organ'.[8]

You all know, Gentlemen, what the pannel thinks of our ancient and glorious institutions. You all heard Anne Fisher testify that he said Members of Parliament should be paid. She overheard him say it! She actually heard him say it! Members of Parliament should be paid thirty or forty shillings per day! And for what? . . . Why, for attending Parliament! Here you have it, Gentlemen! Here you see the cloven hoof! Here you see the heathen French principles made manifest! Here you discover the whole tincture of this man's soul! Can any further proof be required that he means to introduce, in place of our hallowed House of Commons, a National Convention to be run on infidel French principles?

But, the Lord Advocate warned, worse was to come than that frightening prospect of MPs being remunerated for their time.

You heard Anne Fisher further testify that even the poor organist could not pass the door of this, this Demon of Mischief, but he must be stopped and made to play Ça Ira!

Yes, here was crime indeed. *Ça Ira*. Two words used by the

8. Aldridge Man of Reason p142

rebellious Benjamin Franklin in America. Not exactly translatable, but understood to mean that a desired state of affairs would certainly come to pass. Two words now incorporated as refrain in the *Carillon National* of the heathen French Republic. Need a Lord Advocate say more? Well, yes; Robert Dundas certainly thought so.

> *Ça Ira! That clarion call of the French rabble! That sans-cullotte signal for blood and carnage on the streets of Paris and now played on the streets of Glasgow at request of this man! For what purpose was this done? What nefandous end can he have had in mind? Can any now be left with even a shadow of doubt as to how that question must be answered?*

It may safely be assumed that all the jurymen to whom this question was addressed, bar one, were by now quite disumbrous.

> *Gentlemen, having finished my remarks upon the evidence, there are only two topics on which I must beg to make a few observations. The pannel has said that he was unwillingly detained in France and that he always wished to come forward to this trial. I should have made no objection to his proving this. It would have argued some degree of honour. But these false assertions are all clearly refuted. He fled from this country under the impression of guilt and now he is returned to be again The Pest of Scotland, with the same diabolical intention as before! But, gentlemen, what was the reason of his going to France? I was never more surprised at anything than the evidence of Skirving, appearing for the defence, when he told us the pannel was sent to France by persons styling themselves the Friends of the People, because it was believed he might have influence in saving the life of the King of France! Did that witness know, did he recollect, he was accusing the pannel of High Treason?*

Once again the Lord Advocate's desire to implicate Muir in the highest of crimes had driven him to deliberate dishonesty. He knew from the spy report of 21st January that Muir was not 'sent' to France, neither did he go as any kind of emissary.

> *But why were these people so much interested in averting this event? That witness has informed us. It was thought such an event would hurt their common cause. What common cause? The design of overthrowing the Government of this country! Gentlemen, I postponed this trial much longer than I ought to have done because I was willing to give the pannel every opportunity of returning, and I inserted the adjournment in the public papers in the expectation that it might find him while roaming through the world. Observe the shipmaster's receipt; it*

is dated the sixteenth of May; what became of him all the time from that date till the thirty first of July, when he was apprehended? Nobody was informed of his intention of returning.

The macers were unable to identify one single source of the angry protests at this. Everyone else in court knew that the outbreak of war had made it impossible for Muir to declare an intention of travelling to England without risking the guillotine.

Nobody was informed. How unlucky, that not one solitary letter was wafted by the winds, or impelled by the waves, to his friends here, and inserted in the Edinburgh Gazetteer or Caledonian Mercury, to give notice of what he says was his earnest wish. But the very reverse of this was the case. By his father's letter we find him in Ireland, and who knows how he was employed there! No, we know nothing of him all this time except what we may discover from his diploma of the Society of United Irishmen! Gentlemen, you may know a man by the company he keeps. Among the accused's papers there is a letter addressed to the Reverend Thomas Fyshe Palmer, a man who in a few days is to be tried at Perth. The seal of that letter is remarkable. It is a Cap of Liberty on a Spear, and under it is the motto Ça Ira! You see, Gentlemen, the pannel returns to this country with even the insignia of Sedition about him!

Perhaps about here the standard Courtroom dramatics would be employed to excite sympathy for the Crown Prosecutor's great endeavours and facilitate a rapid conclusion; the back of the hand to the forehead and a wee stagger to one side. A brave recovery, though; with the jury secure in his pocket from the outset, the situation did not demand a staged fainting fit.

I trust, Gentlemen, you will view this case in the same light as I do. You will protect your King from the attacks of his enemies, and you will guard this Temple of Freedom from all the attempts of the factions. You will not allow this Temple of Freedom to be violated by that person at the bar; and you will now, Gentlemen, prevent his attempts in future.

Gentlemen, . . . I conjure you to do justice to your country, and honour to yourselves, by returning such a verdict as shall stop that man in his mad career. That man who has been sowing Sedition . . . in every corner . . . with so liberal a hand.

Thank you, Gentlemen, all.

* * *

Strive to make the victory of the accusers less glorious
than the defeat of the accused

For the second time that day the Court heard ten sonorous strokes toll out from the steeple of St Giles. However long it took, the Trial must come to its conclusion at this one sitting. Muir must have been feeling this pressure acutely but he began his defence with apparent composure.

> *Gentlemen of the Jury. I now rise in my own defence. Like the Lord Advocate, I too have long looked foward with joyful expectation to this day. All that malice could devise, all that slander could circulate has been directed against me. Gentlemen, I speak with pride and triumph. After an inquisition perhaps unexampled in the history of this country my moral character stands secure and unimpeached. With the paid and anonymous assassins of public reputation, with such mean and worthless adverseries, I disdained to enter the lists. I reserved my vindication to this day when, before you and in view of Scotland, I should manifest my innocence. But I shall not imitate the example of the Public Prosecutor. Histrionics and hollow declamation are unsuitable for you and unworthy of me. The eyes of this country are fixed upon us both; the records of this trial will pass down to posterity; and Gentlemen, when our ashes shall be scattered by the winds of heaven the impartial voice of future times will rejudge your verdict.*

Those words confirm that Muir was using the Court as a national platform and they were probably the cause of some openly hostile reaction, to which he responded.

> *Gentlemen, I supplicate no favour. I demand justice. You are bound to grant it.*

> *Ye're no here t'tell the Jury their duty, Sir.* [Braxfield sourly] *Gang oan wi yir defence.*

> *Gentlemen, there are two circumstances which have been strongly hinted upon by the Public Prosecutor, though they have little or no connection with the general nature of the evidence he has adduced. He maintains that, conscious of my guilt, I fled from this country. Gentlemen, I admit the fact of my departure. When the whole strength of Arbitrary Power is exerted against one individual would it be commendable in him to expose himself as a sacrifice? When his sufferings might be of no service to his country, and would only present posterity with an addition to the vast catalogue of the victims of despotism?*

A choice of words aimed quite deliberately at his principal accusers. The received wisdom is that Braxfield never failed to dominate all who appeared before him, but at the trial of George Smith and Deacon Brodie a few years earlier, Muir's friend, John Clerk of Penicuik, had brandished a fist in Braxfield's face and stunned this same High Court with the challenging roar – 'Hang ma client gin ye daur, m'Lord, withoot hearing me, his coonsel, in his defence![9] Nor did the career of this fiery new member of the Faculty of Advocates thereafter suffer. Much later, as Lord Eldin, he himself sat on the Bench and is also, almost certainly, the same John Clerk later recommended to the French Foreign Office by Muir as a source of accurate information on the readiness of Scotland for revolt.

After pointing out there had been no attempt to conceal his appearance at meetings in London, Muir went on to refute the Lord Advocate's invention that he had thereafter acted as emissary to a foreign power.

> *In Mister Skirving's evidence respecting a letter he received from me before I left London, he has said that I proposed to go to Paris, as it was the advice of some friends I might be of service in mitigating the fate of the late King of France. Those words, 'some friends', have been ingeniously represented to be members of that truly respectable society, and it is now boldly argued that I went as a missionary from that body. No person can, or dare say that I went as a missionary to a foreign power! But, building then upon this unsubstantial basis of words never uttered by Mister Skirving, I am accused of a species of High Treason. The charge is as ridiculous as the misrepresentation on which it is founded.*

At the same time as making clear his reasons for going to France, Muir revealed that radicals now harboured few illusions over likely future developments.

> *Has not the Prosecutor himself lamented the execution of the late King? Will he not excuse a man who wanted to prevent it and who, with many friends to humanity, of every nation, and of every party, exerted their abilities to ward it off because they considered it pregnant with evil to this country and foresaw that it would introduce years of bloodshed and sorrow?*

The next of the Lord Advocate's suggestions was then dealt with, the one which hinted he may have been in Ireland sometime between

---

9. Clerk Appendix D

the date of receiving his French passport and that of his final sailing
date from Le Havre, a period of two-and-a-half months. There is as
yet no evidence for this perhaps unlikely proposition but it could
conceivably have been true. As Hamilton Rowan soon after proved,
all that was required for such travel was a fishing boat and a friendly
skipper.

> *We all know there have been recent insurrections in Ireland. The*
> *Prosecutor insinuates that the Demon of Sedition as he calls*
> *me, was probably the cause of these insurrections! Gentlemen, I*
> *smile at the ridiculous accusation.*

In the circumstances, a display of open contempt for Dundas was
certainly not wise, but Muir was probably still smarting over the fact
that he had let himself be very seriously outmanoeuvered in one vital
area.

> *The Prosecutor has said I came from Ireland to Scotland in a*
> *private and clandestine manner. I am extremely sorry that the*
> *respectable magistrate at Stranraer, Mister Ross, is not here. In*
> *the list of witnesses adduced against me, I saw his name and the*
> *name of Carmichael, the person who first recognised me on my*
> *landing at Portpatrick. I therefore expected to have found them*
> *inclosed with the witnesses for the Crown, and I would have*
> *adduced them to prove that, so far from concealing myself, I*
> *announced myself publicly and without disguise. But the*
> *conduct of the Public Prosecutor is uniformly marked with*
> *disingenuity. Citing Ross and Carmichael as witnesses for the*
> *Crown seems to have been an art to prevent me citing them at*
> *my own instance. It has succeeded. I am now precluded from*
> *the benefit of their testimony. You will judge of the rectitude of*
> *the Prosecutor's conduct in thus declaiming upon a fact which*
> *he shrinks from proving, and which his artful contrivance now*
> *prevents me from disproving.*

From student days, Muir had been noted for humourous mimicry
in debate and it is clear he did not restrain himself on this occasion.

> *Gentlemen, the Prosecutor has talked of the danger the people*
> *of this country were in last winter, of the deep-laid plots and*
> *treasonable conspiracies. And I am the man whom he charges*
> *as the author of the whole; whom he represents as similar in*
> *malignity to the* Demon of Mischief *and whom he honours*
> *with the title, the* Pest of Scotland! *Well then, let it be supposed*
> *that an attempt was formed to overthrow the Constitution, to*
> *kindle the torch of civil war, and to lead to rapine throughout*
> *the land. Where, I ask, has the proof of this design been found?*
> *Everything has been explored. An inquisition unknown even in*

Spain has been carried on. Everything transacted within the walls of private families has been industriously inquired into; and to prove this mighty crime which is to convulse the State, which is to tear the Constitution from its basis, the principal witnesses are a hairdresser and a scullion girl. . . . Could not some ruffian be procured who could at least give a manly testimony to our atrocious purposes? But to adduce a girl and a hairdresser, the domestics of a private family, to prove a crime which required the co-operation of many thousands of bearded men, . . . while it excites the frown, it must likewise call forth the smile of contempt.

It is not recorded that Robert Dundas returned the smile. He probably had growing realisation he was sitting on something rather unpleasant.

Let us be candid, Gentlemen. Let us advance upon fair and open ground. Let us throw away miserable pretexts. If my standing forward for an equal representation of the people in the House of Commons is the impelling motive of this prosecution, and I judge that it is, in that case let it be acknowledged and I shall give little trouble. I will plead guilty to the charge. I will save you, Gentlemen of the Jury, the wretched mockery of condemning a man for a trifle while the principal cause of condemnation cannot be declared and must be concealed!

The outburst was probably caused by some mutterings that only Muir was meant to hear, and this reaction is likely to have been cause of further, more or less *sotto voce* sarcasms from some Jurymen.

Yes, gentlemen, I do plead guilty! . . . I have boldly contested for an equal representation of the people in what I shall ever call the House of the People, because I consider it to be a measure essentially necessary to the salvation of the State, and to the stability of our boasted Constitution!

After reminding the jury that both the commander-in-chief of the British Army [the Duke of Richmond] and Prime Minister William Pitt had both been recent advocates for reform, he ended this passionate outburst with a direct challenge to Dundas.

And pray, m'Lord, what term of super-eminent distinction will you, the Public Prosecutor, the Lord Advocate of Scotland, claim for yourself? Ehh? You also were, not many months ago, a Reformer. Every charge in your indictment against me recoils on yourself!

He waited till the reaction subsided before conceding the objection raised.

> *Yes, the subject is too ridiculous to be dwelt upon.* [Back to Dundas] *If it was lawful for you and your friends to meet in Societies and Conventions for the purpose of obtaining Reform, it cannot be illegal in me and my friends to meet and to act on the same principle.*

On the subject of official bribery, a witness had testified that Muir said the Duke of Richmond got twenty-thousand or thirty-thousand pounds slipped into his pocket in return for promise of future right-thinking behaviour.

> *And what though I said so? I again say that money was the salutary opiate which calmed and cooled the Reforming fever of the Duke of Richmond's brain!*

After the applause had died away he returned to what remained of the Lord Advocate's now very tattered prosecution case, the charges relating to promotion of Paine's publications.

> *Is there a person upon the Bench, upon the Jury, or in the audience who has not purchased, borrowed or lent the treatise upon the* Rights of Man*? Was there a judgement of any Court in England or Scotland against this book at that time? No! Can you, therefore, now suppose there was any felonius intention in my lending this book?*

The Jury clearly believed the book should have been illegal and it is doubtful if they had much time now for hair-splitting.

> *Gentlemen! If, whether right or wrong, you have come here determined to find me guilty, say so boldly, openly and, let me add, honestly. Resort not to idle pretexts and expedients. The unprejudiced eye will soon penetrate into these pretexts and the determination will soon receive the contempt and indignation of mankind.*

Public debate on political matters was no longer possible in Scotland and this prosecution was proving that it might no longer be safe even within one's own home; but the records of this trial, though edited and distorted, would not be erased and so Muir now indulged himself by launching out on a lengthy analysis of the purely speculative nature of Paine's politics, followed that with a homily on the role of the Press in Constitutional improvements, then continued with an erudite summary of historical parallels to the present situation. All of which he ended with an explanation as to why he had not recommended Paine's book to the Friends of the People meetings he had addressed in Scotland.

> *Mister Paine is a Republican, and the spirit of Republicanism breathes through all his writings. This is his darling system. Whereas the object of these Societies was, by Constitutional means, to procure a reformation. Not a revolution.*
>
> *... Having explained the principle on which I refused to recommend the works of Mister Paine, I again ask ... was it ever before held criminal in an author to publish what speculative systems of government he pleased, provided he confined himself to mere speculation? Was it a crime of Plato, under the Athenian Republic, to compose his beautiful system? Was it high treason in Cicero, under the Roman Commonwealth, to write those renowned works which have been lost in the darkness of the Gothic night, and of which a few fragments only could be found when the morning of letters began to dawn upon Europe? Was Sir Thomas More led forth to the scaffold for composing his Utopia? Harrington proscribed for his Oceana? Or Hume expelled for his Commonwealth? No, Gentlemen; these authors indulged themselves in a liberty which, if we are now to be deprived of it, must leave this land in darkness and despair. I trust you will not attempt to annihilate political science. In this country where our chief glory has arisen from literature, I hope you will not limit her researches but indulge her unbounded flight into every region where the materials of human happiness and human improvement can be collected.*

No doubt there would have been necessity in the course of these long proceedings for what might accurately be termed *discomfort* breaks and it was probably after one of these, long past midnight, that Muir began dealing with the testimony of his parents' one-time scullery-maid, Anne Fisher. Whether alcohol was a factor or not, it is obvious Muir delighted his supporters with mimicry of the Lord Advocate, whose exultation over the evidence of this 'domestic and well-tutored spy' had amused him.

> *Here you have it, Gentlemen! Here you see the cloven hoof! Here you see the heathen French principles made manifest! Here you discover the whole tincture of this man's soul! As I say, I smiled at this behaviour. But next moment I pitied him when I reflected he was a lawyer and Chief Counsel for the Crown in Scotland. Can there be any who has opened the volume of the History of the Constitution who does not know that, until a very*

*late period indeed, Members of Parliament received their wages
from the hands of the people alone?*

Dealing with the charge that he had caused *Ça Ira* – which he
described as a *Hymn to Freedom* – to be played on the streets of
Glasgow, Muir took the opportunity to vaunt his knowledge of the
arts.

> *If I had caused to be recited one of those noble choruses of the
> Grecian drama, in which the enthusiasm of Liberty, the glories
> of the Republics of Athens or of Sparta were displayed in
> language more than mortal, my offence would have been
> deemed the same. If it had been possible for me to have caused
> to be sung upon the streets of Glasgow one of the Psalms of the
> Hebrews in the original language, in which the triumphs of the
> people and the destruction of tyrants are recorded in a strain of
> the highest poetical inspiration, the criminality would have
> been the same as listening to Ça Ira!*

The mood changed considerably over the matter of his uncle, Alexander Muir, not being called for the prosecution.

> *Why is Alexander Muir not brought forward as a witness?
> Certain it is that he was closely interrogated before the
> inquisition held by Sheriff Honyman. But the Lord Advocate
> says that his feelings would not permit him to examine the
> uncle against the nephew. Goodness ever to be remembered and
> extolled!* [Rounding on Dundas] *Did you not advise and direct
> the whole proceedings against me? And will you have the
> effrontery to maintain that Alexander Muir was not dragged
> like a felon from his home by the myrmidons of power, carried
> before your friend Sheriff Honyman, and that every art was
> employed to wring from him every domestic secret? Speak, then,
> to us of your humanity! Ay! Continue to speak to us of your
> feelings!*

There is no record that Braxfield attempted to interrupt this attack
on his Lord Advocate. No doubt he would be lost in his proverbial
line of thought – *Ay, ye're a verra clever chiel; but like monie anither,
ye'll be nane the waur o a hingin.*

> *Gentlemen, if your libraries are extensive, as you have heard
> mine is, lock them up. There is no crime in the whole decalogue
> of which, by the testimony of your own servants, you may not be
> found guilty. The possession of Plato, of Harrington or of Hume
> will mark you down for Republicans. The misfortune of having
> the Koran of Mahomet will cause the shipwreck of your faith*

*and stigmatise you as the disciple of the conqueror of Mecca! ...
Can it be believed that in the close of the eighteenth century,
that this night, the servants of a man should be examined
concerning what particular books he may have had in his
house, and that proof of possession of particular books may
ruin his reputation, sweep away his property, and deprive him
of his life? Gentlemen, if you possess the common feelings of
men, every sentiment of indignation must be excited, not
against Anne Fisher, for she is rather to be pitied, but against the
manner in which this crime of Sedition has been attempted to
be proved. Fisher heard me read Volney's* Dialogue between the
Governors and the Governed *in the presence of my mother, my
sister, and some other people. Who were these other people? Her
accuracy, so much extolled by the Court, totally fails her here.
But the propagation of Sedition must not be confined to a
mother and sister! It must have a wider range! Founding upon
his beloved generality, the Prosecutor has reason to argue that
there might have been a full company present ... a numerous
meeting ... nay, an immense congregation!*

There would have been enthusiastic responses to such harangues
but as subsequent private publications made clear, even to refer to
them was to risk prosecution.

*Gentlemen, I hasten over the evidence of the remaining
witnesses against me. I am overcome by the exertions of the day,
and you must be greatly exhausted.*

*... Of only two more of the prosecutor's witnesses will I make
particular mention. The first is John Barclay, that old and
venerable person who informs you that we were elders in the
same parish, the parish of Cadder, in which the lands of my
father are situated. The Lord Advocate, in speaking of this
virtuous and venerable old man, exclaimed with insolent
contempt, 'such men as these are the companions, and such
men as these are the friends of Mister Muir!' Yes; I tell the Lord
Advocate, I tell the Aristocracy of Scotland, I glory more in the
friendship of such an old, poor and virtuous man than in the
friendship of the highest titled Peer who derives the sources of
his guilty grandeur from the calamities of the people!*

*... The last witness of whom I will take notice is William Muir,
the person whose religious principles at first induced him
rather to suffer, according to the elegant expression of the Bench
'eternal imprisonment' than to take the oath. William Muir
swears that in my father's house, at Huntershill, I gave him
eleven numbers of The Patriot. I maintain that every passage
from these quoted in the libel is highly constitutional, though
the sentiments advanced may not sound musically sweet to the
ears of corruption. They call upon the people to arise and*

> *vindicate the purity of the Constitution, to vindicate their long-lost rights; and, Gentlemen, if my feeble voice could extend to the remotest corners of Scotland, I should resound the same sentiment, in the same language!*

This summing-up ended on the third article of the indictment, the kernel of the whole affair, the public reading of that Irish call for united action.

> *The Lord Advocate has represented to you in general terms, that that Address amounts almost to treason, but he durst not attempt to point out in his speech a single passage which could support the aspersion. I maintain that every line of that Address is strictly constitutional. You must carry the whole of it along with you, and not judge of particular passages scandalously mutilated in the indictment. Gentlemen, I will read over many passages of this Address, not merely because they are the production of an immortal pen, but because every word is regulated by the spirit of the Constitution.*

The essential legal pretext thus established, the rallying-cry from Ireland was made to resound once again in Scotland's highest forum.

> *We honour a nation eminent for men of genius, and we trust that they will now exert themselves, not so much in perusing and penning the histories of other countries, as in making their own a subject for the historian. . . . If we be rightly informed, there is no such thing as popular election in Scotland. The people, who ought to possess that weight in the popular scale, which might bind them to the soil and make them cling to the Constitution, are now as dust in the balance, blown abroad by the least impulse, and scattered through other countries, merely because they hang so loosely to their own. . . . If Government has a sincere regard for the safety of the Constitution, let them coincide with the people in the speedy reform of its abuses, and not by an obstinate adherence to them drive the people into Republicanism.*

The lengthy rehearsal of the Address ended with Muir making clear his own relationship with its authors and their Society.

> *I am a member of that Society and in the last moments of my life to have been so shall be my honour and my pride. If ever after ages shall hear of my name I wish it may be recorded that to these men I had the happiness to be known. To have it said that I was the friend of Doctor Drennan and Mister Hamilton Rowan I would consider as the passport to the only acquaintances whom I value* [again directly to Dundas] *those*

who found their claim to distinction upon the only true basis, their own true virtues.

... What, then, has been my crime? Not the lending to a relation a copy of Mister Paine's works. Not the giving away to another a few numbers of an innocent and constitutional publication. My crime is having dared to be, according to the measure of my feeble abilities, a strenuous and active advocate for an equal Representation of the People in the House of the People. Gentlemen, from my infancy to this moment I have devoted myself to the cause of the People. It is a good cause. It shall ultimately prevail. It shall finally triumph!

Sixteen hours of unremitting effort ended with a final challenge to that choice band of proper-principled brothers.

The time will come when men must stand or fall by their actions, when all human pageantry shall cease, when the hearts of all shall be laid open. Gentlemen, if you regard your most important interests, if you wish that your conscience should whisper to you words of consolation, not speak to you in the terrible language of remorse, weigh well the verdict you are about to pronounce.

As for me, I am careless and indifferent to my fate. I can look danger and I can look death in the face for I am shielded by the consciousness of my own rectitude. I may be condemned to languish in the recesses of a dungeon. I may be doomed to ascend the scaffold. Nothing can deprive me of the recollection of the past, nothing can destroy my inward peace of mind, arising from the remembrance of having discharged my duty.

In the profound silence that followed, with the final words seeming to hang like a banner above the heads of all present, Muir turned to confront the Bench and meet Braxfield's fixèd stare with his own silent challenge. He remained rigidly unmoving for a long moment, then the formal bow. The silence hung by a thread till Muir sat down, then the Court-room erupted. The wild applause was taken up by the crowd still present in the Great Hall. They did not yet know the reason, but it was obvious their man had scored a great triumph.

Three cheers for Tam Muir! Hip-hip! ...

The roar of approval from outside was an amplified echo of the hurrahs in the Court itself.

Hip-hip! ...

Another roar, and the Bench could only sit stupefied at this violation of their authority.

HIP-HIP-HIP!...

From the much-trodden flagstones to the overhead forest of hammer-beam rafters, that third outburst shook the fabric of the Great Hall of the Old Scots Parliament as never before; and instead of ending, the cheering, whistling, stamping and clapping seemed to grow ever more intense.

Macers! [Braxfield's voice was not heard at first above the din] *Macers!... MACERS!*

... M'Lord?

Arrest every man that's cheerin, stampin his feet or clappin!

But that's jist it, m'Lord. [from the much-harassed Senior Macer] *It's perfect impossible t'tak them aw intae custody!*

Unopposed, the disorder in Court did eventually die away. Braxfield waited till it was no more than excited chattering before informing the Jury that, though the indictment against Muir was the longest he had ever seen, there was need only to find the prosecution case established on any one charge for the guilt to be the same as if all had been proven.

This is the question for your consideration. Is the panel guilty o sedition or is he no? Afore this question can be decidit Ah hae twa things t'say that require nae proof. First; the British Constitution is the best that ever wis since the creation o the warld, and it is no possible t'mak it better. Is no every man secure? Does no every man reap the fruits o his ain industry, and sit safely under his ain fig-tree?

... The next thing for yir attention is his rinnin awa f'Justice. Yon's aye a mark o guilt! And whit wis his intention? T'be an ambassador? The pretence o bein an amabassador tae a foreign country, withoot lawful authority, yon's rebellion! He maks pretence o influence wi thae wretches, the leadin men yonder, and whitlike folk are they? Ah never liked the French aw ma days and noo Ah hate them. In ma conseedered judgement, the French are monsters o human nature!

Braxfield seems to have been noted for having a hard head for alcohol, so this may have been a reasonably sober judgement, one that would certainly have a very sobering effect on most present.

Maister Muir harangued ignorant weavers aboot their grievances. He micht hae saved his braith. Ah could hae tell't them Parliament wad never listen t'them. Whit richt has sic a rabble t'representation? Government is made up o the landit interests, which alane has the richt t'be representit. As for the rabble, wha possess naethin, whit hold does the nation hae on them? They may pack up aw their property on their backs and leave the country in the twinklin o an ee, but landit property cannot be sae removed!

His hale defence is that he advised consitutional measures only. Ah say he wis bidin his time. Tumult, too soon, wad ruin his cause. The tendency o his conduct was plainly t'promote a spirit o revolt. If whit wis demandit was no given, it wad be taen by force. By a general insurrection. Ah hae not the smallest doot that ye, Gentlemen o the Jury, like me, are convinced o the panel's guilt. Ah desire that ye return sic a verdict as will dae ye honour.

Thank ye, Gentlemen. Ye may retire for some lang owredue rest. This Coort will hear your verdict when it sits again the morn, twal o'clock, mid-day.

The trial had commenced at 10am on Friday, 30th August. At almost 2am on Saturday, 31st August, Lord Braxfield set off to walk the mile or so back to his town-house in George Square, the lantern held forward by his elderly manservant providing but a puddle of wan light to guide their steps. Tradition has it that Braxfield wanted 'some caller air' after birstling nearly sixteen hours in the tiny courtroom. When fears for his safety were expressed, he is reputed to have hefted his heavy blackthorn stick.

Wi this thing in ma twa hauns, Ah believe Ah'm a match for onie man in Scotland.

Rightly or wrongly, Braxfield has been allowed courage as a virtue.

CHAPTER 5
The Verdict

Saturday, 31st August. 1793
Twelve o'clock, noon

Braxfield enacted the pretence of having to wait for the written result of his jury's deliberations, and the reaction in the Court-room to the Guilty verdict was immediate, but subdued. Few present had not, reluctantly, anticipated this outcome all along. After thanking the jury for their attention, diligence and a verdict of which the Court highly approved, Braxfield invited Lord Henderland's comment.

During the whole course of last winter, month after bitter month, this country was in a most alarming situation. The most alarming that my experience recalls, [Henderland informed the Court]. *So alarming, indeed, that history may well recall that period as the most alarming of an alarming century. The alarms of that period, inevitably, gave rise to feelings of great uneasiness in all thinking men. As one such, I am now arrived at the most disagreeable part of the duty incumbent upon me; to wit, to fix the punishment due to the crime.*

The 'melancholy example' of a neighbouring country rendered it quite unnecessary for Henderland to dwell upon the evil consequences of the crimes committed by the prisoner.

In that country the consequences of measures such as the pannel was promoting have produced every kind of violence, every kind of rapine, every kind of murder known to man.

Most in court would have thought those the sanctioned evils that had given rise to the French Revolution in the first place.

The indecent applause which was given to Mister Muir last night, within these walls, such applause is unknown before in this High Court, is inconsistent with the solemnity which ought to pervade the administration of Justice, and is insulting to the laws and dignity of this Court! All of this proves to me that the spirit of Sedition has not yet subsided!

The voice of more than one distinguished lawyer was heard to protest at this line from the Bench and Henderland raised the level of his in response.

> *However! I shall not seek to aggravate the offence committed by the pannel by the misconduct of others in order to increase the punishment! The punishment to be inflicted is arbitrary. There is a variety from which to choose. In my opinion, though, banishment would be improper.*

Another threatened interruption.

> *Banishment would be improper,* [Henderland responded to the reaction] *for it would only be sending to another country a man where he might have the opportunity of exciting the same spirit of seditious discontent! Likewise; I feel it would be too severe and disgraceful, particularly to a man bearing the prisoner's character and life, to order a public whipping.*

He waited till Braxfield's threatening glowers had restored silence.

> *... Which leaves only two possibilities. Imprisonment I consider to be unsuitable. It is but a temporary punishment, when the criminal would be again set loose and so again disturb the happiness of the people. There remains but one punishment, in our law, and it wrings my very heart to mention it. I consider it a duty, owed to my countrymen, in the situation in which I sit, as punishment due to the pannel's crimes, to pronounce for transportation.*

Henderland raised his voice over the reaction as he addressed Muir directly.

> *It is extraordinary that a gentlemen of your description, of your profession, and of the talents you undoubtedly possess, should be guilty of a crime deserving such punishment! But I see no alternative! What security can we have against his future operations but his removal from this country to a place where he can do no futher harm?* [His Lordship waited till some sort of order had been restored.] *Given the foregoing, I am of the opinion the pannel should be recommitted to prison, there to remain till a proper opportunity should offer for transporting him to such place as His Majesty, with advice from Privy Council, might appoint. For the space of fourteen years from the date of the sentence.* [Almost having to shout the last sentence] *Not to return within that period under pain of death!*

Though no doubt alarmed at the reaction he had caused, Lord Henderland remained defiant. This was the one moment in his life of lasting notice; he had done much more than overturn a hornet's nest, he had gone on to boot it, fearlessly, towards the far shore. Any who hoped this might be a case of sentence in haste, relent at pleasure were quickly disabused of such notion when Lord Swinton had his say.

> *The crime with which the pannel is found guilty, by a Jury of his countrymen, is the generic crime of Sedition. . . . This crime consists of many gradations. It might run from petty mobbing over wages even unto High Treason itself. Punishment should always be adapted to the crime. The question, therefore, becomes – what is the degree of the crime of the pannel? . . . Well, sadly, the crime appears to me to be of the most heinous kind. There is scarcely a distinction to be made between it and High Treason. And for why? Because by the dissolution of the social compact it made way for, and so might be said to include, every sort of crime. Murder, robbery, rapine, fire-raising; in short, every species of wrong-doing, public and private. This is no theoretical reasoning. Have we not had it exemplified before our very eyes in the present state of France? . . . Punishment adequate to this crime is sought. There can be no punishment in our law sufficient for the crime in the present case now that Torture is happily abolished.*

Shocked and disbelieving silence had probably replaced voluble protest as Lord Swinton now resorted to mouthfuls of Roman Law to further convince the *hoi-poloi* of Muir's great criminality, quotations from *Paulus* and *Baldus* ending with Swinton leaning heavily on *Emperor Leo* himself – '*Subdandos autem pœnis eis quas de seditionis et tumultus auctoribus vetustissima decreta sanxerint*'. After leaving everyone to puzzle over this a time he concluded in simpler language.

> *The sole object of punishments among us is only to deter others from committing the like crime in time coming. All that is necessary is that it serve as an example and terror to others. In the present case, I judge transportation the lightest punishment that can be assigned; and that for the space of fourteen years.*

In response to Braxfield's invitation, Lord Dunsinnan stirred himself, allowed a few moments to clear his thinking, then braced himself to speak 'in so low a tone of voice' that only his conclusion is recorded.

> *I perfectly coincide with everything my learned colleagues have said. . . . Perfectly.*

Lord Abercromby also coincided, but made the effort to be more specific.

> *I do not think it necessary to say much as to the enormity of the crime, not after what has been said already. By our law, it might well have amounted to Treason. Even as the law now stands it comes very near to it. One point I must stress, though. Last night, while conducting his own defence, Mister Muir stated, – and I observed, marked, and gave great weight to this, and I quote – that the people should be cautious, and by all manner of means avoid tumults and disorders; for, through time, the mass of the people would bring about a revolution.*

> *'I deny it, m'Lord!'* [Muir shouted, rising angrily to his feet.] *'That is totally false! That is a falsehood!'*

> *'Sit doon, Sir,'* [ordered Braxfield, appearing to show something like benignity now in victory] *'Ye, abune aw men, should hae mair sense o decorum.'*

After commenting on Muir's 'mission' to France and the pleasure he had expressed at meeting 'those monsters' there, Abercromby ended in perfect agreement with his colleagues. 'I can only coincide with their other lordships in regard to the punishment which they think Mister Muir deserves'. In the silence that followed, Braxfield, as presiding judge, sat head-bowed for a long moment. The look he eventually raised towards Muir was that of a mildly disappointed grandsire.

> *Ah'm considerably affectit t'see ye, a man wha had a liberal education, tried like this for Sedition. For ye were a member o respectable society, in possession o considerable talents, and hae hitherto sustained a respectable character. That said, Ah maun alloo that Ah consider even the lowest species o this crime t'be heinous, and it is aggravatit accordin t'the object in view.*

> *In this case, the object is important; for it entailed the creation o disloyalty and dissatisfaction towards Government in the lower classes o people. This, amountin t'the highest sort o Sedition, is borderin oan Treason. Jist a verra little mair wad seen this pannel staun trial for his life.* [Then turning to Muir in all benignity.] *Ah cannot find it in me t'disagree wi the proposed punishment.*

> *Ah micht hae been persuadit itherwise, but the undecent applause which wis accordit the pannel last nicht has convinced me that a spirit o discontent still lurks in the minds o owre monie people. It wad be dangerous t'alloo this man t'remain in this country. That circumstance has nae little wecht*

*wi me in the question o whit punishment Maister Muir
deserves. Ah never had the slightest doot in ma mind but whit
transportation is the proper punishment for such a crime. Ah
hesitate only whether it should be for the term o fourteen year,
or for life. Ma final preference is that it be the former. This, Ah
hope, will gie the pannel time t'reflect owre his past conduct.
Time t'recognise the impropriety which he has comittit. Thus it
may be that if he ever should again be restored to this country,
he micht still hae the opportunity t'show himsel a guid member
o that Coanstitution which he seems, even yet, t'despise sae
muckle.*[An affirmative nod to the Clerk-of-Court.]

Transportation for fourteen year.

As his defence speeches demonstrate, Muir had ability to put class-
ical and historical references together in telling, witty and sometimes
rather too self-indulgent oratory. Now, as he rose to deliver his last
words, it was as if he had been advised that the time had come to be
guided by the wisdom of his ancestors.

Abair ach beag is abair gu maith e.

Which his friend James MacKintosh, from Aldourie on the shores
of Loch Ness, might have translated for him as:

Say little, boy; but say it well!

Muir did exactly that; head high, and straight into the teeth of his
accusers.

*I shall not animadvert upon the severity or the leniency of my
sentence. Were I to be led this moment to the scaffold, I should
feel the same calmness and serenity which I do now. My mind
tells me that I have acted agreeably to my conscience; and that I
have engaged in a good, a just, and a glorious cause. A cause
which, sooner or later, must and will prevail, and by timely
reform save this country from destruction.*

The Macers would not grip and hurry such a prisoner below. He
would be allowed to choose his own moment. When the sentence was
officially documented, the conclusion of its final paragraph contained
the warning that was to carry much weight in Muir's future decisions.

... if after being so transported he shall return to, and be
found at large, within any part of Great Britain, during the said
fourteen years, without some lawful cause, and be thereby

legally convicted, he shall suffer death, as in cases of felony,
without benefit of clergy, by Law of England.

Writing to a friend, the reaction of the reforming English lawyer,
Samuel Romilly, is typical. 'I am not surprised that you have been
shocked at the account you have read of Muir's trial; you would have
been much more shocked if you had been present at it, as I was'. The
blatant and unprecedented abuse of Law had produced similar
feelings in almost everyone present. *Authority* had been prepared, of
course, for some reaction but what probably took it most by surprise
was the speed with which it happened and the source from which it
first came.

Barely minutes after the sentence had been announced, amidst
much horrified bewilderment and confusion in the Jury-room,
Captain Inglis's call for a petition against the sentence found immediate support. Perhaps the only 'innocents abroad' during the trial had
been the men who had pronounced the guilty verdict and who were
now sharing the seafarer's feelings of much anxiety. Before anything
could be put on paper, however, Gilbert Innes intervened to advise
caution. They would all do well to sleep on the matter; such serious
business required reflection. They should all meet again on the
Sabbath, he suggested, to give solemn consideration to the draft that
Captain Inglis would thus have a great deal more time fully to consider.
It is not known if the decision to heed this counsel was a unanimous
one, but heeded it certainly was; the majority bowing to the unden-
iable fact that a Jury Chancellor one day could, for the remainder of
the year, be a highly influential – perhaps even grateful – Lord
Lieutenant of the County.

As he walked the short distance from the Court down into North
Grey's Close, then up the narrow stairs to his wife and bairns, Robert
Watt would have had very little time to reflect on his own part in these
events. Just sufficient time, perhaps, to re-assure himself that, once
accepted by the Lord, nothing that an elect and justified person does
can ever be really sinful.

* * *

The Jury did re-assemble to consider the scrupulous petition that
Captain Inglis had drafted but there is no record that any debate took
place. Gilbert Innes opened proceedings by placing before his jurymen
the death-threat he had received overnight – as Chancellor of the Jury
he had been chosen first to hang from a rope – and even the noble

Law Lords were now under threat of assassination. Such proof that barbaric French practices were about to be adopted in Scotland's capital made clear that Muir and his desperado associates deserved quite the opposite of mercy, and this instruction, delivered in the stern warning-tone of a Lord-Lieutenant-designate, was sufficient to bring proceedings to a permanent close. When that news reached Robert Dundas, who had left Edinburgh immediately after the trial for an unspecified period in the hunting lodge of his uncle's estate near Dunkeld, he would have experienced a great sense of relief and possibly even some sense of gratitude towards whoever had drafted that death-threat to Gilbert Innes. Any sense of complacency, however, would have been dispelled by the almost daily stream of *JB* transcriptions that began to reach him thereafter.

> Sept 4th, 1793.
>
> Sir, Last night we had the most numerous meeting of the Canongate Association that we have had for a considerable time past. Above 30 were present but many of them were visitors from other Societies, particularly the New Town and Calton.
>
> Some particular business, not of the most agreeable kind, has prevented me from going up to see Mr Muir since his sentence – which by the bye – almost everybody, even the most loyal subjects, think by far too severe. Two years imprisonment would have been thought lenient. If even a fine had been added, few would have complained, but fourteen years to Botany Bay! You yourself I suppose will allow it is rather too much. I am told, however, he keeps up his spirit amazingly.

Watt finished by relaying what he had been told; that because of the presence of strangers, of whom they were all very suspicious, Muir's friends could get not a word out of him about his time in France. Two days later, the spy's news was more disturbing.

> 6th Sept, 1793.
>
> Sir, The severity of Mr Muir's sentence, instead of extinguishing the spirit of the Associations, seems to have given a new life & vigour to them. Last night there was the most numerous meeting I ever saw in the Canongate Lodge. There was no possibility of numbering them, so many were standing for want of seats. I once counted 160 but many came in afterwards so that there must have been considerably more than 200. The room was indeed nearly as full as it could hold, and some say it holds 300.

This meeting, according to Watt, was well aware it was being spied upon; but he reported that calls for a membership check were rejected, and there had been loud applause when it was pointed out it did not matter if even half the company were government spies, since they themselves were doing nothing illegal. The meeting had also expressed surprise when informed that 'incendiary' letters had been sent to Judges and Jury.

> All present expressed disapprobation of such measures, which none but blackguards or those who wished to hurt a good cause would be guilty of.

The conclusion of this *JB* report, with its suggestion of possible threat to the Procurator Fiscal's intelligence operation, would be the most disturbing of all.

> I must not close without mentioning that it will be necessary that I should see you tomorrow afternoon sometime. Let me know whether 6, 7, 8 or 9 will be most convenient. But don't write any more from the General Post Office. A certain sharp-sighted Gentleman might observe the subscription at least – and indeed there is hardly a chamber in the office where somebody does not know.

In his Highland retreat Robert Dundas also received a copy of the letter Lord Provost Thomas Elder had sent to Henry Dundas at the Home Office.

> I have the honour to write you this at the request of the Magistrates & several of the Gentlemen of the Goldsmith's Hall Association to state to you that Muir's sentence has revived the frequency of the meetings of the Society called FOP, and in considerable numbers, and that his remaining here tends very much to keep up the Spirit of Sedition. We therefore earnestly entreat you may get him removed from this Country as soon as possible.

After reporting on inflammatory posters all over the walls of the capital and the insufferable number of visitors to Muir in the Tolbooth, the Lord Provost's letter ended:

> I hope you will rid us of this grievance as soon as possible. If you think it proper to send a couple of trusty men to conduct Muir in a post-chaise to London, where his confinement {till an opportunity of transportation} will not be attended with the same inconveniences as here, the expense will be no object.

Matters were serious indeed when Lord Provost Elder could pen such a final six words. Copy of another Watt report reached Dundas the following day and at least confirmed that Procurator Fiscal Scott continued to drive his man as hard as was reasonable, or even unreasonable.

8th Sept. 1793. 6am.

Sir, Notwithstanding my present employment, which is none of the most honourable, {and for which I have to thank our friend more and my own misfortunes} I make it a point to adhere strictly to Truth upon all occasions. As for my not writing yesterday afternoon according to promise, the inclosed will plead my best apology. You know not the immense loss of time that is occasioned by having to hunt for articles of this kind, when you have different people to apply to for them, and when at the same time it is absolutely necessary that you must hardly appear to have any desire after what you are most anxious to obtain. A variety of general and common conversation is necessary on such occasions before one hints at the object wanted. Detection would otherwise be unavoidable – and it will be so if you do not take care to make no imprudent or precipitate use of what I now send you.

And always the afterthoughts.

PS. I was up at Muir with the Committee on Friday afternoon but found him as usual crowded with company – Ladies & Gentlemen.

We saw Sturdy Russell too, who was in good spirits.

Send what you promised. Yours & etc., J.B.

PPS. 7.30am. I find I will not have time to transcribe the whole of my report before 8am. If you could send your servant about 11 or 12, I shall have them completely ready. No porters can be got on Sunday and Spouse is not well. J.B.

Then a copy of Sheriff Pringle's letter to the Home Secretary in London arrived at Dunkeld.

Sept 9th 1793.

Dear Sir, You will have received a letter from the Provost signifying the wish of the Magistrates to have Muir removed from here as soon as it can conveniently be done. As the minds of the lower class of people will be kept in a ferment while he remains here I take the liberty to concur with the Magistrates in earnestly requesting that you will be so obliging as to take the proper measure for having him immediately removed from this Country.

I have the honour to be with much regard, Dear Sir, Your much obliged, faithful, humble Servant, John Pringle.

Apart from the anxiety it caused his elderly parents, Muir may almost have enjoyed this stay in the Tolbooth. He now had a room to himself and his closest friend, William Moffat, was in regular attendance, often accompanied by his wife, who with fresh-cut autumn flowers and some linen quickly transformed Muir's immediate surroundings. To ensure he was allowed due privileges, it was arranged that two members of the Canongate committee would dine with him each day, and there was wine and good food on the table when friends such as Samuel Romilly, Lord Daer and David Dale Junior visited. During this period he was able to edit his closing speech and thousands of copies were already printed and distributed as pamphlets. Then, within nine days of it ending, the complete *Trial of Thomas Muir* was published in book-form, priced two shillings, with a preface note from the editor – 'The profits were left to be disposed of in any Charitable manner which Mr Muir might direct; and he has desired them to be given for the Relief of Poor Prisoners'.

Other versions of the Trial quickly appeared, most with editors' cautious disclaimers and excuses for ommissions necessary to avoid arrest, but one proclaimed his work 'a debt which we owe to the cause of Liberty and Reform', going on to refer to previous 'Reform Gentlemen' who had 'under the mask of public virtue, and the semblance of patriotism, obtruded themselves into the higher offices of state, basely abandoning the cause of reason and the people.' This ended with the admonition – 'TRUST TO PRINCIPLES AND NOT TO MEN'.

A sold-out transcription of the trial, published in America, was shortly afterwards into a second edition, while in Paris the unbelievable corruption of Scottish justice suffered full exposure in *Le Moniteur* [1] – all of which amounted to a great deal more notice than the world would ever have taken of an apologetic and trimming defence by the eminent Henry Erskine. With more than a month of continuous and stressful effort behind him, Muir was now able to lie late in the mornings, reading meeting reports and formulating advice for the crowded late-afternoon debates. He may even have had a hand in the Friends resolution from Blackfriar's Wynd, dated 4th October,

1. Bewley *Muir of Huntershill*

one that must have left Robert Dundas even more dissatisfied with public life when he received his transcribed *JB* copy.

> Conscious of the purity of their motives and the legality of their proceedings, which have been solely confined to that great object of national justice, a parliamentary reform; the Friends of the People have heard, with mingled astonishment and contempt, the false and injurious aspersions bestowed upon them in the course of Mr Muir's trial. In their own vindication, and to show the world that neither the imbecile ridicule of a crown lawyer, nor the unconstitutional opinions of a judge can make them desert the great and important cause in which they are embarked, a numerous and respectable meeting resolved:

> 1) That this society is determined to adhere to the original principles of its institution – 'an equal representation of the people, and a shorter duration of parliamentary delegation.'

> 2) That without reflecting on a verdict of the country, the meeting consider it their duty to return thanks, in this public manner, to Thomas Muir, younger, of Huntershill, for his manly and honourable exertions in the cause of Parliamentary Reform.

> 3) That this meeting likewise consider it a duty to express their thanks to the Revd T.F.Palmer, for his exertions in the same important cause.

> 4) That this society calls upon the people of Scotland to unite in promoting the happiness and prosperity of their country by assisting to obtain a reform in the Commons House of Parliament; the only measure that can secure to them and to their posterity, the inestimable blessings of peace, check an increasing and oppressive system of taxation, and prevent the baleful influence of that corruption which has proved so inimical to public virtue, and so destructive to private morals.[2]

The Revd Fyshe Palmer was also now in prison, at Perth, he too having been found guilty of Sedition and sentenced to seven years transportation, but many remained convinced these sentences would never be carried through, pointing to the case of Alexander Lockie, the King's Birthday rioter Muir had defended. It was more than a year now since Lockie had been sentenced to fourteen years transportation, yet not only was he still in the country but rumour had it he now entertained expectation of release from jail at no very distant date.

---

2. *State Trials*

The Home Secretary was certainly as determined as ever to crush every last vestige of democratic influence on British politics, but in this, as in all else, he strove to achieve maximum effect with minimum repercussion. A very considerable repercussion threatened if, as advisors now warned, all the sentences of transportation might actually have been illegal. The possibility was aired of side-stepping a dangerous legal challenge by mitigating these, but when the Home Secretary suggested this to his nephew, it was rejected out of hand for fear such leniency would be read as a sign his conduct of the trials was being criticised in Westminster. The Lord Advocate insisted neither Muir nor Palmer should be granted any leniency at all unless they first petition for it; he too had received a death-threat, copy enclosed, as proof of the continuing dangers.

The Lord Advocate knew Muir never would petition, not after that closing speech. In any case, the possible illegality of the sentences was under investigation, north and south of the Border, and if proven might be used to expose a great deal more than judicial incompetence. Home Secretary in London, Lord Advocate in Edinburgh, Reform leader in the Tolbooth; a triangulated game of political chess that might have progressed unhurriedly, as in Lockie's case, had it not been that news now arriving from France served to quicken every personal prejudice. Reformers, hailing the imminent end to feudal wars against the rights of man, took heart from the French Army's recent victories over foreign invaders and *Authority*, already dismayed at Admiral Hood's failure to hold Toulon for the Royalists, reacted with horror to Marie Antoinette's execution and vowed ever more vehemently to crush all things tainted by French-Republicanism. Sheriff Pringle added his capital voice to the warnings that had been cascading onto the Home Office desk.

> The minds of the lower class of people will be kept in a ferment while Muir remains here. His visitors have been very numerous!

A few days earlier the Lord Provost of Glasgow had again been in alarm.

> The Friends of the People remain indefatigable. I believe the general principles of it have taken very deep root and are making daily progress. I am at a loss to conjecture why Government has allowed the building of Barracks in the City to be so long delayed. It seems to me a measure of much immediate necessity.

A week after this the Lord Advocate wrote his uncle again, warning that Lord Lauderdale had visited Muir in the Tolbooth to plan an official appeal to Parliament against the legality of the sentence, with all that might imply. Worse, every one of the Friends of the People clubs of yesteryear had now revived and were daily finding new heart. So much so their most dangerous Convention yet was about to open. A *British* Convention! In the capital of Scotland! And of course;

> the bad consequences of Muir remaining here become every day more apparent. Although it is still my opinion that, if possible, no distinction should be made between him and any other convict, yet rather than allow him to remain here, I consider his removal to London to be essential for the peace and quiet of this city.

For the Home Secretary, all this was then greatly aggravated by an item of disturbing family news; Archibald Hamilton Rowan, the United Irishman, had announced that he would shortly be arriving in Edinburgh to challenge the Lord Advocate to a duel.

Midst all this escalating hubbub the Reformer worked long hours each night in his candle-lit corner of the Tolbooth, drafting papers his friends would collect the following day and convey to the Convention; papers which, while outlining his thoughts and advice on tactics, constantly stressed the necessity to avoid any action which could conceivably, or even inconceivably, be judged contrary to constitutional procedure. The founder of the radical *Gazetteer*, Captain Johnston, who had served his three months in the Tolbooth but was still liable to forfeit the £500 bail demanded as surety for good behaviour, also felt need to write cautionary letters to William Skirving, now the leading organiser of the Convention.

> ... In the immature state in which the societies are at present, it would be infinitely more politic to soften, than to exasperate by hasty denunciations. If you do denounce, from that moment you will be considered as pursuing a similar conduct with the *Jacobin clubs in France*. ... I am convinced that we have the ball at our feet, if we can manage with common address; but should we proceed to violent denunciations, the next course to be adopted will be violent measures.

Some very sound advice on strategy in this difficult time is followed by a statement of his own continuing commitment to reform. Johnston, whose talents had caused him to be described in one of Robert Watt's reports as 'the modern Demosthenes', appears to have been a man of considerable sagacity as well oratory. Another letter, warning that aristocrats like Lord Lauderdale were too committed to political *Party* to be any real assistance to the *principles* that must guide the people, gives his reasons for not being personally more active at present.

> I have sacrificed health, friends, and more money than I can afford, to a cause which I am ready to lay my life down tomorrow, to see obtained; my peculiar situation renders my attendance impossible, – you know it, – I hope the world knows it, – take my advice, – mind no body, – go on, – let– Magna Charta and the Bill of Rights direct your conduct, – don't waste your time in weak and trifling debates – be dignified and constitutional.

Johnston's next letter warned Skirving that the proposed reconvening of the *British* convention would create a great deal of official bustle, and from the conclusion of Watt's report a few weeks earlier [29th October] it seems that bustle had by then already reached a level where even the *agent-provocateur* was being provoked.

> It is now 11pm. Yours half-asleep, J.B.

That of the 31st began:

> 10 minutes past twelve midnight.
> Sir, This is the proper hour for works of darkness.

Then in his first report of November, referring to the fact that the previous night's Reform meeting had ended with a prayer, Watt ended his letter cheekily:

> So you see, my good friend, we are not all French aethesists, altho we ape some of their peculiarities – and altho some of us condemn ourselves in that which we allow. Wishing you nevertheless a good morning, I am, Sir, yours ever respect'ly,
> J.B.
> PS. This is rather severe for both soul and body. When is it to be at an end?

Spying by day and writing reports by night was taking its toll. Watt's burden had been greatly added to when the much anticipated British Convention of the Friends of the People opened on Tuesday, 29th October, though it turned out at first to have been much too ambitiously titled. There were upwards of 150 delegates in attendance on the first day but none was from England. Despite this, Convention business proceeded, and by the time it adjourned four days later resolutions had been passed calling for annual Parliaments, the universal right to vote and a petition to oppose the war with France. When the delayed delegation from England finally did arrive in Edinburgh, it was decided to call a second Convention and two of the late arrivals, Maurice Margarot and Joseph Gerrald, who had been nominated by Thomas Hardy of the London Corresponding Society, then began to take a very active part in proceedings. Contingency plans were drawn up to deal with any Government measures raised against them, and a secret committee was set up to monitor and act when necessary.

In the midst of receiving reports on all these matters, the Home Secretary had to pause and take quiet steps to prevent that duel taking place between his nephew, now returned from Dunkeld to Edinburgh, and Hamilton Rowan, the United Irishman, now arrived in Scotland's capital from Dublin. The Home Secretary wrote the Solicitor General arranging to have Rowan arrested on a political charge, but Colonel Macleod, despite having previously written the Irish leader to express disapproval of an action he considered politically unhelpful to 'the public cause of liberty', put up the demanded bail and the Irishman was released from custody. Robert Dundas, who had referred to the United Irishmen during Muir's trial as 'infamous wretches who had fled from the punishment due to their crimes' now insisted he could not be held responsible for remarks made in the course of a Court trial and Hamilton Rowan – declaring Robert Dundas to be a liar and a coward – celebrated by having a merry dinner two days later with Macleod and Muir in the Tolbooth cell, during which he presented the prisoner with a pair of the pistols intended for the duel.

The disdainful labels that the privileged had been using were now enthusiastically incorporated in radical toasts, and as the wine flowed they would no doubt be used to make Edinburgh's old Tolbooth resound.

The swine of England!
The rabble of Scotland! The wretches of Ireland!
The three United nations!

But that was to prove the last light-hearted meeting anyone in Edinburgh had with Tom Muir. The Lord Advocate's anxious letters to his uncle had finally produced the desired result, and on 10th November Muir wrote a letter of farewell to his closest friend.

I leave you and Mrs Moffat perhaps for ever, but your
remembrance never shall be effaced from mine. In public I can
act the part of a man – I can meet everything with fortitude;
but in private I must give way to the feelings of nature. My
dear and valued friend, in the remotest corner of the world
your remembrance and that of Mrs Moffat shall soothe my
afflictions, but my tears shall flow over the remembrance. I am
really unwell. I cannot write much, nor have I time, but neither
of you shall be wiped away from my heart.[3]

Throughout that week Muir was said to be quite ill, was seen by
very few, and at the end of it was escorted down to Newhaven to be
put aboard the Revenue cutter *Royal George*. He was bound for
Campbell's Academy, as bitter irony had named the prison hulks at
Woolwich. But this removal of the ringleader did not prove to be the
expected final solution. Before the month was out, the essential core
of Dundas power in Scotland appeared to be under threat.

RD, Edinburgh, to HD, London. 11th December 1793.

I understand that the general feeling of the inhabitants here
is that Muir and Palmer ought only to have been confined until
opportunity of transporting them offered, and that their being
handcuffed or obliged to work like other felons is made the
handle of some clamour, and which may have a bad effect. If
you think it proper to show them any distinction from the case
of other convicts, it appears to me your doing so would be of
service. If the juries here take it in their heads that more is
done to these gentry than is absolutely necessary, they may
aquit where they would otherwise have convicted.

It seems that even the Lord Advocate's hand-waled fifteen men
'of proper principles' could no longer be relied upon to have entirely
unscrupulous minds.

* * *

3. Insh Papers. National Library of Scotland. Dep. 344.

Loose Ends

> Procurator Fiscal Scott to Lord Advocate Dundas. 22nd Dec, 1793
> From the minutes of Convention & other papers seized it is
> evident that JB's information has been very full. Conviction of
> the Ringleaders is unavoidable, the good effects of which I
> hope will be long felt.

It is not surprising that Robert Watt's recent reports via the Fiscal had
been of such value. He was now serving on Friends of the People
committees, with free and immediate access to all their resolutions,
some of which he actually helped compile. He had received one of
those Extra payments to cover the dinner he had with delegates to
the 3rd British Convention, amongst whom he reported James Wilson
from Strathaven, probably the same radical leader executed in 1820.
Other delegates had come from Linlithgow, Stirling and Dundee, two
from Glasgow were listed as United Scotsmen and the spy noted that
Lord Daer had been addressed as Citizen Douglas. But making all this
information available to Procurator Fiscal Scott, so soon after taking
active part in late meetings and dinners, involved very hard labour.

> 10 at night. Tho' I finished my last this morning at 3 o'clock I
> did not get it put in the office till one – but I hope you got it
> soon after.

He noted that the writing of this current report took till 2.15am,
and the following day complained about such official pressure.

> Half-past 12am. Is not this a degree of the slave trade?

Next night he was too late home to write, he explained, but had
made up for it on the morrow by working till half-after-midnight,
completing an unusually informative report; so informative he was
constrained to end this letter with a reminder that his own safety was
now at stake.

> If you wish to investigate the nature of their secret business
> judicially, do as you please, but do not be too precipitate or
> hasty in your inquiries – for the sake of, Sir, yours etc., J.B.

Procurator Fiscal Scott would recognise they were pressing their
man very hard indeed, but these were hard times and so with Sheriff
Pringle's blessing he pressed even harder, the immediate result of
which was a sarcastic rejoinder from Watt in which he refused to be
regarded as 'omniprescent'.

That could be ignored. More perplexing to the Procurator Fiscal would be the letter Watt sent addressing him as Citizen Scott. It was probably just another example of the man's wry humour, mocking the style adopted at the Conventions, but it must have caused the Fiscal to conjecture on just how much more pressure he could usefully apply. For some time now Watt had become rather over-familiar in his letters and it remained unclear whether his skewed personal observations were being addressed at the Procurator Fiscal, Sheriff Pringle or, via the transcriptions, the Lord Advocate; possibly all three.

In the following week, however, any such concerns would be set to one side; the quality of information received had allowed Sheriff Pringle to organise a raid on a Convention meeting and he now had sufficient evidence on the arrested ringleaders, Skirving, Margarot and Gerrald, to ensure they would shortly receive similar sentences to Muir and Palmer. To this good news, sent to Lord Advocate Dundas, once more in London, was added the information that Lord Daer was ill, not likely to be active for some time, and Colonel Macleod had now publicly dissociated himself from the British Convention. At long last *Authority's* sword seemed ready to deliver the *coup de grace* on the hydra-headed monster that for so long had haunted its nightmares, and in very large measure indeed this success had its origins in all Robert Watt's works of darkness in the wee small hours of those long October and November nights.

If December was tidy-up time, it was also time for pay-off. The Revd Lapslie surfaced again from Campsie to remind Dundas of his own great contributions to the struggle against democracy, adding for good measure – and quite gratis – some further words of advice. At ground level, he warned, the Friends of the People were as vigorous as ever; but the anti-religious news from France should be put to use, as even Reformers were upset by it. This man of Christ then went on:

> I am highly sensible my Lord that it would be highly improper in me or any person to talk of limiting the Royal Mercy in pardonning criminals – at the same time I am inclined to believe that the community at large do not wish at this critical period that a Seditious person should experience much of the Sovereign clemency. The mob, my Lord, would be apt to mistake the motive from which the government acted – they would ascribe to timidity every mitigation of their sentence – they would boast that the King durst not put the Law in execution. I am confident the lower classes of mankind should never for their own sakes be permitted to entertain such an idea.

However Lapslie may have recognised his 'community at large' from his 'mob', he ended this epistle with the final warning that, for fear they will abandon all order, the lower classes must never be allowed to taste luxury. Meanwhile, Procurator Fiscal Scott had not waited for another begging letter from his spy before giving proof of official gratitude, as Watt's reply indicates.

21st December, 1793.

I beg pardon for not having sooner acknowledged receipt of your repeated favors, particularly your genteel presents to a certain Royal Lady who desires me to return you her best thanks for it. A variety of circumstances that it would only be proper to mention viva voce have occupied every moment of my time since I wrote you. Besides there was nothing new, at least that I could hear of, worth communicating to you.

I mentioned in my last that the Oracle was shut. This requires explanation at meeting. Next week the Spirit of Divination may probably return {since you insist upon it} as I expect to have more leasure soon. Meantime, I am, Sir, yrs etc,
J.B.

Before the end of December Sheriff Pringle, too, had received his just desserts.

Much praise is due to our Sheriff, Mr Pringle, who is now at the close of the labour more deservedy promoted to an office of greater emolument & ease & dignity and which I sincerely wish he may long enjoy.

Having been at some pains to record in writing his own exertions and continuing efforts, particularly with the indispensable *JB*, the Procurator Fiscal added what might have been a hopeful reminder.

Sheriff Pringle's successor will it's to be hoped have little to do in such a business as we have of late been employed in.

I have the honour to remain, my Lord, your Lordship's most obedient Humble servant, William Scott.

Then just before the year was ended, Lord Braxfield made Henry Dundas the present of the crowning news that, in his opinion, Muir's trial and sentence had been quite justified and lawful; despite the continuing protests, transportation could proceed.

Authority's New Year started full of positive thinking. After Skirving and Margarot had duly been found guilty, the Lord Advocate wrote his uncle that he was prepared to go to 'utmost extremity' in tying up any remaining loose ends; the successful outcome of all the Sedition trials, resulting from exercise of that delegated discretion, having proved such a boost to his confidence that he now addressed his uncle much more as equal.

> I need not point out to you the propriety of an early, indeed an immediate removal of both Margarot and Skirving to the final place of their destination. Any reasons which formerly operated against the immediate removal of Muir & Palmer are now at an end. The more decided you are in your treatment of these people, the better for the Country; and to do you justice you have been completely so with the other two; and your conduct here is universally approved.
>
> I will only say the conduct and behaviour of Margarot during his Trial, that it was a scene of insolence, effrontery & petulance unparalleled. His speech, or rather his lecture to the Jury, was in every part Inflammatory & Seditious; in some respects Treasonable.

In ending, the Lord Advocate still seemed a little upset that the man after whom his youngest son was recently named, had been a particular target. 'Margarot abused Mr Pitt most completely'. Then a week or two later, in case London still harboured doubts over the need for that immediate transportation, the Lord Advocate forwarded a copy of the latest threatening letter to arrive in his office.

> 23rd January, 1794.
>
> My Lord, it is impossible for any person to behold with an indifferent eye the transactions which are now carrying on in this country. On the one hand we have Reformers contending for certain principles & certain renovations which everybody allows to be founded on justice. On the other, Government prosecuting in rigorous manner such honest endeavours.
>
> You have the honour, or rather misfortune from your situation, to be the Chief Agent in such prosecutions. But reflect, my Lord, that the trite argument of this being an improper time for reform will be found wanting in the Balance of Posterity.
>
> I remember, and your Lordship knows well, that the Reformers previous to the Glorious Revolution were more few, more despicable, more oppressed than any Reformer now a days. The wanton cruelty, the perversion of Justice, the unheard of oppression employed towards these men soon attached to their cause the feeling of the Moderate. The Nation was roused to fury, it took ample justice on the authors of their wrongs.

Thank God we have not at this day the same causes of complaint; but they are sufficiently strong to excite the murmurs of the People. Your Lordship is perhaps ignorant of the extent to which the principles of Reform have diffused themselves. When I say that two-thirds of the Country are so inclined, I am positive I do not exceed the number.

Do not imagine that because certain Corporations are ever ready to re-echo the self-dictated applauses of the Magistrates & to thank them for their exertions {which in better times would have brought them to the gallows} or because a jury can be found that will vote as your Lordship pleases, that therefore you enjoy the confidence of the People. Very far from it. Corporations in every country are the least numerous, the most servile of the community. They have certain interests which are most closely connected with the Ruling Party. But even among these monopolies, such are the charms of Truth, there are many Friends of Liberty.

Your Lordship is daily losing in the esteem of the Rabble. The sanguinary & harsh measures employed against Reformers are with some degree of propriety attributed to you. Mr Muir & now Mr Skirving's & Margarot's cruel treatment have added to your Lordship's unpopularity; a few more will render you perfectly odious. It will then be reckoned honourable to deprive Society of such a Pest. Some Male, or rather more likely some Female hand, will direct the Dagger that will do such an important service and Britain shall not want a Female Patriot emulous of the fame of M'selle Cordet.

Your less humble Serv't,

Tabitha Bramble.

If the identity of the writer was discovered it does not appear to be recorded. *Tabitha Bramble*, of course, is a character in what was then a popular new Scots novel – *The Expedition of Humphry Clinker* – written in epistolic form by Tobias Smollet. Early editions of that work carried on the title page a quotation from Horace's *Sermones* – '*Quorsum haec tam putida tendunt, Furcifer? Ad te, inquam*' – for which the 1998 edition gives the translation: To what object are these disagreeable facts directed, you rogue? To you, I said.

Both the style and content of *Tabitha's* letter have some echoes of Robert Watt at this stage in his activities but perhaps it is too fanciful to suggest his characteristic wry humour had led to *Jeremy Bramble* being chosen as *nom-de-guerre* when first recruited to begin his own long series of epistles.

Though removal of Muir and Palmer from Edinburgh had greatly eased matters for the Lord Advocate, their transfer to the Hulks at Woolwich seems to have created one problem after another for his uncle. When it became known the pair were being shackled into convict-gangs every day and made to labour on the river banks, the outcry in London proved rather more serious than would have been politic to ignore, but when the Home Secretary then decreed that the pair should simply be confined to quarters all day, they began to enjoy prolonged visits from a great many influential English supporters, the kind who could raise damaging debates in Parliament.

Like his nephew before him, the Home Secretary decided there would be no end to the trouble this pair attracted until they were removed, out of the kingdom, once and for all. They were to sail without further delay, he ordered, and the the transport ship *Canada* was made ready. Then *Canada* was found to have a rotten hull. Then Muir became very ill again. For all his great powers, even Henry Dundas might not survive such a death in custody and this ever more troublesome prisoner was quickly removed from the diseased Hulks to slightly more salubrious lodgings in Newgate Prison. But Skirving and Margarot, having been despatched out of Scotland immediately after their trials, were already lodged there and so Newgate became something of a Reform headquarters, its situation allowing readier access for an increased number of visitors, some titled, all influential, and all demanding a Royal Petition against the sentences.

Added to these cares, and almost every day now, the Home Secretary was subject to what might have been an orchestrated bombardment of alarmist reports from Provosts of Towns all over Scotland.

Armed rebellion can not be ruled out.
Loyal Volunteer Corps must be formed.
To give arms to the Militia is to arm Reform!
The army must not be billeted with the populace.
Military barracks must be built without delay!

King Harry surfaced through this paperwork, ordered a replacement for *Canada* to be made ready at once, and by mid-February the transport *Surprize* was off Woolwich. Long before dawn on the day after she anchored there, the reformers in Newgate Prison were roused from their sleep with neither ceremony nor warning and shipped on board. Then, as soon as tide and loading permitted, *Surprize* weighed anchor and set sail for Botany Bay. But just as it seemed these troublesome men were at last out of the Home Secretary's wig, bad weather delayed the ship as she attempted to round North Foreland

Head, allowing news of her departure from the Thames to spread, news that even reached Paris, where officials ordered all measures be taken to intercept the transport and restore Muir and his colleagues to freedom.

For Robert Dundas, the thought of his prime adversary being snatched to safety by a vessel despatched for the purpose by the revolutionary French, would be about the worst possible outcome he could ever imagine. That and other very serious matters drove him to depart once more, poste haste, for London.

Though the now storm-damaged *Surprize* was still limping along towards Portsmouth, many believed the sentences on the four political prisoners – barbaric if not illegal – simply could not or would not be carried out. The Hulks, where about one in three convicts eventually died, had been bad enough, but it was known that in the voyage to Botany Bay as many as a quarter could die before even reaching there and half as many again shortly after landing. Though the Royal Petition vote in Parliament had been lost by more than five to one, with the usual block vote for Henry Dundas by all the Scottish MPs excepting Colonel Macleod, there were still those thirty-two English MPs who voted in favour and who remained active in the campaign for a review of the sentences.

Large meetings in a number of English towns had demanded justice for the reformers and all redoubled efforts when *Surprize* was found to require repairs that would keep her lying at the Mother Bank for almost six weeks. Even at this remove the reformers remained the focus of much attention. Friends, well-wishers and activists travelling down to Portsmouth to stay long hours in conversation and have meals with the four men, and the sculptor, Thomas Banks of Soho, took a cast of Muir's face for a future bust. Thomas Hardy of the London Corresponding Society was there to tell of the high hopes he had for the great open-air meeting planned in London; it would be an important affair, also involving the Constitutional Information Society, and it would take place on Thursday, 24th April, at Chalk Farm. Much was expected of this meeting, and much that was unexpected arose out of it. In its immediate aftermath, the Westminster Secrets Committee of both Houses of Parliament – guided in very large measure by uncle and nephew Dundas – ordered the arrest of all the English-based ringleaders, followed by a suspension of *habeas corpus*.

No doubt having managed till now to put a brave face on things, the four political prisoners aboard *Surprize* must have been shattered on the morning of the first day of May to hear the sailors chant the capstans into rotation and feel the creaking, clanking thuds as the ships great anchors were finally weighed. But it would be more than their own immediate situation – just a week after the Chalk Farm meeting – that finally caused the heart to be temporarily knocked out of them. During the weeks at the Mother Bank they had been taunted by some officers about the news being received hourly from across the Channel; unbelievable news, but news their visitors had later confirmed. The list of utterly incomprehensible disasters in France, daily increasing in frequency, must have had a devastating effect. In January, Tom Paine had been made a prisoner of the Republic he had given so much to create.

La Guillotine lui attend!

Then the twenty-two Girondist deputies from Caen, several of them men Muir had known and liked; men who had assisted at the fall of the Bastille

Guillotiné!

Madame Roland too, in whose home he had dined.

Guillotinée!

The heroic and greatly-admired Danton

Guillotiné!

Desmoulins and his young wife.

Guillotinée!

As the sails filled and *Surprize* began to surge up and over the water they could not have felt other than that everything, the whole world, had been turned completely on its head. But it would be a long time before they learned just how completely and utterly everything had been reversed. Two weeks after *Surprize* sailed from Portsmouth, uncle and nephew Dundas were still together in London, busily preparing for the final trial in their long-running series. Appropriately, this promised to be the most impressive of all. For the first time in several generations the High Court in Edinburgh would be sitting in judgment over an accused charged with the capital crime of High Treason. Best of all for the Dundas Duo, this final trial promised to tidy up for ever all the dangerously loose ends that had lately been causing them much increased concern. The wry-humoured *JB* of the epistles, their most diligent and successful of spies, had penned his last tongue-in-cheek postscript. His alter-ego, Robert Watt, was just about to be arrested in Edinburgh on a charge of plotting armed revolt against the State.

Lord Braxfield who sentenced Muir to fourteen years transportation

Chapter 6
Exile

Thomas Muir de Hunters Hill
Gente Scotus, Anima Orbis terrarum Civis Obtulit.

This was the inscription Muir wrote on the flyleaf of a book left at the Monastery of San Antonio, when Surprize lay for a short time off Rio de Janeiro, taking on board supplies.

Thomas Muir of Hunters Hill,
by race a Scot, in Spirit a citizen of the World, has made this gift.

The voyage to Australia occupied almost half a year but though it was to prove a far from uneventful passage, nothing of any political significance has been noted. The two French frigates despatched in the rescue attempt appear not to have located the convoy of which *Surprize* was part and so all on board the transport remained effectively isolated from European events. They were, however, very much involved in what might be described as domestic problems. Muir, Palmer, Skirving and Mr and Mrs Margarot shared the vessel with the normal crew, two officer's wives, three young children and a small number of voluntary settlers. Also on board the 430 ton vessel were an ensign of the New South Wales Corps, twenty-one other ranks – some of whom had been deserters and one a mutineer – plus twenty-three male and sixty female convicts.

> None of the female convicts exceeds 40 years of age and there can be no doubt that they will be the means, by intermarriage, of rendering the men more diligent and laborious, and with greater satisfaction to themselves, in proportion as the object or motive of their labour will thereby be increased and enhanced.

That, at any rate, was the optimistic view of Home Secretary Henry Dundas. In practice, *Surprize* became something of a hellship. The crowded holds were miserably wet and cold by day, steamy and suffocating by night under battened-down hatches, and always pervaded by the stench of livestock close-confined with the humans below decks. Alcohol fuelled every excess, from officer brutality to sexual licence, and no doubt played a part too in the alleged mutiny that had to be suppressed under threat of swivel-mounted blunderbusses. The Captain, during this alarm, was 'accoutred like a perfect Robinson Crusoe. He was girt with a sword and dagger and carried pistols in all his pockets'.[1]

There are contradictory accounts of individual behaviour during this troubled half-year at sea, such a guddle of accusation and counter-accusation that, despite the captain's document-laden charge to the colony's Governor at the end of the voyage, no proceedings were ever raised against anyone. Muir had offered to act for those accused of plotting mutiny, but amidst all the recriminations no one records that he was otherwise involved. He seems to have kept very much to himself during the voyage, having paid for a small cabin which he left no more than was necessary. Suppositions that he may have taken to drink, a liaison with one of the female convicts, or both, are no more than that; suppositions not yet based on any real evidence. Were they true, however, many would surely judge it a fairly understandable way for anyone in his situation to thole a hellish voyage.

The Latin verse on the flyleaf of that book presented to the monastery was translated as:

> O Scotland! O my country for long blessed and proud above others, most holy land of heroes, rich in resources, fertile in men, most fortunate in its rich plains!
>
> Who could ever relate thy afflictions and the extent of thy troubles, and find words to match our sorrows and base disgrace and those barbarous laws!
>
> We leave behind the frontiers of our fatherland and its sweet fields.
>
> Tomorrow we shall journey again over the vast ocean.[2]

It seems likely a great deal of Muir's time on that voyage would have been spent in study, he having indicated that intention in a letter written just before *Surprize* left behind the last of what most considered to be civilisation.

> I am perfectly resigned to my situation. A man who dreads dishonour as the greatest of all possible dangers should never use the term – suffering. The book of mankind is shut to me, but the volume of nature is widely opened. I am preparing my

---

1. Appendix A.

2. Bewley Muir of Huntershill p115

124

mind to those studies, whose object is the investigation of her animal and vegetable productions, for an innocent, if not useful amusement. My imagination sometimes whispers to me that I shall not be a spectator of inanimate nature merely, but that I may contemplate an infant empire, a new Europe in embryo.[3]

But while the New World might present great opportunity for an enquiring mind, the Old World was now going to even greater lengths in that scorched-earth policy against growth of new ideas. After the London meeting for reform at Chalk Farm, Thomas Hardy of the London Corresponding Society was arrested with others and held without trial, while in Edinburgh the last of what were to become known as the Scottish Martyrs, Joseph Gerrald, had also received the now standard fourteen years transportation. Procurator-Fiscal Scott continued to keep the Dundas Duo in London fully up-to-date with events in the north via his continuing stream of *JB* transcriptions.

> A mild winter, a cold spring,
> A bloody summer, and no king!

At the beginning of the year, Watt had reported this Thomas the Rhymer prophecy for 1794 to be on every Reformer's lips, then in his report dated 18th April he told of events that had occurred the previous night at a production of *The Royal Martyr* in one of Edinburgh's theatres. It had been billed as a chance to compare the similarity of circumstances which attended the two kings, Charles I and Louis XXVI – 'A proper lesson at this juncture to be held out to warn mankind from stepping out of the paths of virtue and religion'. The publicity succeeded in attracting more bums, perhaps, on seats than it had bargained for; the attempt at *God Save the King* being swamped by their bellows of '*God Save the People!*' – '*Ça Ira!*' – '*The Soo's Tail to Geordie!*' The show, it seems, was a riot. The local radicals had been reinforced in their protest by Irish medical students and the young [Sir] Walter Scott, now himself a member of the Faculty of Advocates, lent the weight of his stick on the side of those supporting *Authority*. In a letter to Patrick Murray a few days later, Scott recorded that he was one of five bound over to keep the peace and obliged to post bail for future good behaviour.

With the Lord Advocate's return to Scotland a month later, political events then took that even more dramatic turn that was to prove beyond the powers of Robert Watt to put on record. Partly because of

---

3. Ibid. p103.

that, the truth underlying what transpired may never be established with complete certainty, but a number of facts very damaging to the marble-white images of uncle and nephew Dundas in Old Parliament House are beyond dispute. Just one month after that fracas in the theatre, Home Secretary Dundas wrote Prime Minister Pitt to commence putting on record what he clearly hoped would henceforth be the public version of events in the north.

> Whitehall, May 19, 1794.
>
> Sir, I have received this morning, from the Sheriff-Depute of the county of Edinburgh, authentic information of an accidental discovery made on the 15th and 16th inst., the general report of which I feel it proper to state to you, as it seems materially connected with the enquiry which the Secret Committee of the House of Commons is now engaged.
>
> The creditor of a bankrupt having received information that part of his goods had been embezzled, and were secreted in the house of an individual, the usual warrant was issued, authorising a search to be made in the suspected place; and, in carrying it into execution, on the afternoon of the 15th, the officers discovered in a private place where they appeared to be concealed, twelve pike or spear-heads.[5]

Mr Lockhart, Depute Sheriff-Clerk in Edinburgh, had been involved in that search for some goods of a bankrupt when some unrevealed source had provided information that these 'embezzled' goods were likely to be found *chez* Robert Watt. In the trial record, Watt swore the goods were sent to him from Musselburgh, some eight days previously, 'under the pretext of their being forwarded to Glasgow'. Mr Lockhart appears to have lost all interest in the search for these goods because, to his amazement, he found in a locked cupboard in Watt's home those twelve new-made pike-heads. The dutiful functionary hurried with this news to the Sheriff Clerk's office and Robert Watt was arrested. Some time after midnight, having returned to make the arrested man's home secure, lo and behold another four pike-heads were found in another cupboard; all of which, when combined with broom-handle shafts, were seen to form efficient revolutionary halberds. Among the finds this time was a copy of that first letter Robert Watt had written to Henry Dundas, two years previously, together with the Home Secretary's reply. Lockhart, of course, had a witness to all these great revelations; a Sheriff's officer, William

---

5. *Scots Magazine* Aug. 1794. Report of the Secret Committee

Middleton, had accompanied his visits. At the trial, Middleton was asked if he had ever searched the premises of a man named Orrock, who had a smiddy at Dean. He had made such a search, after the first search of Watt's house, though no explanation is recorded as to what drew him to the location. At the smiddy, they found a few more finished pike-heads and a larger number unfinished. By another of those strange coincidences it seems that a servant of Lord Swinton, one of the judges who tried Muir, had by chance arrived at the smiddy just some days previously when Watt was present and urging the blacksmith to increased production. The explanation given to Swinton's servant was that the pike-heads were decorations for a gentleman's gate.[6]

After arrest, Robert Watt's behaviour suggests he was convinced he would soon be set free. He declined to give the Sheriff any answers at all other than that he communicated with the Home Secretary and the Lord Advocate about 'certain circumstances'. Those circumstances were almost certainly the cause of some further urgent correspond-ence from the Home Office, to which Edinburgh's Lord Provost replied immediately.

23rd May, 1794.

I have received the honour of your letter dated 20th instant signifying His Majesty's pleasure that, in case any well grounded suspicion should fall on any person or persons in this city or neighbourhood, having in their possession such arms or weapons as mentioned in your letter, I shall cause diligent search be made for and seize all such arms or weapons, together of the persons to whom they belong, and any papers of a treasonable and seditious nature which may be found in their possession that such person or persons may be dealt with according to law. I beg you will do the Magistrates of Edinburgh the honour to assure His Majesty of their utmost exertions and vigilism obeying his comands on all occasions.

So, on the 20th of May, five days after Watt was arrested, Home Secretary Dundas had written the Lord Provost to say His Majesty would be pleased if Edinburgh would keep an eye open for anyone behaving like Robert Watt. The Lord Provost's reply to this instruction went on to explain that, just nine days previously, the day Robert Dundas had returned to Edinburgh from London, he himself had received just the very information required by King George. Strangely,

6. *State Trials*

though, the Lord Provost's letter makes no mention of any bankrupt's embezzled goods.

> On Wednesday se'enight, [14th May] I had good information from a private person that such weapons were making in different places without the Jurisdiction of the City. I immediately communicated to the Solicitor General and to the Crown Agent, and the day after, [15th May] by warrant of the Sheriff and Magistrates, several of these weapons and those employed in making them were seized and are detained in prison, and a general search made the suspected houses both in the city and suburbs, but the Sheriff before whom these persons have been examined has wrote you regularly the particulars, I thought it unnecessary to trouble you to the same purpose.

Unnecessary, except perhaps to acknowledge instructions regarding how Watt was to be dealt with and to put on record an explanation for him being held incommunicado.

> Our jail is so excessively crowded with these and other prisoners that an order of Government to send to the Castle such as are taken up for treasonable or seditious aggressions would be of great consequence. I have the honour to remain with the most perfect respect and esteem, Sir, Your most faithful and most obedient Serv't, Tho, Elder.

A more elaborated explanation of these transactions was recorded in a pamphlet published the following year. From this it appears that one Neilson, of Musselburgh, having despatched a trunk of goods from his premises after being declared bankrupt, found a creditor demanding immediate payment of what was owed him. The Magistrate involved established that the missing goods had gone to Robert Watt's home in North Grey's Close and, out of a sense of civic duty, passed this information on to the next creditor who sued; more, he assisted this second creditor to get official participation in that search of Watt's home which revealed the deadly pikes. After all of which, it seems almost *de trop* that the pamphlet ends by recording that the bankrupt Mr Neilson of Musselburgh, whose financial misdemeanours had proved so useful to *Authority*, left Scotland within the week to become a preacher in England.[7]

If a ruthless official fit-up to silence Robert Watt be discounted, along with the notion he actually *was* commander of nascent

7. Pamphlet. National Library of Scotland. Ref 3.855[3]

revolution, two other possibilities remain. Either he may have been creating revolutionary evidence in hope of personal reward, or he was officially employed in the role of *agent provocateur* when some minor sheriff's employee accidentally stumbled over the pikes and banjaxed the contract. A third possibility can not be discounted; Watt may finally have flipped his own lid to the extent that his left hand kneweth nothing of what his right hand did, though in that case subsequent events do not heap credit on his employers. The trial records give the date of Robert Dundas's return to Edinburgh as 15th May, the day Watt was arrested, so there probably was time for the Lord Advocate to brief Lord Provost Elder of decisions made in London. As things turned out, however, it seems that not everything in Edinburgh went quite to plan. There is something like alarm in the Home Secretary's next letter to his nephew.

> My dear Advocate
> I wish to God you would come down to us. This damnable news renders your presence indispensible. This is not a time for punctillios and much as I esteem & revere the Solicitor, his character fits him beyond all men for the office of a judge but not for a minister.

Which raises the interesting question what sort of character Henry Dundas thought a government minister ideally should have. There were other problems, too, now that the Lord Provost was no longer the Post Master General.

> 27th May, 1794. Lord Provost Elder
> to Henry Dundas, Home Office.
> Mr Sheriff Clerk, thinking your letter to me of 20th authorising the seizure & detention of the persons & papers of those suspected on good grounds of Treasonable or Seditious practices sufficient to stop at the Post Office letters directed to such persons, he and I applied to the Secretary in absence of the Post Master General to stop letters directed to certain persons who are now prisoners & others who have absconded. After deliberating, Mr Kerr did not think your letter to me warranted the Postmaster or his inferiors in the Post Office to take this strong measure and therefore by the advice of Mr Clerk & Mr Kerr I now write you & submit to your better judgement . . . you may think it proper to send an order for the purpose to the PMG to stop all letters addressed to such persons as the Lord Justice Clerk, Lord Provost or Sheriff or any of them you think most proper, shall direct . . . The Sheriff thinks it very material in the investigation at present going on to have your authority for stopping letters.
> Yours etc – Tho. Elder.

From these last two letters it appears the Dundas's were no longer getting things quite their own way in Edinburgh; though within the week, Lord Adam Gordon, Commander-in-chief Scotland, wrote the Home Office agreeing to the Castle being used, as requested, for selected prisoners.

As was the case after the 1745 Rebellion, the Lord Advocate now had a country-wide network of Lords Lieutenant instructed to organise local surveillance capable of separating loyal sheep from radical goats. Lord Provost Elder was now to be so appointed and a draft document from the King specifically indemnified him, while in pursuit of HM's service, 'of all blood, slaughter, mutillation, or any other inconveniences whatsoever'.

By way of delivering a *coup de grace* to the monster that was *British* Reform, the Dundas plan now was to link London's Chalk Farm detainees with all treasonable activities discovered north of the Border. For this and other reasons, a normal Scottish trial was not desirable. On 20th June, nephew wrote uncle – *entre nous* – that he would prefer a Commission of Oyer and Terminer, the principal benefit of which being that it would not require involvement of the hitherto highly serviceable but now apparently 'violent and intemperate' Lord Braxfield.

The Lord Advocate did not have to put on record that this would also mean that, with an English judge presiding over a case conducted according to English Law, he would not have to act as Crown Prosecutor in face-to-face accusation of his erstwhile co-conspirator. Though some might protest that the Treaty of Union was thus being broken, there would be little real protest if the public at large was massaged into a suitable state of alarm over the dangers from which they had just been rescued. The Home Secretary to Prime Minister correspondence necessary for that purpose, carefully worded, was about to be made public.[8]

A series of letters during May and June of 1794 first of all indicated the need for magistrate's reports from Edinburgh to be placed before Westminster's Secret Committee, recorded that only a happy accident had discovered that pikes were being manufactured and warned that 'artful means' were being used to incite mutiny in the Fencible Regiments that had just been raised. There was oblique reference to Watt's activities as co-ordinator of these revolutionary proceedings and a statement that all previous suspicions concerning the nation-wide nature of the planning had now been confirmed 'by every

8. e.g. *Scots Magazine* Aug 1794

account and information which the magistrate's have received'. In case anyone should ask awkward questions about all this, there was a concluding paragraph to this official version of the relevant correspondence.

> Your Committee have, for obvious reasons, omitted to annex
> to their Report the evidence of particular witnesses, by whom
> the facts above stated are supported; and for the same reasons,
> they have studiously forborne to mention the names of
> persons and places, in all cases in which they could be omitted
> with a proper attention to the general object of their enquiry,
> and to the information which the House has a right to expect
> upon so important a subject.

With all the preparatory pieces now securely in place, there remained only one thing left to do, and the man for a final proof of Scots loyalty was Edinburgh's leading wine-merchant. Lord Provost Elder's letter to King George, in July, placed at the foot of his Majesty's throne tributes of zeal and affection 'to the person and government of one of the best princes that ever ruled over our nation'. Pledging every assistance of the nation's burgesses 'in support of the civil power and the maintenance of the executive government of this country', and expressing gratitude for the action Westminster was taking 'in this juncture of national danger', this most solemn of tributes ended on an upbeat.

> Permit us, Sir, at the same time, to join our voice to that of the
> great body of the nation, in presenting our most hearty
> congratulations on the late glorious success of your Majesty's
> arms in the great naval victory obtained under the command
> of the gallant Earl Howe, over the enemies of this country, and
> the foes of the human species. We anticipate with joy the
> happy effects of this signal success, in hastening that
> conspicuous period when we shall once more enjoy the
> blessings of a lasting and honourable peace.
>
> Signed in our presence, and by our appointments, at
> Edinburgh, the 9th day of July, 1794 years.
>
> THOMAS ELDER, Lord Provost of the City of Edinburgh, and
> Preses of the Convention.

Robert Watt – the spy who came to a sticky end in the Royal Mile at the hands of his masters

Chapter 7

Works of Darkness

R obert Watt's trial for High Treason, under Commission of Oyer & Terminer, began on 21st August but due to the non-appearance of cited witnesses, many adjournments proved necessary and it was September 3rd before evidence began to be heard. Employees of the Edinburgh Sheriff's office then duly repeated the tale of pike-heads discovered by accident, but the copy of that introductory letter Watt had sent to Henry Dundas two years earlier was not allowed as evidence, since there was no proof it was a true copy of any actual letter despatched. A reply at that time from Henry Dundas to some such letter was accepted but the prosecution had already taken steps to limit further probing into this aspect of the business.

> Horseguards, August 29, 1794.
>
> Sir: I have the receipt of your's of the 26th instant and lose no time in informing you that having made a distinct search I do not find that I am in possession of any one of the letters adrest to me by Mr Watt, or the copy of any one of my letters to him; to the best of my recollection, all Mr Watt's letters were put in the hand of the Lord Advocate.
>
> I am, sir, your obedient humble servant, Henry Dundas.[1]

The Lord Advocate, appearing in this Treason trial as a witness for the prosecution, rehearsed quite factually and in some detail how Watt had come to be employed as an informer in 1792, but resorted to lengthy waffle when William Erskine, for the defence, asked if he had received a letter from Watt while at Dunkeld. Erskine then asked a very direct question.

> *Does your Lordship recollect any communication with respect to the plan of seizing the Banks?*
>
> *Never . . . Please to repeat your question.*
>
> *Whether your Lordship received from Mr Watt any communication with respect to a plan for seizing the Banks*

---

1. *State Trials*

while you were at Dunkeld in September 1793?

I was at Dunkeld in September 1793. I do not recollect having received any letter from Mr Watt, or having seen Mr Watt, since June or July 1793. It may be otherwise, but I do not recollect it.

Which reply may or may not be truthful.

Do you remember having seen any letter from him when you were in London?

In February 1793, before going to London, I saw Mr Watt at night once or twice. I cannot tell the number of times . . . I heard that a good deal of money was going amongst those people. I thought the money must come from some concealed quarter. I was desirous to know, and I stated that I was pretty positive it must come either from France or London, and I desired him to direct his attention particularly to that object. In March, about the end of it when in London, I received a letter from Mr Watt; he stated that he had been in company with certain individuals, their names I shall not mention, unless the counsel desire me to do so; two of them were of that description whom he watched, and whose proceedings he communicated. He wrote me that two of them had given him reason to believe that something of a very serious nature was going on which they were acquainted with, and which they were inclined to divulge, but which they would not discover unless they received a thousand pounds sterling down, or some very large sum I am sure it was.

Dundas then stated that, concurring with the advice of his uncle and the Chancellor of the Exchequer, he wrote Watt that such a sum could not be advanced without firm proof of the true value of the intelligence. He heard nothing further and on return to Scotland met Watt and had him reimbursed thirty shillings for out-of-pocket expenses incurred in dealing with these would-be informants. Erskine then asked if the Lord Advocate had any letter written by Watt to Henry Dundas.

After receiving my subpœna, I searched every place where I thought it possible, and ordered my clerk to do the same. I searched every place where I thought any correspondence with Watt could exist. I wished to get every correspondence between us, and there is what I have been able to find.

Though the prosecution tried to hurry Erskine on from this line of enquiry, the Lord Advocate was forced once again to search his memory.

*I do not think I have seen or heard from Mr Watt since June or
July last year; I may have received a letter from him at Dunkeld;
if I did, it has escaped my recollection completely.*

The defence, clearly briefed otherwise by the accused, refused to
leave this line of enquiry.

*Did I understand your Lordship right, when you said that Mr
Watt, in the month of March last, had made an application to
you, stating that some persons would make a disclosure,
provided they could receive a sum of money?*

In March 1793.

That was not accepted?

I wrote to him declining it.

*Have you had, to the best of your recollection, any letter from
him, or any meeting with Mr Watt since the meeting of the
British Convention that met in October 1793?*

Dundas was forced to give a little more ground.

*I mentioned already, I think I have not seen him, nor received
any letter from him, since June or July 1793, and I was asked if I
received a letter from him at Dunkeld, to which I gave for
answer that I do not recollect having received any such; but I
am positive I have neither received any information from him
nor seen him since October 1793.*

Which was, at best, a very economical truth. Transcribed *JB* reports
continued to arrive on the Lord Advocate's desk till the end of the year
and the Procurator Fiscal continued to receive his spy's reports up till
four weeks before his arrest. When pressed by the defence over the
'seizing of the Banks' letter that had been sent to him while in London,
'in March last', Dundas pointedly insisted it had been March 1793,
but no record was found in the official correspondence to confirm
this. The defence reluctance to abandon this line of questioning, taken
together with the behaviour of Robert Watt when apprehended,
suggests the spy had either lost the plot completely or had indeed
been in direct communication with the Lord Advocate on some matter
of great import. But with no written evidence being produced, the
Lord Advocate's statements had to be accepted and the outcome had
to rest on those twelve gate-decorations accidentally found in Watt's
home and a supposed but never demonstrated plan for their
distribution by the thousand throughout Scotland. The Jury took all

of ten minutes to find Watt guilty of High Treason. In a trial immediately following, David Downie, alleged accomplice of Watt, was also found guilty of High Treason and execution day was fixed for 15th October. The sentence on the pair was reported in the *Edinburgh Advertiser.*

> You and each of you, prisoners at the bar, are to be taken from the bar to the place whence you came, and from thence to be drawn upon a hurdle to the place of execution, there to be hanged by the neck, but not until you are dead; for you are to be taken down, your heart to be cut out and your bowels burned before your face, your heads and limbs severed from your bodies and held up to public view, and your bodies shall remain at the disposal of His Majesty; and the Lord have mercy on your souls!

Watt immediately petitioned King George III on the grounds that throughout February 1794 he had served on the Radical committees to gather information to give the Lord Advocate on his return from London. He complained that the Court which had convicted him did not consider 'the encouragement I had to do it'. He went on to state he had received the detailed plan for insurrection from Angus Cameron and had sent it immediately to the Lord Advocate – who was by then with the Duke of Athole at Dunkeld, but – 'it appears never to have reached his Lordship.'

A question mark hangs over Downie. His involvement may or may not have been genuine. He may have turned King's evidence to save himself. One source states he was freed because he was judged to be of unsound mind. Whatever the truth, the Jury 'on account of certain circumstances' unanimously recommended mercy, which was granted, and Downie shortly afterwards left to settle in America. By another of those minor ironies, US President Ronald Reagan was recently reported as being descended from Downie on his mother's side.

Walter Scott had been particularly eager to witness the conclusion of Watt's trial. He was in court from 7 o'clock in the morning, equipped with cold meat and a bottle of wine, and remained there till the verdict was given at 2am the following day. In a letter to Miss Rutherford shortly afterwards he described the trial as 'the most interesting I ever was present at' but also recorded that 'the *peuple* seem to interest themselves very little in the fate of their *soi-disant* friends'. That fact, which suggests the *peuple* had long since seen through Robert Watt and the charade of a trial, does not seem to have triggered the critical faculties of the future historical novelist. No effective protest arising over this cynical disregard for Law in Scotland, the Home Office seemed to feel confident a similar disregard might produce similar results in England, especially if those incommunicado prisoners held in the Tower of London since May could now be shown to have been deeply involved in the revolutionary conspiracy hatched in Edinburgh.

Trials for High Treason of some of these men, including Horne Tooke, John Thelwall and the Revd Jeremiah Joyce were now prepared, with Thomas Hardy, long the organising Secretary of the London Corresponding Society, first in the dock. Despite their dark hours in Westminster's Secret Committee, the Dundas Duo's efforts to establish incriminating links between Hardy and the Edinburgh decorative-ironwork wholesaler failed abysmally. England, effectively still with its own government, still had its own opposition able to ensure that some semblance of law and justice remained and a unanimous not guilty verdict was returned. Horne Tooke's defence team then went on to make successful use in the English court of Tom Muir's own defence arguments, to the extent of actually citing the Prime Minister and the Duke of Richmond to witness that they too had been reformers and therefore as guilty, or otherwise, as their man. Horne Tooke was freed and the case against the remaining accused was abandoned, at the outset, when exactly that same defence, pioneered by Muir, was offered.[2]

When Hardy exited from court, his supporters freed the horses from the coach waiting for him and themselves pulled it in jubilation through Fleet Street, Strand, Pall Mall and St James Street. The procession stopped in sudden silence opposite 9 Piccadilly, Hardy's former home. In June, while he had been held in the Tower, some loyalist thugs had attacked the house, breaking windows, attempting to break down the door and threatening to set the place ablaze. Hardy's wife, heavily pregnant, was injured when neighbours hauled her to safety through a small rear window. At the end of August she gave birth to a dead child and herself died. After those moments of silence outside his now ruined former home, Hardy was taken to live with his brother-in-law in the Strand.

* * *

2. Howitt *History of England* Vol 2

Execution!

> On Wednesday, about half past one o'clock, the two Junior
> Magistrates, dressed in black, with white rods in their hands,
> white gloves, & etc, the Reverend Principal Baird, and a
> number of constables, attended by the Town Officers, and the
> City Guard lining the streets, walked in procession from the
> Council Chamber to the east end of Castlehill, when a message
> was sent to the Sheriff in the Castle, that they were waiting to
> receive the prisoner.

Thus began the official reports on Robert Watt's last hour on earth.

> The prisoner was immediately placed in a hurdle, and the
> executioner, with a large axe in his hand, took his seat
> opposite to him at the further end of the hurdle. The
> procession then set out from the Castle, the Sheriffs walking in
> front, dressed in black, with white rods in their hands, white
> gloves & etc, a number of County Constables, surrounding the
> hurdle, and two hundred of the Argyleshire Fencibles keeping
> off the mob, walking the dead march from the Castle to the
> Waterhouse.

According to this report the now emaciated Watt, stockings hanging loose but bible in hand and eyes fixed on heaven, presented 'a
most melancholy spectacle'. When the procession arrived at the Old
Tolbooth, the prisoner was taken inside for prolonged 'devotional
exercises', then brought out onto the platform where some more time
was spent in prayer and singing psalms, at the end of which he was
'launched into eternity'. The more gruesome parts of the sentence
having been remitted, however, the body was left hanging for about
thirty minutes.

> When the body was taken down, it was stretched upon a table,
> and the executioner, with two blows of the axe, severed off the
> head, which was received into a basket, and then held up to
> the multitude, while the executioner called aloud, 'There is the
> Head of Traitor, and so perish all Traitors!'

The report is identical in both the *Edinburgh Advertiser* and the
Caledonian Mercury, down to a final sermon directed at any remaining
non-believers.

> May this great national example strike deep into the minds of
> those who inculcate the principles that induced this man to
> commit the crimes for which he suffered! and may Britons of
> every denomination, made sensible of their own happy state,

138

by a comparison with that of other nations, unanimously unite in supporting a Constitution under which alone they can expect a continuance of the happy enjoyment of Freedom & Security!

But the shared statement that Watt had behaved 'in a most penitential manner' from the hour of his sentence is a blatant fabrication, and the same seems true of the 'confession' published shortly afterwards, though it was attested by the Revd Dr Baird, Principal of the University, and the Revd T.S. Jones of Lady Glenorchy's Chapel. These two gentlemen may or may not belong in the sad list of the nations's justified sinners. An editorial appendix to the official record of the trial states that, soon after it ended, visiting ministers were promised a written confession by Watt; but one month later, still appearing 'easy in his mind', he had not even begun the work and in the following week wrote only one page, which later disappeared. 'By what he said afterwards, it is plain, his hesitation arose from the vain hope of a reprieve'. Over the weekend before the execution date he became 'much agitated' but on Monday, 13th October, calm again, he said he had at last determined 'to declare all he knew'. That same evening, the order for his execution on the Wednesday was delivered to him. On Tuesday he continued writing and by evening the required *confession* was sealed, addressed by himself to the Sheriff's Office, and handed over to the commanding officer of Edinburgh Castle for safe delivery. Enclosed was an accompanying letter, requesting the Sheriff to transmit the contents to Principal Baird and the Revd Jones, 'to do with them as they may find proper'. The two ministers may have transcribed verbatim from a document given them, but if they were not present when it was written they had only the word of some Lord Advocate's employee that it was genuine.

Though the personal details on childhood and youth in the published 'confession' are in general accurate, the tone of the whole is much too measuredly tendentious to be at all convincing. There are lengthy moralising paragraphs, some religious metaphysics, sermonising to parents on how to bring up children and a great many outbursts of Christian guilt over the temptations of a tortured soul. Penny's *Traditions of Perth* confirms that Watt was well-known in Perth in his youth and noted for religiose behaviour. He was thought to be the illegitimate son of a gentleman of some wealth and there are indications that his birth father continued to take an interest in his well-being before Watt's own ambitions caused him to plunge into the drumly waters of Dundas politics.

Two reasons induced me to this unhappy conduct. One, a love of the peace of society, – I apprehended, that if they were permitted to continue their meetings, the public tranquility would be interrupted. This opinion was founded on my ignorance of the many abuses in the administrative – the offspring of corruption in the legislative branch of government. For when the legislative becomes more corrupted than the executive, there is an end to true liberty.

The other reason, to obtain Mr Dundas's favour, that I might the sooner arrive at that station in society to which my views were directed. Some may imagine that I had a personal hatred at some of the Friends of the People, but this was by no means the case.

Mr Dundas wished me to correspond with the Lord Advocate, and accordingly recommended me to him. My correspondence with him continued to August or September 1793, when it was discontinued.

Having provided religion with what it required, this last section would be the important one for *Authority*, though further self-incrimination would make it easier for the Lord Advocate to go to that 'utmost extremity' he had promised his uncle at the beginning of the year. Again Watt appears to have provided exactly what was necessary. He takes full responsibility 'my mind being then changed in favour of reform' when he says his ambition and enterprise soon had him main instigator and leader of all the subsequent plans for armed insurrection, reports from a network of *his* intelligence agents buoying the great enterprise.

The first movement was intended to be made in Edinburgh, London, and Dublin; while every town throughout the kingdoms were in readiness to act, according to the plan, on the very first notice, which was to be given by couriers despatched by express.

It is simply not credible that the above and what follows were part of any hurried, eve-of-execution confession.

The nature of the plan was this: – A body of men, to the number of four or five thousand, were to be assembled in a place to be fixed on. These were to be armed with pikes, guns, grenades – to be properly divided, with proper leaders. In regard to Edinburgh, these were to be placed at the Gaelic chapel, head of the West Bow, Tolbooth, or head of the High Street, – that when the Castle soldiers came out, they might be surrounded. In order to prevent bloodshed, means were to be used to gain as many of the soldiers as possible over to their side. The regiment was to be enticed out by companies. But, previous to this, the Magistrates, Lords of Justiciary, Commander-in-Chief, and many others in town to be selected, were to be apprehended; but to be treated, in every respect, becoming their station in life, and detained till the mind of the ensuing Convention, or rather Parliament, was known. There was no intention whatever to put any to death; but if found guilty of oppression and injustice to the patriots, to share a similar fate with them, viz, transportation.

The manner in which the soldiers were to be induced to leave the Castle, was by means of a letter, either signed by the Lord Provost or Commander-in-Chief, previously in custody, ordering the commandant to send a company, without any ammunition, to a fire that was to be kindled in St Andrew's Square, under the pretence of its being a house on fire; and the said company to be secured and disarmed in the mean time. The most of the remainder to be drawn out in the same manner, by means of fires kindled in succession in other quarters of the city. But in case they either could not be drawn out of the Castle, or had obtained information of what was a-doing, they were to be compelled to surrender, by being deprived of victuals; – the incarceration of the Commander-in-Chief, and the influence of Party among themselves favouring the plan.

The public offices and the banks were to be secured, by placing proper persons as sentinels over them, till the proprietors and managers appeared the next morning. The same were to be consulted with by qualified persons, to be previously chosen. The property of such persons, either residing in town or country, deemed inimical to liberty, in the hands of bankers, was to be sealed up, but what was necessary for their maintenance, till their fate was known. The post-office was to be taken possession of; as thereby all intercourse would be cut off between such as were hostile to the patriots, while the channel of communication was left open for them.

After these things were effected in Edinburgh, London, and Dublin, in one and the same night; and which was expected to be accomplished about six or seven o'clock in the morning, – couriers were immediately to be dispatched throughout the whole nation, to the leaders in other parts; while troops were to be marched from places to be fixed on, that could spare them to the assistance of such as would be deemed necessary. No sooner was the plan executed in the three metropolisses, than proclamations, previously prepared, were to be issued to the landholders, and officers under government, as did not cordially unite with the patriots in their views and designs, not to go above three miles beyond their dwelling-places, under pain of death; – to farmers, not to conceal or export any grain;

– to ship-masters, not to carry any person coast-ways, without giving intimation of the same; place come from, and where going to, of such person or persons, within a reasonable time after such intimation was given, to the nearest justice of peace, that the same might be called to an examination, under a similar penalty; – to such persons as were authorised to levy men, to deliver up their commissions and men to persons to be nominated, under the same penalty.

There was preparing an Address to be made to the King at the same time, consisting of a long catalogue of abuses, both in the legislation and executive branches of government; and requesting of him the dismissal of his present servants, and a dissolution of Parliament, the same to be replaced by men in whom the people could confide.

We are to suppose that this detailed, intelligent and eminently practicable three-nations revolutionary strategy was the creation of a man who for some time had been much distressed by serious family illnesses, who spied on meetings by day and evening then worked the wee small hours to write them up and who, only weeks before his arrest, could find time to visit the theatre and provide Procurator Fiscal Scott with a criticism of both actors and audience? Then get a dozen or so pike heads made 'for sale' to his revolutionary forces? There seems every possibility the thousand pounds worth of 'serious' information involving 'a take-over of the banks' referred to in the trial concerned exactly this revealed plan, which has all the hallmarks of being based on a genuine and long-debated strategy aimed at bloodless overthrow of a corrupt regime. At the conclusion of this discordant mid-section, we are probably back to something based, more or less, on Watt's own words.

My views were the good of society; and not robbery or murder. I will not say but my own interest was blended in these views; for who is he, that if he serves society, but will naturally expect a reward?

There follows advice to leave reformation of abuses to those who mind only earthly things, and a plea to be forgiven for having left a few debts unpaid. It seems Watt had hopes of an imminent improvement in his finances, 'but in this situation it would be improper to mention what those views were'. Perhaps he had expectations of a family legacy but now sought not to identify his origins. As likely, perhaps, he could not identify the source of the expected windfall without contradicting this *confession*, the ending of which again suggests much editorial input.

O God! soon shall my body be given to the dust, and my soul will ascend to thee. Thou knowest my sincerity in the narrative I have given; thou seest my sorrow for all my sins. Hear me graciously. – And for the sake of the Lord Jesus Christ, receive my soul to everlasting glory.

– Amen.

This is the truth, and the whole truth, as far as I recollect, I declare as a dying man.

(Signed) Robert Watt. Tuesday Evening, Oct. 14th, about 8 o'clock at night, 1794.[3]

For reasons given as 'the good of the public', one source states that only ministers of religion had ever been allowed to visit the condemned man.[4]

As the published Trial records, from the hour of his arrest Robert Watt had continually demanded to see the Lord Advocate and during his incarceration in Edinburgh Castle, after being sentenced, held out from putting a confession in writing for a month in belief his life would be spared. The price demanded for such mercy would, of course, be a comprehensive document clearing the Dundas Duo of any complicity whatsoever in any of it. Once such confession was delivered, however, there would remain the problem of arranging safe and permanent anchorage of such a loose cannon. If Watt's fate had not been quite certain from the moment of his arrest, it was certainly sealed at exactly the same moment as his *confession*.

Whether there was any family relationship between Walter Scott and Procurator Fiscal William Scott is not known, but the future novelist delayed a Highland holiday and travelled to Edinburgh specially to be present at the climax of the Edinburgh official's endeavours, recording his impressions in another letter to Miss Rutherford. 'It was a very solemn scene, but the pusillanimity of the unfortunate victim was astonishing considering the boldness of his nefarious plans.' Perhaps Scott's astonishment should have caused him to question those bold and nefarious plans. The official indictment had constructed Watt's revolution around a handful of pikes found in his home, together with plans for larger numbers to be manufactured at some future date and offered for sale. According to Carlyle, when the French people decided to set about the Bastille, fifty-thousand pikes were hammered out in thirty-six hours.

---

3. *State Trials*

4. Pamphlet. National Library of Scotland. Ref 3.855[3]

Though details of all the circumstances involved in this sorry episode may never now come to light, it seems certain a serious revolt was being planned, if not imminent, and – one way or another –Watt's involvement triggered the opportunity, or necessity, for *Authority* to act as it did. The last *JB* transcription found in the official records is dated 19th April, 1794, less than four weeks before Watt was arrested. From some very recent research it appears that his handler, Procurator Fiscal William Scott, continued to serve as the Lord Advocate's diligent spymaster for at least a further three years, operating with some efficiency against the genuine revolutionaries then regrouping under the United Scotsmen banner.[5]

David Downie who escaped execution with Watt and emigrated to America. President Ronald Reagan was recently said to be descended from Downie, on his mother's side

5. McFarland *Ireland and Scotland in the Age of Revolution*

CHAPTER 8

Botany Bay

On the evening of the tenth day after Robert Watt's troubled life came to its even more troubled end, the transport *Surprize* rounded the headlands at Port Jackson and began threading a passage up the broad channel towards the final anchorage at Sydney Cove. Botany Bay, named at the time of Cook's explorations and frequently used to describe the convicts' final destination, was a few miles south of the actual penal colony. One result of the American Revolution was that undesirables could no longer be sent to labour on the other side of the Atlantic and after failure to deal with prison overcrowding by establishing a new penal colony in Gambia, where almost half the transportees died and a majority of the survivors escaped, Westminster had sanctioned the use of pensioned-off naval transport ships – *The Hulks* – as temporary prisons. Proposed in the first instance for a period of two years, eighteen years later these expedients had themselves become the problem, and increasing numbers of convicts began to be transported to the other side of the world in conditions little different from those in the slave trade. Some early shipmasters reduced convict rations below subsistence level and this, combined with the danger of rotten vessels foundering at sea and brutally short lives once ashore, caused a passage to the New World to be widely regarded as little less than a death sentence.

By the time these political prisoners were despatched from Britain, however, there had been one very important change. The Navy Board, recognising that this new colony must also fail if deprived of labour, now paid one guinea to the ship's officer concerned for every reasonably healthy convict decanted into it.

The first arrivals had landed in 1788 to establish a small clearing in the bush and now, little over six years later, there was a recognisable township spreading out on both banks of the stream that flowed into the head of Sydney Cove. On one bank was the two-storey government house, its gardens already cultivated down to the shore, and behind that a scattering of officials' houses dotted the rising ground where the newly-completed church was another noticeably white-washed construction. The barracks for the unmarried men, on the opposite bank across the wooden bridge from government house, was still the only other large building to be seen but there were numerous simple brick or white-washed-wattle terrace rows straggled up both banks of the stream. These thatched or shingle-roofed bothies were home to the convicts and also served as married-quarters for members of the New South Wales Corps. Total population at the time was about 1500, with about the same number again divided between adjacent farms and the nearby village of Parramatta, all interconnected by rough and narrow tracks through the bush.

By now, cattle were thriving in the ever-widening clearings, grain was ripening in fields of 40-acre extent, and in the fenced gardens around the huts, fruit and vegetables achieved 'almost tropical' luxuriance. It was an early-summer morning when the political prisoners got a first clear view of all this from the deck of *Surprize* and though letters home shortly afterwards do convey some sense of relief, it can not have been long before they became aware of a few blots on what at first sight seemed a not too unpleasant prospect.

Major Francis Grose, commander of the New South Wales Corps, had been appointed Lieutenant-Governor two years previously and had immediately substituted military for civil authority.[1] The men of his Corps were in large part rejects from other regiments, or deserters and mutineers delivered in irons to the transports, and with such now enforcing law-and-order it is not surprising the colony had an unpleasantly brutal side. David Collins, Secretary as well as Judge-Advocate, recorded in his diary that burglary and theft were continuous, drunken riot frequent, and gang-rape not unknown. Punishments ranging from 300 to 1000 lashes and a few hangings seemed to have had little overall effect. Official corruption controlled all trade, all use of convict labour, and every sale of land, with the result prices were now being 'forced up to ruinous levels'. Against that, however, a 21-gun salute was always fired on the Prince of Wales' birthday, so in one way at least it may all have seemed quite like home.

Grose had been advised from London that he could not demand labour from the political detainees but that they should not have any supplies from settlement stores unless they 'performed tasks as directed'. All four special prisoners had personal funds, sufficient to have convicts allocated to them as servants, and seem to have determined from the outset to remain as independent as conditions permitted. When they disembarked early in November, brick huts on the east side of the cove had been allocated to them, but shortly afterwards Palmer and Skirving purchased small existing farms a little

1. Grose Appendix D

further inland. Muir, having choosen to work a piece of mainly virgin land on the north shore of the harbour, wrote his old comrade William Moffat that he was now perfectly well, apart from being separated from all he loved and respected.

> I have a neat little house here, and another two miles distant, at a farm across the water. A servant of a friend who has a taste for drawing has etched the landscape, you will see it.

This letter also indicates that the urbane young lawyer had adapted very rapidly indeed to the traditional ways of the beach-comber. Within a month of coming ashore he could quote the going price for a healthy goat in gallons of more or less drinkable hooch.

> When any money is transmitted, cause a considerable part of it to be laid out at the Cape or Rio Janeiro, in rum, tobacco, sugar, etc. etc., which are invaluable, and the only medium of exchange. We bought some rum at Oris for 18d the gallon, and can sell it for 30 shillings. In a country like this, where money is really of no value, and rum everything you must perceive the necessity of my having a constant supply by every vessel. For a goat I should pay in money £10 sterling; now, for less than 8 gallons of spirit, at 18d the gallon, I can make the same purchase. Tobacco at Rio sells for 3d per pound, here at 3/6d. That too is an article to be considered.[2]

The New World was benefitting from those childhood years behind the counter of the grocer shop at Glasgow Cross.

Skirving, the experienced and innovative agriculturist, had called his land-holding *New Strathruddie* and Muir's sandy beach and wood-land at the North side of the harbour was named *Hunter's Hill*. Muir may have chosen this relatively isolated location for purposes of study, or for putting some distance between himself and the drunk-and-uncatchable criminal fraternity of the township, but he may already have been contemplating the possibility of escape, a small boat being essential transport over the two miles between Sydney Cove and Cockle Beach.

Among the books available to these new arrivals were most of the volumes of the 3rd edition of the *Encyclopædia Britannica*, which had been presented to Fyshe Palmer by his friends before leaving England. It is recorded that Palmer greatly benefited from an article on boat-building in these volumes and it is tempting to think that Muir too learned to build his own boat from that same source. James Tytler,

2. MacKenzie *Life of Thomas Muir*

the man he had left Glasgow to defend before being arrested at Holytown, that mortal who had 'drudged about Edinburgh' in his leaky shoes and skylighted hat, had edited all and composed the major part of this work that was now the first, the principal, indeed the only do-it-yourself manual in Australia.

Though Muir, Palmer and Skirving remained on good terms, they all kept some distance from Margarot. Whether this was solely related to that mutiny on the voyage from England, or in some way also connected to political events prior to leaving Scotland is not yet clear, but a letter written by Muir after he left the colony said of Margarot 'I can speak with little certainty, but I believe he is greatly to be pitied'.[3] Margarot had sided with the Captain of *Surprize* against Skirving and Palmer and while these two remained in partial confinement for the remainder of the voyage he became Captain Campbell's close assoc-iate. Muir, who from the commencement of the voyage seems to have distanced himself from all three, did nevertheless take steps to defend Skirving and Palmer against the Captain's allegations. The truth behind it all may never be known. Captain Campbell got no satisfaction at all when he hurried to Major Grose with his tale of mutiny-on-the-high-seas and though lurid reports were despatched back to London, the whole matter was eventually allowed to fizzle out.

Now that there was neither scope nor occasion for political activity, Muir channelled a part of his many abilities into some service to the rough-and-ready community deposited around him. He may have operated the first printing press in the colony, at first to distribute selected biblical texts to those who desired them, and at least once offered his services as a lawyer, successfully, to one of the free settlers who had been asaulted by the military. Much of the rest of his time appears to have been spent in study, writing commentaries on the recent political trials in Scotland as well as completing a work on Scots Libel Law.

The overall impression is that these political prisoners or 'specials', so long as health permitted, adapted to their new circumstances quickly and surprisingly well, though at first they were certainly buoyed-up in the firm belief their exile would not be of long duration. Shortly after being sentenced, the Revd Fyshe Palmer had written Hamilton Rowan that he remained 'sanguine enough to hope that the time is not far distant, when I shall be recalled with honour to my country.'[4] There had been, from the outset, this general expectation

---

3. To Dr Joseph Priestley, from Monterrey, 15 July, 1796

4. 7 Nov. 1793

that one day soon a ship would arrive with news that political action in Britain had caused the required change in government, and they all had the promise from leading Whigs, in both Lords and Commons, that their sentences would automatically be quashed and immediate repatriation organised. In line with the outlook that had led to the trials the year previously, it would appear there was genuine belief such blatantly corrupt government simply could not and would not survive much longer.

It would have taken at least six months for the news of Robert Watt's trial and execution to reach Botany Bay and so it was probably April/May 1795 before the event was known about. There is no record of reactions but they are not difficult to imagine. Margarot and Skirving had been in close contact with Watt at Reformers meetings in Blackfriar's Wynd and Muir may well have conversed with the man at meetings as far back as the end of 1792. Given the wit, geniality and education of the spy, it is likely that on more than one occasion they all had exchanged a few *bons mots* with him on the politics of the day. Latterly though, Muir had become very guarded, constantly warning his colleagues against informers and it is a question whether he ever came to suspect the man who visited him with the Friends committee in the Tolbooth.

The one certainty is that news of the fate of the pleasant, humorous and self-effacing man who had attended their meetings and dinners would have had a very profound effect on them all; on Muir most of all, perhaps, given he knew Robert Dundas had been desperately trying to establish the same Treason charge against himself. In the circumstances, it would be surprising if his previous somewhat dismissive scorn for the Lord Advocate did not now take the form of a rather bitter personal enmity, and justifiably or not, he may also have been feeling just a bit scunnered with his immediate associates at this time. Together with Captain Johnston and Colonel Macleod, he had continually warned against giving *Authority* any grounds for increased repression, never more so than when himself incarcerated in Edinburgh's Tolbooth, and yet Skirving, driven on by the London delegates Gerrald and Margarot, had breenged straight into the trap set for them all.

It was known in Sydney Cove that the executed Robert Watt had been on friendly terms with Skirving and had visited him at his home to obtain the information sought by the Lord Advocate, whilst Margarot had almost invited prosecution by his behaviour at that third [British] Convention, later described by Muir as 'a miserable plaything of the English Government'. Muir certainly had sufficient ego to believe that had they listened to him they might all still be in Scotland, preparing and organising, but in his letter to Hamilton Rowan after the trial there is expressed some acceptance of the role for which he, above most, was best suited. 'The cause of truth and freedom derives strength from persecution . . . the apathy of the public mind is fast melting away'. Muir was sufficient of a realist to acknowledge that every ground-root political movement requires at least one potentially self-sacrificing banner-carrier, what is known in modern parlance as the kamikaze speaker. Chambers Dictionary gives kamikaze as Japanese for *divine wind*.

In addition to their hopes for a change in government at home, the four 'specials' seem to have had growing expectations of some kind of rescue attempt, probably by an American vessel charged specifically with that mission, and Muir's decision to transfer himself from the watchful confines of the settlement at Sydney Cove to the isolated dwelling just above Cockle Beach could be connected to this. Though attempts at escape inland had almost always ended in disaster, there was already the precedent of some convicts using a lug-sailed, six-oar boat to reach freedom at Timor, and after about the middle of 1795 the news reaching the colony from Britain would gradually have resulted in the possibility of such escape becoming the only real hope of freedom.

The political battle in England now appeared all but lost, and in Scotland anyone known to be even remotely sympathetic to reform was now finding it impossible to earn a living. An example of official attitudes is given by an advertisement in *Glasgow Mercury*, 15th July, 1794, when magistrates of Dunbarton were seeking a new schoolmaster.

> None need apply who have the most distant view towards the Ministry, or who cannot produce paper certificates of their moral character, success in teaching, and ATTACHMENT to the PRESENT CONSTITUTION, in CHURCH and STATE.

This applied to every stratum of society. Artisans judged to have the wrong political opinions were sacked by loyalist employers and blacklisted, while troublemakers of the officer class could usually be sent into distant empire service or, as a last resort, cashiered. Whig lawyers became all but unemployable at this time, it being widely understood that decisions of the ruling judges, even in civil cases, would not favour any who employed such in their pleas.

Cockie Millar's son, himself a lawyer, sought refuge across the

Atlantic while Muir's closest friend, William Moffat and his Edinburgh agent, James Campbell, could continue working in law only by losing themselves in the relative anonymity of London. Developments in the arts, of course, were also badly affected. Though not completely silenced, Robert Burns was forced to make public show of greatly altered opinions while his friend, Alexander Nasmyth, gave up a lucrative career as society portrait-painter rather than give up his political opinions. The Paisley poet, Alexander Wilson, finding the situation impossible, walked to Greenock to find passage in a ship there to America. The most able and creative minds in the country were being systematically silenced or forced into exile by a regime that could tolerate only the greedily servile.

> *My name's Jamie Lapslie, I preach and I pray;*
> *And as an informer expect a good pay.*

That chilling political wind from Britain coincided with the onset of cooler winter weather on Australia's south-east coast, and by all acounts the four 'specials', on the face of it resigned for the moment to life in Sydney Cove, used the skills they had brought with them to make the best of the situation. William Skirving, with a reputation in Scotland as an innovative agriculturist, launched himself into getting the best out of the fertile soil on his *New Strathruddie* farm, while the Revd Fyshe Palmer became something of an entrepreneur as well as part-time farmer. Together with his friend James Ellis and the free-settler, James Boston, Palmer engaged in various manufactures and eventually set up *Boston & Co*, a trading firm with its own seagoing vessel.

> My imagination sometimes whispers to me that I shall not be a
> spectator of inanimate nature merely, but that I may
> contemplate an infant empire, a new Europe in embryo.

In one of the most pleasant climates the world has to offer, Muir was devoting much of his time to this study; but he was also, day by day, sailing further and further out in his small boat to explore the many creeks leading off the broad passage from Sydney Cove towards the open sea beyond.

* * *

New Broom

On the seventh day of September, 1795, the colony braced itself for what promised to be a vigorous and possibly painful Australian Spring cleaning. Though Major Grose had departed the previous Christmas his replacement, delayed by bad weather, had only just arrived. The two ships *Endeavour* and *Fancy*, in harbour for some time now, were joined by *Reliance* and *Supply*, the two new arrivals from Britain. *Supply*, it would be observed with enthusiasm, was very low in the water. Throughout winter the colony's stores had been running down towards danger-level, but with that immediate worry over, it would be on *Reliance* that most attention turned now for a first sight of the new Governor.

> *Name o Hunter. Cap'n John Hunter.*
> *King's Navy, what you expect?*
> *Bloody 'ard-nosed Scotchman.*
> *Aberdeen.*
> *Leg-irons and cat-o-nine-tails!*
> *Sort you bastards out in no time.*

At first those on shore had to make do with distant glimpses of the new man as he surveyed, by telescope, the principal features of the colony he was to control. Captain Hunter, it seemed, would not set foot on shore till all the formalities due his rank were in place.

> His Excellency did not take upon him the exercise of his authority until the 11th; on which day his Majesty's commission was publicly read; after which his Excellency, in a very pertinent speech, declared the expectations he had from everyone's conduct; touching with much delicacy on that of the persons lately sent out for a certain offence {some of whom were present}; and strongly urging the necessity of a general unanimity in support of his Majesty's government. He was afterwards sworn-in by the Judge-Advocate.

Fifty-eight years old, with some forty hard years at sea behind him, Hunter was by all accounts rather a crusted old salt to be burdened with the problems of a remote and rumbustious penal colony. Nor did he have his troubles to seek. A week after that inauguration ceremony, a significant number of his convicts took the opportunity to liberate themselves when *Fancy* and *Endeavour* left Port Jackson bound for India.

> It was found after their departure that, notwithstanding so many as fifty persons, whose transportation had expired, had

been permitted to leave the colony in the *Endeavour*, nearly as many more had found means to secrete themselves on board her. This was the more vexatious, as the loss of even one man's labour has become an object of consequence at this time.[5]

In the New World, as everywhere else, the Governors could not survive without the labours of and a dialogue with the Governed.

Before leaving England, Captain Hunter had been well-briefed on the heinous behaviour of the four political prisoners, full details of their attempted 'murderous mutiny' on *Surprize* being fed to him and he had prepared himself to confront that particular problem head-on. The result was not at all what he had expected.

16th October 1795

The four gentlemen, whom the activity of the Magistrates of Edinburgh provided for our colony, I have seen and conversed with separately, since my arrival here. They seem all of them gifted in the powers of conversation. Muir was the first I saw. I thought him a sensible young man of a very retired turn, which, certainly, his situation in this country will give him an opportunity of indulging. He said nothing on the severity of his fate, but seems to bear his circumstances with a proper degree of fortitude and resignation. Skirving was the next I saw; he appeared to me to be a sensible, well-informed man – not young, perhaps 50. He is fond of farming and has purchased a piece of ground and makes good use of it, which will, by and by, turn to his advantage. Palmer paid me the next visit; he is said to be a turbulent, restless kind of man. It may be so – but I do him the justice to say, that I have seen nothing of this disposition in him, since my arrival. Margarot seems to be a lively, facetious, talkative man – complained heavily of the injustice of his sentence, in which, however, he found I could not agree with him. I chose to appoint a time for seeing each separately – and, on the whole, I have to say, that their general conduct is quiet – decent – and orderly. If it continues so, they will not find me disposed to be harsh and distressing to them.[6]

In this letter to a friend in Leith, Captain Hunter makes observations rather than judgements, but the phrase 'activities of the Magistrates of Edinburgh' might suggest he now at least partly understood events from his prisoners' point of view. Reassured by what they had learned of Hunter at their interviews, possibly even encouraged by what may have been communicated *viva voce*, Muir prepared a petition to his

5. Collins *Account of the English Colony in NSW*

6. Historical Record New South Wales, Quoted Insh Ms.

Excellency in which he argued that banishment having been achieved by transportation, their sentences should now be considered as completed, quoting for evidence a statement made by Lauderdale in the House of Lords.

> ... the Lord Justice Clerk since the trial had declared: that in sentencing these persons to fourteen years transportation, in consequence of which they were to be sent to Botany Bay, it was not in his contemplation that they should be confined to that place, or that they should be prevented from going to any other, provided they did not return here, or that they should be kept in servitude and subjected to controul.

Nothing that Hunter recorded suggests the normal official antagonisms of the time; quite the contrary, as his letter within days to the new Home Secretary, the Duke of Portland, suggests.

25th Oct. 1795.

> I have examined with care and consideration the respective sentences of these people, I have perused their arguments in favour of and against these sentences, and I am obliged to confess, my Lord, that I cannot feel myself justifiable in forcibly detaining them in this country against their consent. I am the more inclined to this opinion in considering the manner in which they have been sent out. It has been customary to have the servitude of other convicts assigned over to the Governor of the settlement for the time being, in order to their being disposed of for the benefit of the public; but this has not been the case with respect to these men. They appear to have been particularly cautious of not giving the public any claim upon their labour, had it ever been desired, for they have not accepted of any provision from the public store since their arrival. They have lived quiet, retired, and as much at their ease as men in their circumstances can be supposed to be; yet they do not appear satisfied with their situation here considered as compulsory. They can have no other cause of dislike. Although they have it not in their power to return to any part of Great Britain but at the risk of life, they probably might have a desire to pass their time in Ireland. I hope I may receive his Majesty's instructions upon this subject.

That Hunter should suggest Ireland rather than the potentially much more officially acceptable America is noteworthy. Within weeks of Captain Hunter writing that letter, Joseph Gerrald, the fifth victim of Scottish injustice, arrived at Sydney Cove. Gerrald had spent a year in Newgate Prison before being put aboard the transport ship and would therefore arrive with the latest information on the political situation at home. He cannot have been the bearer of any good news, able only to confirm what they already probably knew – an effective alliance between Irish and Scottish radicals now offered the only way foward for British democracy. However, since it would be at least a year before Captain Hunter could expect to receive His Majesty's instructions, life in Sydney Cove just had to go on.

As he fished the ten-mile stretch of water between Sydney Cove and Port Jackson, Muir must have found much fascinating material for his new studies. Though some dangerously large sharks had to be avoided, there was an abundance of other fish, both familiar and exotic, while ashore there were the hitherto unknown marsupials – wombat, bandicoot and kangaroo. Duck, quail and other gamebirds were there for the taking and like most of the settlers he probably developed a liking for the kaleidescopically-colured lorikeets and cockatoos, served up as parrot-pie.

But there were also some man-made problems developing in this, at times, unexpectedly pleasant exile. 'The soil is capital, the climate delicious. . . . I never saw a place where a man could so soon make a fortune and that by agriculture'. The trouble was that too many of the settlers agreed with that opinion expressed by the Revd Fyshe Palmer and the more the land was cultivated and shot over during the first six or seven years, the more the aborigines were deprived of traditional foodstuffs. To add to the problem, escaping convicts stole from the aborigines, sometimes taking prized hunting tools and fishing nets, which caused the aborigines to retaliate by taking some of the settler's cultivated crops, along with some of the convicts' lives. Under Governor Grose's military regime the solution to this problem was increased official violence, which resulted in aborigines previously friendly towards the new inhabitants spearing more of them to death. It may be, though, that subsequent official brutalities were not the result of specifically racist attitudes. The colony's convicts still worked in chain-gangs, watched over by guards with ready-loaded muskets and the soldiers themselves could be hanged or flogged nigh to death for stealing from the stores. In his behaviour towards the native Australians, Major Grose may simply have been following guidelines judged necessary to maintain military discipline even in Great Britain and Ireland.

Despite those initial forebodings, the replacement of Grose by the grizzled Captain Hunter had proved to be the beginning of some very welcome improvements in the colony, and as 1795 drew towards a warm December close the settlement expanding on both banks of the stream was beginning to acquire some quite Old World characteristics; carpenters' workshops were busy, iron was hammered to purpose in new forges and the first of some very drinkable wine was being pressed from increasingly abundant grape harvests. Viewed from seaward, though the geography was greatly different, some of the similarities with his home town of Glasgow must now have been apparent to Muir. Like Sydney, Glasgow's origins had been as a tiny settlement straddling a stream where it flowed into a larger waterway, with the rising ground behind offering further development and similar distant mountains as backdrop. If Muir, as a child, had ventured no great distance from his home at the Cross, he would have seen the foundations of Miller Street being laid out over open fields where cattle still grazed, and while he was at university the hunting grounds to the west of Queen Street were being cleared and advertised as building plots in what was proposed to be named Buchanan Street. Surprisingly rapid urban development had been a familiar pattern of his youthful years and so he may not now have been at all surprised to witness work nearing completion on Sydney's first purpose-built theatre; already it had been announced that the curtain would rise on its première production – *The Revenge* – just two weeks into the New Year.

As always, though, midst great and rapid change, there is a comfort to be drawn from some old and apparently simple things. The sight of aboriginal bairns swimming in the shallows around Sydney Cove, or happily scliffing stones out across the water must have been a poignant reminder to Muir of his own barefoot days on the sandbanks at the foot of Glasgow's Saltmarket, and every sabbath morning the four 'specials' would congregate to lead a service of worship, their voices lifting up in the old psalms in such pleasing harmony that Governor Hunter made a habit of placing himself within earshot at the appointed time.

After a second experience of the somewhat unreal celebration of Christmas and New Year in days of long, hot, blazing sun, the main event the colonists had to look forward to was that grand opening of the new theatre, built at a cost of over £100. The opening night, January 16th, 1796, proved a great success for all concerned and the box-office takings – '1 shilling for the gallery; or flour, meat and spirits in lieu' – fully met the producers' expectations. The takings on the second night were even better, when the colony's criminal element, responding enthusiastically to this burgeoning of the arts, siezed the opportunity to empty the homes of every absent drama-lover.

Then, quite unexpectedly, just exactly a week after that profitable second night in and out of the theatre, everything changed for Muir. The flurry of increasing excitement began with the arrival of another store ship being signalled from Port Jackson, and when she dropped anchor in the bay, it was revealed that *Ceres* was carrying more than much-needed supplies from home. She was also carrying some unusual passengers, picked up during the voyage. While sailing before the Westerlies across the South Indian Ocean, *Ceres* had been driven close to *Ile d'Amsterdam*, a volcanic upthrow in the middle of the Southern Ocean, on which her crew found four men who had been living a Crusoe-like existence. These four castaways increased the normal bustling interest created by the arrival of any vessel but then next day another ship, *Experiment* from Calcutta, entered the bay; and before the excitement from all this had time to subside, the flag at Port Jackson was run up again to signal the approach of a third vessel. This last arrival turned out to be a three-masted trading vessel, *Otter*, out of Boston, and though Muir would not be aware of it immediately, the bizarre series of events linking the first and last of these arrivals would go on to have the most profound effect on every aspect of his future life.

* * *

Pierre François Péron

The story of how Péron came to be on board that first ship, *Ceres*, made him the focus of attention in the colony. Born in Brest, at the extreme north-western tip of France, he was a young ship's officer who had been left in charge of four seamen on *Ile d'Amsterdam*. Not without some misgiving, he had volunteered for the task of heading the party that would collect and cure sealskins while their ship *Émilie* continued the voyage to the northwest coast of America, eventually to return via Canton. Captain Owen, the American master to whom Péron had been first mate, was confident he could return within fifteen months and assured his men they would have two years worth of supplies. He had just learnt from another ship, off the island to retrieve its own seal-hunting party, that there were several fortunes to be made in such a venture. Fur-seal skins, much in demand for fashioning high quality clothing in China, were attracting unbelievable prices.

When Péron's ship left France, in mid-1792, the war between France and Britain still had not broken out but was looking more and more likely, so to avoid difficulties with the British Navy in any part of the world they might find themselves, it had been arranged that only half the brig's crew were French, the remainder mainly American. As it turned out, two of the seamen who volunteered to go ashore on Amsterdam Island with Péron were French and the other English, the fourth member of his party to be supplied by the ship just about to leave. However, only part of what should have been twenty four months supplies was landed with the volunteers in the first boat ashore and though the sea remained calm, it was after nightfall before the promised 'very experienced guide' was ferried across from the other ship. Péron flatly refused to accept a man he described as 'almost a skeleton, moribund, emaciated and blemished' but the officers refused to take their man back, leaving Péron and his motley and partly-mottled crew standing on shore the following morning to watch both vessels hoist sail and depart. Captain Owen may have behaved callously, but he may have decided the hunters would have more chance of picking up extra supplies from passing vessels than he would himself. Though Amsterdam Island was nothing but a rock projecting some 800 feet into the air out of the depths where the South Indian and Southern Oceans become one, over 2000 miles from the nearest landmass on either side and only a little less from Antartica, it was on the direct route from Cape of Good Hope to New Holland and traders from Europe to China used sight of the island to indicate when they should begin heading north.

Despite an acknowledged moment of despair, the twenty-three-year-old Breton was clearly a man of some character. After calling his men together in prayer, he explained without evasion the difficulties of their situation, issued a good tot of rum all round and suggested they get to work. They had inherited a rather dilapidated hut, judged adequate for a climate Péron compared to summer in Bordeaux, and when the man expected to die – an English seaman named Godwin – made a surprising recovery, they learned that water from the island's hot springs was not only palatable but could be used to cook freshly caught fish in a matter of minutes. Though at first they managed to kill only a few seals daily, Godwin assured them this was due to it being the wrong season; October, November and some of December being the time whales were in these waters and smaller creatures kept well out of their way; things, he promised, would be much better by the end of the year. In one way they got better even sooner. During a brief stay in November, the carpenter from *Le Canada* assisted with repairs to the small boat they had inherited; then about eight weeks later, by which time the piles of marketable skins had begun to grow quite dramatically, two British vessels – *Lion* and *Hindustan* – arrived in convoy, giving Péron his first opportunity to show distinguished guests over his new domain. Lord Macartney, accompanied by Sir George Staunton, was on route to a post as Ambassador in China, but when Péron returned from taking some of them to the summit of the island, he found that seamen from the two ships had got his men drunk on free rum, prior to sculling off with 800 of his hard-won skins. Despite promises from the officers, no restitution was made and both ships set sail again that night. Péron's bitter feelings over this incident can not have been lessened when he later learned that his own ship *Émilie* never could return because she had been captured by the officers of *Lion* shortly after they had been his guests on Amsterdam Island. Following the visit of one other ship, in September 1793, the castaways were on their own for two years.

From a combination of diminishing foodstocks and a growing sense of despair, disagreements in this tiny community grew into armed mutiny, then into some violence that left Péron seriously injured. To save the young Breton's life, his compatriots carried him to a refuge named *Cave du Milieu*, after which that remote volcanic rock in the middle of nowhere had its own Anglo-French war raging till, by a ruse, the Frenchmen recaptured both weapons and hut and sentenced the Englishmen to a life restricted to the cave and its foreshore. The three Frenchmen continued to kill seals and cure skins during the third year of their stay on the island, but by now all had to clothe themselves in the skins of the animals whose meat had become almost their sole means of survival. The resultant poor nutrition eventually caused the death of one Frenchman and Péron's *Mémoires* record that when he died, after a long and painful illness, the two Englishmen were as affected by his passing as the others. This was the tale that made Péron the focus of all attention in Sydney Cove and it ended by his recounting how, the week before Christmas, he had been gloomily and rather hopelessly brooding by the dead man's grave when he heard the wildly excited cry of *Navire! . . . Navire!! . . . Navire!!!* at sight of the first sail for nearly two years.

Though the arrival of *Ceres* had heralded a joyous release for the four survivors, it was yet a bittersweet moment. The store-ship could take the men on board but, for reasons not explained, nothing else. Whether because of bad weather, or the vessel already being overloaded, that so hard-won fortune in sealskins had to be left lying abandoned on the shores of *Ile d'Amsterdam*. To stand on deck of *Ceres* and watch nearly three-and-a-half years of his life's effort slip out of sight beyond and below the ship's wake must have imposed new demands on Peron's inner resources, but for all that he took time to assure Cook and Godwin, the two Englishmen, they would face no penalties for the attempt on his life. Once landed at Sydney Cove, they would be free men again.[7]

In the shaping of their creations, writers of fiction are commonly forbidden resort to coincidence, despite the fact that for those who lead less than humdrum lives the most extraordinary coincidences seem to occur with quite remarkable frequency. No ship had visited Amsterdam Island in two years, yet just two days after *Ceres* left, the American vessel *Otter*, out of Boston, arrived in search of wood and water. Captain Ebenezer Dorr must have thought it Christmas indeed when he stumbled over that fortune in cured sealskins, neatly stacked near the jetty, and not an owner to be seen anywhere on a 360° horizon. The fact that *Otter* then followed *Ceres* almost 5000 miles across the Southern Ocean and into harbour at Sydney Cove is less of a coincidence, there being at that time no other port available en route to America's northwest coast. For all that, the arrival of Dorr with those two thousand seven hundred cured sealskins just twenty-four hours after Péron had arrived to tell of his great loss must have had the two principals momentarily speechless.

> He kept an accurate and neatly-written journal of his proceedings, with some well-drawn views of the spot on which he was so long confined.

So the colony's Judge-Advocate and diarist, David Collins, wrote of Pierre Péron, for whom he clearly had much admiration. Collins was witness to the subsequent very heated dispute over ownership of the skins between the hard-nosed Boston skipper and the young Frenchman, but Captain Hadley of *Ceres* took Péron's side in the confrontation and a deal had finally to be struck. Dorr, reluctantly acknowledging that the sealskins properly belonged to the other party, offered Péron the position of first mate on his vessel, with profits from sale of the sealskins in China to be equitably split. Péron accepted and *Otter* prepared to put to sea again.

For many generations after the event, it was repeated that Muir had been rescued from Botany Bay by a ship sent specifically for that purpose by George Washington. Later research proving that *Otter* was

7. Péron *Mémoires*

in fact an ordinary trading vessel on a rather less than ordinary trade route resulted in both the myth and its propagator, Peter MacKenzie, being roundly debunked. Pehaps the objections are overstated. David Collins recorded in his diary at the time that he suspected Captain Dorr had 'some other motive' for his arrival, judging him peculiarly reluctant to trade anything, and Margarot later supported the view that Dorr had knowledge of the 'specials' prior to his arrival. *Otter* was cleared to sail from Sydney Cove on 18th February, 1796. After dark on the evening of 17th February, Muir pushed his fishing boat off from Cockle Beach and began rowing quietly and steadily down the two-mile wide channel leading from the colony towards the headlands at Port Jackson. On board he had his two servants and a compass supplied by Péron. The plan was that once clear of the land he would head out to open sea, holding as close as possible to an agreed course, which *Otter* would follow after leaving Port Jackson next morning. Weather, as always, must be a player in such a game and as the small craft headed into darkness and the expanse of the Tasman Sea, those on board must have acknowledged some misgivings, silent or otherwise.

Suppose the compass prove erratic?
Suppose the mists continue for days?
Suppose we drift and Otter fails to find us?
Suppose another violent squall? Suppose . . . ?

But the British navy had patrols liable to board and search vessels entering or leaving Port Jackson, so the first leg of any voyage towards liberty demanded of Muir that he be master both of his own fate and of his own small craft. Once more the die had rolled.

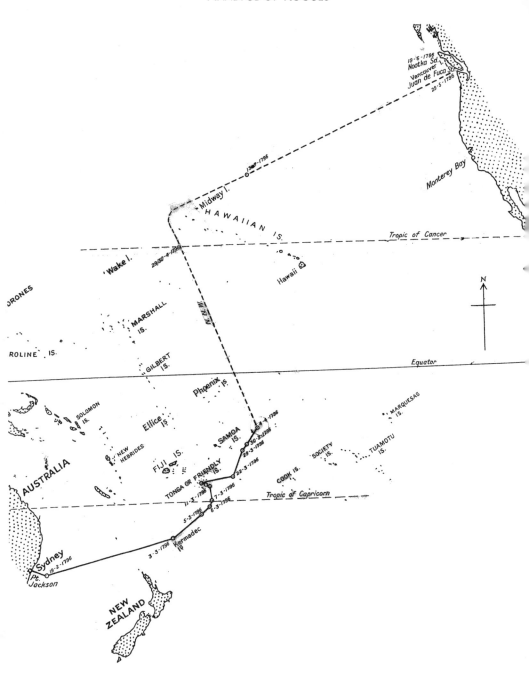

The *Otter* chart – taken from the log of Pierre François Péron – shows the voyage of Muir across the Pacific

CHAPTER 9
Freedom!

> The Captain agreed to give me a passage to Boston provided I
> could effectuate my escape . . . without danger to himself. . . .
> About the middle of the next day, we were received into the
> ship, at a considerable distance from land.

Taken from a subsequent letter from Muir to George Washington, this makes clear the American President was in no way involved with *Otter*, politically now an unlikely proposition in any case, but it does not rule out the possibility that Dorr had been briefed by sympathisers at Boston to look out for the 'specials'. The fact that Muir was able to take with him those two 'servants', one of whom may have been the only female on board, suggests Dorr agreed in advance to accept the three, though it is unlikely he would have done so as a gesture of political goodwill. From what is known of the American skipper, it seems certain he would have demanded prior payment for any transaction, either cash-on-the-barrel, or via some New England promissory-note as copper-bottomed and water-tight as the craft he commanded.

From a long-established and successful ship-owning family in Boston, Dorr had left that port in Autumn 1795, on a trading venture whose possibilities had become apparent only a few years earlier, when it became known the native Indians of America's northwest coast were eager to trade their abundant sea-otter skins against woven cloth, copper, worked metal tools and powder for their guns. Dorr's ship, launched that same year, was a good one for the purpose. Built at Amesbury, Massachusetts, she is given as a square-stern three-masted craft of 168 tons, 77 feet length and 22 feet beam, her deep hull provided with fore-deck, quarter-deck and mounted with ten guns.[1] The guns were a necessity; apart from the risk of piracy anywhere in the world, many ship-masters judged the Vancouver Island Indians to be quite unpredictable, and already many seamen had been killed among Captain Cook's Pacific islands that had to be negotiated on the passage there. Against these dangers, successful trading offered

---

1. Insh Papers. NLS. Dep 344

high rewards for any enterprising mariner; sea-otter skins were in as much demand as fur-seal in Canton and could be exchanged there for tea and silks that were sold at great profit back in Boston. According to the Australian researcher, John Earnshaw, the only thing Dorr lacked on this enterprise was a sufficient number of crewmen for the possible dangers to come. He gives *Otter's* complement on arrival at Sydney Cove as just fifteen men but when she sailed, apart from Muir's trio, she had a further eighteen on board, made up of both time-expired men and some escaping convicts.

Muir had taken time to leave a note for Governor Hunter, thanking him for his kindness and outlining hopes for his own future in America, and though this may have been no more than a typically courteous gesture, it might also have been aimed at providing evidence Hunter could use to prove he had absolutely no prior knowledge of the matter. The Governor's support for Muir's petition would not have gone down well in London, despite the fact that arguing a distinction between transportation and banishment was by this time redundant. Less than two months after Muir's escape from the colony, Lord Colchester made a note in his diary.

31st March, 1796

> A certain circumstance occurred to me today demonstrating the absolute necessity for a complete register of expiring laws. Shelton, Clerk of Arraigns at the Old Baily, . . . mentioned the instance of the Act 25, Geo.III, cap. 46, for removing offenders in Scotland to places of temporary confinement, which was suffered to expire in 1788 . . . Muir and Palmer were actually removed from Scotland and transported to Botany Bay, though there was no statute then in force to warrant it.

Even if Lord Colchester had thought to bring this official oversight to the notice of government, it is certain no more attention would have been paid to it than to Captain Hunter's previous petition. In a letter to his nephew two years earlier, while Muir was still confined in Scotland, Henry Dundas had made his requirements crystal clear; if Scotland's Lord Justice Clerk would write assuring him the sentences were legal, he would have them carried out immediately and face any subsequent outcry in Parliament 'without dismay'. Lord Braxfield's reply was worded, quite cynically, to conceal that the letter had been requested by the Home Secretary in the first place.

> In writing to you it would surely have been unnecessary to say much, as you are as well acquainted with the criminal law of Scotland as any of us. But as it occurred to us that others who

had not the same opportunity of being acquainted with the law of Scotland might wish to be satisfied, we have therefore given our opinion at considerable length in a report signed by me by the appointment of other judges, which I herewith transmit to you, and from a perusal thereof I apprehend it must be obvious that transportation was known in Scotland prior to the Act of 1703, at the date of it, and down to the present time.

Thus were some rather watery English scruples thoroughly emulsified by Scottish oil. The evidence supports Muir's opinion that *Authority* was determined he and the other radicals should end their days in Sydney Cove, and by now he seems to have been the only one left able to challenge that.

> Now for my colleagues – The situation of the whole of them, even at best, is mournful. Palmer enjoys the best health, Skirving is in a failing state, & Gerrald, Alas, I left on the bed of death. He urged me to this enterprise. My youth, my situation, demanded superior exertions. I now have the prospect of being of essential service to all my colleagues. I know the situation of all, & can inform concerning it all.

This was in the letter Muir wrote to *Cockie* Millar's son five months later. In fact, Joseph Gerrald died four weeks after *Otter* sailed from the colony and three days after that Skirving's health finally gave way too, releasing him from more long, empty years of pining for his family.

From Pierre Péron's *Mémoires* it is clear that he and Muir found they had much in common. With Muir now thirty and Péron three years younger, both men were in their prime, had similarly enquiring minds concerning the world around them and shared an enthusiasm for revolutionary French politics. The fact that each was quite fluent in the other's language would be another factor that increasingly drew them together and away from Captain Dorr's rather narrow mercantilist company. Péron, now navigating officer in *Otter*, kept a detailed and informative log on the subsequent voyage across the Pacific.

> 19th February, am. 153.60E, 34.56 S. 107 miles from Port Jackson. Noticed sandbank, or coral reef, about 300 feet circumference in 15 to 20 fathoms of water.

On 2nd March, after variable winds, he recorded that the sea became suddenly like a mirror, lead-white in colour, the surface covered in phosphorous material which caused sufficient illumination to read by on a dull day. From this and his observation of the behaviour of seabirds, Péron believed they had passed in the lee of an unknown island, one of the Kermadec group.

> 7th March. 2am – Tropic of Capricorn. Light N'ly winds perfumed by flowers on nearby island – still unseen.

The sightings of land birds and floating marine plants increased up till the 11th of the month, when his noon-observation gave their position as 186.30E and 20.53S, about 40 miles Southeast of Rotterdam Island [*Annamouka*] placed according to Captain Cook.

> 12th March. 11am. Still on tack NNW, sighted 22 islands and 3 dangerous reefs – one WSW, one N, one SE, 3 or 4 miles out from land.

> Mid-day 183.30E, 20.22S – Rotterdam Island about 8 miles NW – with a small island between – great many native canoes came out.

The winds making it impossible to round that first island, which they understood from the natives was called *Mongo-Lahi*, they had to tack eastwards again for two hours before making another attempt to reach the centre of the group on a westerly course. Once again a canoe came out to meet them, this time offering cooked fish served on coconut leaves as a much appreciated gift of welcome, and when they announced their immediate destination as *Annamouka*, the delighted local chief sent his men ashore and stayed on board to assist Péron navigate *Otter* to the northern tip of the island. During the subsequent, slow, three-hour passage down *Annamouka's* west coast, they were joined by a large number of canoes, single and double, each loaded with edibles.

> All the time we were searching for an anchorage we continued a very lively bartering with the natives. By 8 o'clock that night the bridge was covered with five or six types of banana, watermelons {the lightest weighing about 12 lbs} oranges, yams, sweet potatoes, pineapples, coconuts, breadfruit and sugar cane.

Though these were indeed proving to be the Friendly Islands, the worldly-wise Péron was inclined to think Captain Cook may possibly have exaggerated that aspect of local behaviour. He estimated the number of Tongans around the ship at about a thousand, described them as tall, vigorous, gallous and noted for helping themselves to whatever they wanted. Quite violent tribal wars, with subsequent cannibalism, were not unknown in the Pacific and Captain Dorr had taken the precaution of storing all swords and guns in the Bridge, handy for immediate use, with the ten cannon already lined up and loaded with grapeshot. However, one thing did seem to be understood and obeyed by all. As dusk approached, a single cannon-shot was the peremptory signal that trading was over for the day and canoes must head back to shore.

> The night passed and at sunrise we again fired the cannon. At this signal the sea became covered with racing canoes, and a most vivid sight opened up. It was a race as to who would reach us first. About a hundred canoes surrounded our ship and bartering began again for scissors and knives. We had seen pigs but the natives were reluctant to part with them unless in trade for axes, which we did not have.

This eagerness for barter was very much a two-way affair. Apart from victuals, the crew of *Otter* wanted a supply of the excellent fishing lines, ropes and mother of pearl fish-hooks on offer, even some of the local clubs, spears, bows and arrows. The only difficulty encountered in another day of fair-trading down *Annamouka's* coastline seemed to arise from the lack of good anchor-ground, the coral retaining one of *Otter's* precious hooks and badly damaging another, but when it finally came to quitting this friendly area the difficulties at first seemed insurmountable; time after time *Otter* set out on a nor'easterly course, only to find a seemingly endless multiplicity of coral-reefed islands barring progress. The following day, after very many *touch-and-go* passages, Péron recorded his reaction when he looked astern to gauge what had been achieved.

> Noon, 14th March.

> I was suprised to count 26 islands, scattered all over the horizon, from Southeast to Southwest by the North, connected by a chain of reefs on which waves broke with considerable force.

They still had not found a clear north-easterly passage by noon the following day, when canoes brought the local men and women back; as many as 80 of them, Péron reckoned, in one large double canoe. This time, as well as fruit, the chief traded a very welcome 250lb pig against some knives and scissors, appearing well satisfied with the deal. Another man who might have been equally well satisfied was the ex-Sydney Cove convict who slipped away here, in a canoe, with one of the local women. Péron recorded no criticism of the man's action; himself considering the women 'very attractive' and not, as he put it, 'cruel'. On 15th March, after a somewhat stormy night, *Otter* was found to be dangerously close to the SW reef of what they knew as Mongo-Lahy island, and Péron attributed their eventual safety to 'a lot of good work by the crew' particularly since 'a violent tempest' that sprang up shortly afterwards would certainly have driven them on to the reefs. Later in the day, the winds having subsided, they found themselves with the island of Eua to the south and the main island of Tonga-tabu to the west. Trade this time included some fine pearls and six very fat pigs, in return for which the visiting ship managed to find two of the much-prized axes to add to the knives and scissors they bartered. *Otter's* first mate now recorded that the attractions of Eua Island included a wonderful climate, fertile inland grain-fields, and a population who seemed to be smiling even when they quarreled. The women he had the opportunity to observe, whether typical or not, he judged to be happily obliging towards any male who took their fancy and the Breton found it not at all surprising that five more of the men from Sydney Cove chose this moment to desert Captain Dorr's command. On 16th March, after four days trading, *Otter* finally found the passage that allowed her to leave the Tonga Islands – and all six ex-convicts – to their Friendly fate. Earnshaw records that soon afterwards, three of them took advantage of a visiting ship to leave the islands and within three years two of the others had met deaths as violent as their behaviour appears to have been. The fate of the one who escaped to another island was unknown.

By the end of March, *Otter* was skirting the eastern fringes of what is now Samoa but shortly afterwards was forced by headwinds on to a course towards the Hawaiian Islands. On this heading they came across some uncharted islands, the behaviour of whose inhabitants suggested they had not previously had any contact with Europeans.

> All the evidence convinced us we had the right to attribute to ourselves the honour of having discovered three new islands. I gave them the name of *The Otter Islands*. In order to distinguish them we named the eastern one *Péron-and-Muir Island*, the one to the north *Dorr* and gave the name of *Brown* to the third, after another of our officers.

The ceremony completed, *Otter* left the islands [identified by John Earnshaw as Pukapuka] but prevailing winds kept them on a course heading more for eastern Siberia than the west coast of America. Throughout April they were carried on that NNWly tack across the

Tropic of Cancer, on till well to the west of Midway Island, and it was into May before Péron was able to plot the new ENEly course that at last had them heading more directly for Vancouver Island. With a favourable wind on that last leg of the voyage, *Otter* began to make a real passage and Péron, who had left France four years earlier, would now have time to learn all about subsequent political developments from Muir. It is likely, though, that it would be the influence of the Frenchman's knowledge on the other man that would have had the most noticeable effect. By the end of this 10,000 mile voyage, it is unlikely the principles of oceanic navigation would retain many mysteries for the former Edinburgh advocate and it would be surprising if he could not now shoot-the-sun and box-the-compass with the best. Spinning the wheel to meet a sea and paying-off when necessary, the wake on that voyage to freedom would tell Muir he had learned to steer as true a course as any man.

* * *

Nootka Agreements

Almost three-and-a-half months after clearing Port Jackson, those on deck with Péron at daybreak, on 29th May, were rewarded with a spectacular landfall when a warm sunrise began to reveal the great snow-capped mountain ranges that backed first sight of Vancouver Island. The wrong coast it still might be, but for Muir that first view of the American continent must have been cause of considerable elation. By noon the same day, making a brisk eight knots with favourable winds, *Otter* was just a few miles off the entry to Juan de Fuca Straits, named as far back as 1592 but still a little-known and at times dangerous area for new arrivals. It was also, somewhat surprisingly, the focus of some very recent and very heated European politics. Spain had long dominated the American west coast up into the region around Monterey, and with the development of the lucrative sea-otter trade had begun to take an interest further north. Britain, too, was interested in this area and conflict soon developed.

In 1788, a John Meares bought some land from the native Indians and laid the foundations of a trading settlement at Nootka Sound, a hundred miles or so north of Juan de Fuca Straits, but almost immediately the Spanish Navy arrived to request his departure. When he obeyed, the Spaniards demolished the settlement, seized some ships and built a fort to control their own trading. The resulting threat of

war between Britain and Spain led, in 1790, to the international
Nootka Convention, through which it was agreed that Spain and
Britain would have equal temporary trading rights north of California,
in return for Spain giving up its base and paying compensation to
Meares. This arrangement led to the fort being formally decommiss-
ioned the year prior to *Otter's* arrival, by which time both Spain and
Britain had naval patrols in the area to enforce the terms of the agreement and at the same time deter Russian fur-traders venturing south
from Alaska. The indigenous inhabitants of Vancouver Island were,
however, signatories to no agreements of any kind and the word was
that any vessel venturing to trade with them had to make policy
decisions on a day-to-day basis.

> Sailing up the west coast after daybreak, a canoe with nine
> Indians aboard came alongside. They were very swarthy, not
> very tall, naked apart from a piece of cloth held at the throat by
> two leather thongs, open at the front and hanging below the
> calves at the rear. Their hair was dressed into spirals, radiating
> out as if from a common centre – like an opera demon. The
> crudity of their canoe and their brusque manners made a poor
> impression. They had nothing to exchange. When we asked for
> otter skins they indicated they would go and get them.
> Another canoe 20 to 30 feet long came out about 7am. They
> offered one otter skin for a fathom of blue cloth.

Péron at first thought the Indians here disinclined to make contact,
a judgement seemingly confirmed later the same day when two
canoes came out to confront them, near the wide bay the Indians
called Out-Cha-Chel and identified as Barkley Sound by Earnshaw.
Twenty-two men in all, eleven in each canoe, they approached the
ship chanting a war-song in 'deep and sonorous voices' at the same
time beating out its rhythm by paddle-blows on the sides of their
canoes. At a distance of about 300 feet, the singing came to an abrupt
end, followed by an apparent readying for battle. The twenty-two
warriors rose to their feet in unison, loosed the neck-fastenings to
wrap robes round the waist, then used the paddles again to speed
directly at *Otter* in complete silence. Once alongside, and after a close
and detailed inspection of the vessel and her crew, their leader stood
up to shout *Can-zi-ca-gan*. Choosing to take this as a sign of friendship, those on deck replied with enthusiasm – *Can-zi-ca-gan* – but all
this brought forth was a long, fierce and quite unintelligible harangue.
The ancient sign language of barter becoming a last resort, *Otter*
offered the warriors some of their obviously plentiful blue cloth. No
interest. Those in the canoes held up sheet-copper to indicate their

main requirement. The entire ship's hull was clad in that material but none could be spared. The Indians wasted no more time and, rather dismissively, turned back to shore.

As experience had shown with the aborigine tribes around Sydney Cove, it needed only the trigger-happy actions of one scared, thoughtless or bloody-minded individual to create long-lasting problems, and more than once in his *Mémoires* the Breton seafarer made clear he deplored such incidents and, though he remained forever vigilant, was of the opinion the indigenous people 'had more good sense and perspicacity than they are usually given credit for'. He tried always to be fair in his dealings with them and had found them usually to be so in return. A practical example of this was his behaviour the evening after the war-party visit. Making way up the coast, with the weather worsening, he came across a canoe well out from land bearing four men, four women and five children, 'some at the breast'. He had a line passed to the canoe, towed it to safety nearer the shore, and before parting company these Indians conveyed the information they were from Tatascou, where there would be an abundance of sea-otter skins available for trade. Despite this desire for generous and straight-foward dealings, Péron also put on record his main strategy. 'Indians seldom undertake anything unless assured of success. Keep them guessing and they keep their distance.'

A combination of mists and heavy seas necessitated a safer distance from shore for a few days and when *Otter* moved closer to the coast again, on 3rd June, it was found she was back from whence she had started. Short of wood and water, they entered Juan de Fuca Strait this time and found a safe anchorage in what Péron's coastline sketches show as Baie des Pauvres, now . While the crew gathered the necessary supplies, attempts to make contact with local tribes further up the creek were unsuccessful. Two canoes the officers came across turned and vanished at first sight of the visitors and at daybreak the following morning the established signal of firing a cannon drew the response of only one canoe.

> It contained 4 men and 3 children, dressed in bearskin, deerskin or coarse cloth. Their faces were as black as any chimney-sweep and the smell of them was unbearable.

Péron's sailors seemed quite happy to negotiate the purchase of three salmon from this fishing crew, who were then followed in the route they had taken up a river running into the anchorage.

> I got on board the dinghy with Mr Muir and four good rowers,

with the intention of visiting the river. At its mouth, a column of smoke caught our attention and we rowed in that direction. Fifty paces from the river a cabin was seen, belonging to 5 or 6 Indians. One beckoned us to approach. He led us to an old man sitting in front of a hut. The old man made many gestures of welcome, then invited us to enter. Inside he unrolled otter-skins and laid them out on hollowed wooden seats, inviting us to sit on them.

The *Mémoires* go on to describe the scene.

Putrid meat, rancid fats, rotten fish, cooking bear-meat and latrines, all helter-skelter in the room they lived in – plus the smell of their clothes, their skin even – produced an unbearable stench.

Despite Péron's sensitive nostrils he did find much to marvel at, such as how a beautifully-efficient canoe, twenty-five feet long and four-and-a-half feet in diameter, could be fashioned out of a hardwood similar to walnut with tools so crude as a piece of iron glued and thong-bound to a crooked stick. By 12th of June, *Otter* was again off Out-Cha-Chel and by the following morning had found a good harbour. They were still exploring the bays of this area by dinghy, trying to establish alternatives passages through the many islands, when another fleet of canoes approached. This time there were women and children aboard, always seen as a good sign, and everything began quite amiably. What was described as 'theft' was the only real problem and though it was recognised that European and Indian views on this were quite different, the rule aboard *Otter* was that if anyone was caught offending, *all* would be sent ashore. When someone was later caught in the act of winning the carpenter's tools, this sanction was applied and one Indian, obviously aggrieved at being punished for something he had not done, resisted the dismissal. Péron admitted that he 'helped him on his way' and was later made to realise that this one act of white-man's justice might well have had fatal consequences for himself and Muir. Two days after the incident, the chief of the district came aboard; he too was named Out-Cha-Chel, though whether the territory was named after him or vice versa was not clear. Of one thing only all were quite certain, this latest visitor was, without doubt, the main man in the area. Described by Péron as about 50 years of age, ferocious of face, squat and heavily built, it was obvious he had domination of all around him. Thinking this an ideal opportunity to carry out mappings and explorations needed to facilitate future trading, Péron arranged with Captain Dorr that the chief would be detained on board as an unwitting hostage against their safe return from shore, and on this understanding he and Muir set off in the dinghy.

The expedition started well. The Breton and the Scot were greeted with friendly cries of *'Vacache, vacache,'* assumed to be a welcome demanding an identical response, and there was general joy when they returned the cry; the only dispute arising among the throng surrounding them being over which hut the visitors should enter first. Péron, ever the chart-maker on potentially profitable coasts, indicated that they wanted first to climb an adjacent height and the pair were guided up a small narrow path to the summit. As expected, it proved to have remarkably extensive views of all adjacent creeks, bays and islands, allowing Péron to astonish his guides with a series of rapid outline sketches.

On return to the village, though they did not wish to be away from *Otter* too long, they had no option but to enter some of the many cabins opened up to them in a spirit of hospitality and in one of these Péron came face-to-face with the Indian he had recently been shoving around. Following gestured attempts at reconcilliation, the man submitted to a brief embrace but still obviously brooding over the incident turned and withdrew from the company. While the visitors were being thoroughly examined 'head-to-toe' by the the other villagers, the man returned and requested an understandably wary Péron to follow him to his cabin. A woman illuminated proceedings with a lighted torch while the man, looking aggrieved and hurt, opened chests and pulled out samples of their contents as if to demand if he could be accused of stealing anything from the ship. Péron tried to explain that he accepted him as 'an honest man in wrong company' and finished by inviting him on board the following morning, when gifts would be given. Despite the language difficulty, sufficient of this apology was understood for the Indian nearly to choke the life out of Péron in fraternal embrace before escorting him back to the main village. Here, despite the desire not to delay return to the ship any longer, the party were pulled in to join the throng hunkered-down round the communal fire. 'The women now became very friendly, trying out a rather naïve coquetterie'. Whether despite or because of this, Péron became very firm in his insistence they could delay their departure no longer, to the extent of now informing his hosts and hostesses they would not get their own chief back till he and Muir had safely returned on board. In the midst of these explanations the squat, heavily-built and ferocious-faced Out-Cha-Chel walked in through the door.

Mr Muir and I remained bewildered; the thought came to us that Mr Dorr wanted to sacrifice our lives by abandoning us to these savage people's mercy. Despite the warmth of greeting and the friendship we had just experienced, we knew there was a general antipathy towards strangers, and the value of our effects could easily drive them to some deadly act. Nevertheless, it would have been dangerous to show our fear.

Péron pulled out all the flattery stops. The beauty of the women-folk was praised to the chief's ferocious face and great regret expressed that his two visitors did not have sufficient command of the language to enjoy the lively spirits they obviously possessed in equal measure. Out-Cha-Chel interrupted Péron mid-flow.

He did so to make it very clear all the women were his, the natives of the village were all his subjects, and that when he went to war he always won.

Fearing a long and possibly dangerous harangue on martial exploits, the first mate launched his own long harangue in praise of the chief's riches and abilities, only to finish rather lamely with insistence he and Muir were already late for the expected time of returning on board. This quibble was dismissed with a gesture and a signal they could not yet leave. Leading them to some large chests, the outsides of which were encrusted with human teeth, the chief indicated his own teeth to make sure his guests fully understood before opening one chest and withdrawing a man's head by the hair. Péron was honest enough to record that he trembled at this 'politesse du Prince'. Apparently enjoying the reaction, the chief lifted another head from the collection for admiration. At this the assembled tribe-folk became vociferous in extolling the courage of their chief, who then assured his guests he had killed all these enemies himself. Muir remarked in an aside that it could well be their own heads would finish up in that same chest. Péron agreed, but counselled further trust in the philosophy of the bold front. After a display by the Indian chief of how armour was worn, together with a brandishing of arrows, spears and daggers, followed by a demonstration of how actual battle was conducted, the Indian chief deigned to release his captive but apparently hugely impressed and appreciative audience. Péron recorded that he and Muir 'curtailed their farewells'.

The Spanish fort at Nootka having been abandoned twelve months earlier, Captain Dorr's expectations of assistance when he reached there were disappointed. All he found in that northwestern inlet of Vancouver Island was the small vessel *Sutil* of His Catholic Majesty's

Spanish Navy, whose commander, Don José Tovar, was in even greater need of help. The Spanish ship, out of San Blas, had been on routine patrol to protect national rights in the area when serious illness among the crew drove them into Nootka in hope of finding a European vessel with a doctor on board. Despite the fact that Dorr could not help with this problem and Tovar, himself short of stores, could do little to assist Dorr, it began to dawn on several of those present that some other co-operations might be negotiated. Of *Sutil's* nine seamen, six were unfit for duty, while Captain Dorr had more mouths to feed than recent fur-trading experience warranted; what more sensible than he transfer five men to the Spaniards, a possible but surely in the circumstances forgivable breech of regulations that forbade foreigners landing in Spanish territory? This proposal appealed to the Spanish commander, particularly after he had been softened-up by tales of Indian attacks on under-manned vessels, and so this became the first of the new Nootka agreements. It is perhaps a comment on conditions under Dorr that five volunteers stepped forward immediately, all prepared to serve 'for keep without pay' till arrival at San Blas.

During these debates, Muir learned to his concern that the British frigate *Providence* had recently been on this coast and was expected to return quite soon. *Providence* had been at Sydney Cove for almost two months in late 1795, so if she now intercepted them he ran the risk of being recognised and re-arrested. In any case, to remain with *Otter* involved at very least another year of his life at sea before reaching Boston, via Canton and the Cape of Good Hope, such a voyage itself greatly increasing the risk of encountering the British Navy and being faced with that 'death without benefit of clergy' the High Court in Edinburgh had decreed. The alternative, which the experienced Péron could confirm, involved an easy voyage safe in Spanish hands down to San Blas, perhaps a month over the mountain roads via Mexico City to the sea again at Vera Cruz, then another swift and easy passage northwards to an American east coast port. With any luck at all, he could be with his friends in Philadelphia inside four months. Don José Tovar still had to be persuaded to risk a further breech of regulations, this time without the excuse of his own pressing shipboard needs, and it turned out to be a last-minute decision. The Spanish commander was working *Sutil* down-harbour towards open sea when Muir scrambled up the rope-ladder from *Otter's* dinghy to begin what was probably the most urgent pleading of his career. Tovar, not it seems the most mentally dynamic of shipmasters, remained dubious but finally agreed and the dinghy was despatched back to pick up Muir's few possessions and some funds apparently in the keeping of Captain Dorr. The dinghy returned at the very last moment with a few articles of clothing lying at the bottom of a very small trunk and no money at all. In a somewhat aggrieved account of this whole transaction, put in writing for his immediate superior, Don José Tovar summed-up the position very succinctly.

> He embarked without any clothes, or money, jewels or any
> other article that could be worth ten pesos.[2]

Whether due to misunderstanding or not, this last Nootka agreement saw Tom Muir set out for that meeting with the first President of the United States of America with not two copper *centimos* to rub together in the pocket of his tarry breeks.

> Among those carried off from Port Jackson was one of whom I
> will always keep a warm memory. Mr Muir, of whom I shall
> speak more later, had been condemned in England, with
> Palmer and some others, for having wished to overthrow the
> existing form of government. An enthusiastic partisan of the
> French Revolution, he had the project of substituting for the
> aristocratic organisation of the English parliament another
> order based on freedom and universal equality. Mr Muir was a
> man of great talent. His altruism and sense of loyalty gained
> for him my esteem and that of all who knew him in his
> adversity.

Such was Péron's assessment of the man who had been his shipmate and trusted fellow-adventurer. It is unfortunate the published *Mémoires* do not, as promised, speak more about Muir. It would appear this was lost when the subsequent editor decided to discard about one third of the Breton's original manuscript, and with it may have gone some information on the two 'servants' Muir took with him on his escape, some explanation of why he did so, and perhaps some indication of intentions when he parted from them so abruptly at Nootka Sound.

---

2. Insh Papers. NLS. Dep 344.

CHAPTER 10
Nueva España

The Spanish government had very strict rules against foreigners being permitted access to their territories in America and Don José Tovar was at pains to convince his superiors that in the case of *'Don Tomas Moro . . . un Caballero Escudero de Escocia'* he found out only too late he had been victim of some deception. Muir may have been embellishing his own *curriculum vitæ* but language difficulties seem to have been at least part of the problem.

> This individual, so far as I was able to understand him, is a high ranking gentleman from Scotland who has been persecuted by the English Government for defending his Mother Country and the Christian States of Ireland, until his ultimate banishment . . . seeing that on my vessel he would be able to arrive in it [America] more promptly, he implored me to take him. As I felt sorry for his misfortune, and his moving petitions, I consented to his passage, as I had no orders to the contrary, and having various precedents.

Precedents there certainly were, Don José Tovar's own 2nd Pilote, the young Boston-Irishman named Joseph Caine being one. An earlier governor of Alto California recorded that Caine and his father were fur traders in the area, the son being hired in 1789 as coastal pilot to the ship that first claimed Nootka for Spain. Some years later this son, by swearing as a Catholic to put his local knowledge at the service of the Queen of Spain, was allowed to remain on the Californian coast and subsequent training in navigation at San Blas resulted in his becoming *Sutil's* mate, under Tovar. The Spanish captain probably hoped to be cleared of any wrong-doing in accepting replacements for his own sick crewmen but in striving to excuse himself for having allowed the penniless Muir on board, he seems particularly aggrieved that expected monies had not materialised.

> During the voyage I was struck by several discrepancies in his story, . . . he told me that [Captain Dorr] was supposed to keep 200 pesos for him and that he could not send these to him because of being separated, this being an evident untruth, first because the said Captain is a man of independent means, the owner of many vessels and who has done a large amount of business in

New Holland; and secondly, having despatched his trunk
and mattress whilst he and I were under sail, it is obvious
he would have sent the money at the same time; so I am
convinced of having been deceived through the sincere
feelings of pity I had for him.[1]

It is possible that Muir was the one deceived. He may well have
expected money to be sent across with his trunk and mattress, perhaps
his own money, or an expected refund on the further year's passage
on *Otter* he now no longer required, and much of that expectation
may have been promised as reward or re-imbursement to Tovar.
Despite an apparent agreement to remain in convoy, *Otter* was out of
sight shortly after clearing Nootka Sound and it seems at least possible
Dorr used the fact both ships were under sail to re-arrange any deal
in his own favour. Later Spanish assessment of the American seafarer's
general behaviour was not complimentary. 'Dorr treats his men very
badly and pays them even worse'.

From Péron's *Mémoires*, and in the various Spanish and American
records where he is mentioned, there is confusion whether *Sutil's* mate
was called Caine, O'Caine, O'Quinn, Quinn, Kein, Kendril, Kendric,
Kenduic or simply *The Boston Boy*. Morrison's *Maritime History of
Massachusetts* gives a Captain John Kendrick, with his son, at Nootka
in 1789. It says Kendrick later lost this son to the Indians and died
himself in 1794, while trading to China. Morrison also refers to a young
Joseph O'Caine who, in 1795, arrived at Santa Barabara and at his own
request asked to be put ashore. Bancroft mentions 'a Boston lad',
carpenter and pilot, who in 1795 was put ashore at his own request
by Captain Moore of *Phoenix*, and was later sent to San Blas. The story
Sutil's 2nd Pilote told Muir and Péron at Nootka Sound suggests Caine,
Kein, Quinn and Kendrick are the same person, that son Captain
Kendrick 'lost' to the Indians.

Some five years earlier he had been in command of his own vessel
on this coast when it was attacked at night by native indians. When
he was discovered hiding in the hold the womenfolk interceded on
his behalf, probably on account of his age, but by then the rest of the
crew had been massacred and he was forced to assist the burning of
their bodies. Péron's *Mémoires* go on to relate that Caine told Muir
and himself he was then forced to don Indian garments, and when
any ship appeared was bound to a tree in the forest till it sailed but
that eventually he gained more and more freedom by pretending to
go along with what the the tribe wished. This was the situation the

1. Insh Papers. NLS. Dep 344

day a three-masted barque dropped anchor nearby. After nightfall, Caine made for the shore and used a canoe to reach the ship, which Péron recorded as American and under command of a Captain Mourre [Moore?], who already knew of Caine. The following morning, as the Indians approached for renewed trading, the ship's cannons opened fire without warning and twenty canoes were sunk.

> He said he saw them eat flesh more than once, usually
> after tribal battles. On one occasion, another Indian
> taken captive was forced to watch all his family being
> eaten. Caine seemed a trustworthy kind of officer and not
> one likely to be given to romance.

It is quite likely Caine was little more than a boy when taken by the Indians. This was a time when New England lads, still in their teens, had begun to skipper world trading voyages.

The arrival of *Sutil* at Monterrey, July 5th, 1796, was the beginning of what must have seemed like a fortnight of bliss to Muir. After four-and-a-half months in the confines of a small trading vessel, he now found himself ashore as guest of Don Diego Borica, the Governor of Alta California. From a military background, Borica, a Basque, was by all accounts a man of culture who along this most northern stretch of coast exercised a benign and quite relaxed influence. Prior to his governorship, a chain of mission-houses, seemingly accepted by the local Indians, had given rise to developments in agriculture and live-stock husbandry that made life more comfortable and more predictable for all concerned. In these pleasant surroundings, Muir quickly became something of a guest of honour, both in Borica's household and among the Mission Fathers who were eager to renew European contact. The Governor was particularly interested in Muir's accounts of 1793 events in Paris, noting particularly his vivid descriptions of principal personages such as Mirabeau, Condorcet, Lafayette, Dumouriez, Brissot, Robespierre, Danton, Tallien and Égalité.

> With a view to being able to inform Your Excellency
> regarding the said Scottish Intellectual, Don Thomas
> Muir, I suggested he write down everything concerning
> himself {translating an extract from a printed Trial which
> he showed me} and I despatch to your Superior Hand the
> original of same with his portrait which he also handed to
> me saying that his followers in England had sent it to
> him, where they were thinking of erecting a marble statue
> to him for his firmness and energy shown in the defence
> of the rights of the Scottish people who had nominated
> him as their deputy.[2]

Despite an amiably relaxed attitude to wine consumption, Borica had not been forgetful of his duties, as this letter to the Viceroy of Mexico indicates. In the two-week voyage from Nootka to Monterey, Muir would have learnt much about Spanish bureaucracy from Tovar's first mate. With the international situation bringing new and more severe restrictions on foreigners into force, even Caine's own situation was now uncertain and in this increasingly xenophobic climate Muir was not above using a little psychology to make a good case for himself. Knowing the letters he wrote at Monterey would be opened and inspected, they all seem carefully worded to disarm suspicion and flatter hosts for whose actions he had, in any case, genuine cause to be grateful.

> The governor of this part of the world, a nobleman of high rank, has showen me such civilities as could not be believed. Every refreshment has been sent aboard for me. Could you imagine, that even his lady, with her own hand, could have employed herself in making some portable soups for me during the remainder of my voyage by sea. I never can be sufficiently grateful to heaven, nor to these people.

This was in the letter Muir wrote his parents. Others were written to the Earl of Lauderdale, the Earl of Stanhope and Charles James Fox, MP at Westminster. In the one addressed to Messrs Lyndsay & Shields, the reason for his hardening attitude towards British *Authority* is made clear.

> From the moment I put my foot on that shore [New Holland] it was admitted in Court & in Parliament I was free to goe where I chose except to G.Britain. But my enemies in that remote & horrid region could laugh at such admissions, could mock at all law & all right, & could unconditionally detain me to the last moment of my life.

Another letter was to Dr Joseph Priestley, the English scientist whose home and laboratory had been burned down by reactionary mobs and who had been forced to seek sanctuary in America.

> I deeply regret I was hurried away from London a few hours before you & Mr Lyndsay did me the honour of calling upon me at the place of my confinement.
>
> . . . I dare not indulge my imagination with the idea of that day, when in America, I shall rejoin the benefactors of

2. Ibid.

mankind. Much yet I may have to endure, & I cannot raise the cup, lest it should be dashed from my lips.

John Millar Jnr., the professor's son, was also in America by this time.

> Poor Gerald told me in New Holland that you too have been added to the numbers of the victims of an atrocious ministry, that in voluntary exile you & your family have been obliged to retire to America & forced to begin the world anew. May God grant you happiness according to your utmost wishes.
>
> ... My life since I left you has been a romance. I have literally circumnavigated the globe. If I publish my voyages and travels, as I think I will, I smile when I think that a man of the gowen must make his first DEBUT to the world as a Navigator.
>
> ... Great God, can I indulge the delicious idea of meeting so soon with the friends of man in America, with Priestley, with Cooper, with Russel & many whose names I cannot possibly know. ... Present my sincerest respects to Mrs Millar – to your father – to all in Scotland. Write them where I am & that I am on my way approximating towards them.

So far as impressing the Spanish authorities was concerned, the letter to the President of the United States would be Muir's trump card.

> Sir; the circumstances of my Trial in Edinburgh, upon the 30th and 31st days of August 1793, & of my exile in consequence to New Holland, are no doubt known to your Excellency. You have likewise perused the debates to which these events gave rise in the Parliament of Great Britain. I have likewise reason to believe that independently of these publick proceedings, if at an earlier period I had reached the United States I would not have remained long unknowen to you.

This is not presumption. Apart from friends involved in commercial and banking contacts between the West of Scotland and the United States, just three years earlier his father had written to George Washington and to many of the 'first people of America' on his behalf. Though Washington would no doubt be as cautious in his dealings with a Scots reformer as he now judged he had to be with those from England and Ireland, Muir knew that many of those close to the President would be outspoken on his behalf.

> I have claimed the protection of your name, I hasten to Philadelphia to solicite it in person.

> . . . I have likewise presumed to draw upon you for what
> necessary expenses may attend my journey. This needless to
> observe that these bills will be joyfully reimbursed in Europe.

> . . . I will unfold to you my future designs. If I cannot re-visit
> my owen country, free and emancipated, if I cannot once more
> contribute towards that object, I will consume the remainder
> of my days in the United States, happy if in the narrow range of
> my abilities I may be able to demonstrate by their exertion my
> devotion & my attachment to the land of my Asylum.

That last sentence is indicative of Muir's thinking and intentions
at this period. If he cannot return to a free Scotland, or 'once more
contribute towards that object', only then will he settle for a new life
in America. Having thus paved the way for some much-needed
American assistance, Muir now addressed himself directly to the
Marquis de Branciforte, Viceroy of New Spain at Mexico City, and in
this letter of 17th July makes the most of the political background to
his present situation.

> The people of Scotland have long groaned under the most
> hideous oppression. Their antiant rights have been ravished
> away from them. Their antiant Lawes have been insulted. Of
> their antiant Constitution at this hour they possess not even
> the shadow. This brave and high-spirited people have made
> exertions to break their chains.

Having outlined his own leading part in the struggle, Muir, probably following Caine's advice, lays stress on Catholic connections.

> The situation of the people of Ireland, if possible, was even
> more deplorable than ours. Three Millions of Catholics were
> denied the rights of our common nature, were excluded from
> all the priveledges of the social state, their properties exposed
> to sanctioned robberies & their persons to insult &
> persecution. With the Presbyterians, who were equally
> oppressed, they have formed an union.

> They turned their eyes to Scotland, to the Assembly of its
> delegates. From mutual co-operation they rationally expected
> an exertion more strenuous & an effect more succesful. They
> transmitted a solemn & pathetic[3] address to the Assembly then
> sitting in Edinburgh. This address came officially into my
> hands. I read & published it in the Assembly & with all the
> energy of my abilities defended its principles.

---

3. In the sense impassioned, now obsolete

His attitude to the trial and reasons for that decision against self-exile before it are made clear.

> The Ministry would have triumphed if I had stooped to solicit their favour. Exile was out of the question. I reverenced my country and I reverenced my name.

The avoidance of another eighteen months at sea is given as reason for transferring to *Sutil* and the letter finishes:

> I have told you all. I have concealed nothing. I know & I feel that I am not unworthy of your protection. To have defended the antiant lawes & constitution of my country – To have contended for the instant & immediate Emancipation of Three Millions of the professors of the Catholic Religion – These are No Crimes. I come into your country with no improper intentions & from no slight causes. I wish to pass through it without delay to an Allied State, & to the Chief of that state, who with open arms will receive me as a friend & as a son. May I therefore, for this purpose, presume to solicitate your permission?

All these letters Don Diego de Borica despatched from Monterey to Mexico City, with his own covering notes and assessments, but the Marquis de Branciforte, Viceroy at Mexico City, was either unauthorised or unwilling to make serious decisions. He kept copies and translations where appropriate and forwarded everything to the Spanish Prime Minister, Manuel Godoy, the corrupt *Prince of the Peace*. None of Muir's personal letters was ever forwarded out of Spain to the addressees.

The frigate *Sutil*, still with Muir and the five ex-*Otter* deckhands aboard, left Monterey on 21st July, 1796 and reached its home port of San Blas on 12th August. Shortly after arrival, Muir was allowed to leave the Spanish vessel to find quarters in the small inland town of Tepic, which enjoyed a much healthier climate at an elevation of 1000 feet above sea-level. Here he met and had assistance from a fellow Scot, Robert Gibson, a businessman on his way to the Phillipines. This stay in Tepic, in which he also received welcome hospitality from a local naval family, was nevertheless a delay imposed on his own still driving ambitions, as a further letter to the Marquis of Branciforte illustrates.

> Permit me in this letter, with the same frankness and sincerity as in the former, to state the cause of my anxiety. Three years have almost passed since I enjoyed a regular and uninterrupted communication with my friends and relations.

In this impending crisis motives the most powerful, private and public, urge me to accelerate my course to resume my station in the scenes of the world.

By long and tedious voyages and by sudden transitions into opposite climates my constitution has been affected and my health impaired. It is to me a material object, soon to breathe a more congenial air.

There are other reasons of no inferior force. I recollect that I am a stranger – a stranger in a land where few have had pretensions to enter, and a stranger in circumstances uncommon and unprecedented. Delicacy and propriety prevent me from applying to private individuals for resources to support my necessary expenses. They can be supposed to have no intercourse with those channels through which reimbursements to them must flow. I have deemed it then most expedient, more suitable to my own character and more honourable to your Lordship, to make, for them, to you, a direct application. In the economical manner in which I propose to travel to the Havannah my expenses cannot exceed seven or eight hundred dollars and probably may be a great deal less. General Washington will duly honour whatever bills I may draw for that purpose in your favour. . . I flatter myself I shall soon have the honour of waiting on you in Mexico and shall be proud to give you every degree of satisfaction.

But the Viceroy remained uncertain of this man who had been sent to Botany Bay '*que es la Siberia de los Ingleses*' for playing a leading role in some '*revoluciones Parlamentarias*' the details of which were still not fully understood. From the letters to his brother-in-law, the Prime Minister in Spain, it is clear Branciforte sought highest sanction for any proposed action concerning Muir, together with certain reimbursement of any expenses this might involve. So far as personal fortunes are concerned, the Viceroy of Mexico and Captain Dorr seem to have had some shared characteristics.

A month was to elapse at Tepic before arrangements were completed for Muir's journey to Mexico City. He was to be escorted 'economically, yet with some distinction' by Don Salvador Fidalgo, commander of a frigate recently reurned to San Blas from Macao, and with the party went Don Andres Salvador, Fidalgo's lieutenant, together with Joseph Caine, *Sutil's* erstwhile 2nd Pilote. Whilst acknowledging that Caine had given no cause for concerns and had for some years served the authorities of Nueva España well, the Marquis of Branciforte had decided the new royal edict against foreigners must now also apply to the young Boston seafarer. Under the pretext he would serve as Muir's interpreter, Joseph Caine was also being escorted out of New

Spain, via Mexico City, Vera Cruz and the Havannah.

The old trail from sea-level at San Blas towards the 18,000 feet peaks of the Sierra Madre, with many Conquistador artefacts and Aztec speculations along the way, must have been of immense interest to Muir but it also involved a journey to further test his patience and endurance. With his ultimate goal almost in sight, a further twenty-three day's of slow travel on horseback up to Mexico City was necessary before he could learn if he was to be allowed to continue on this chosen path to freedom. No doubt the courteous attentions of Don Salvador Fidalgo when showing him round places of interest on the journey would relieve the long monotony of the treck, but his interest in the many ancient wonders must have come second to his eagerness to have that interview with the Viceroy. He would have no way of knowing that, just days after he had set out on horseback from Tepic, the Viceroy had already written to inform Madrid of his decision to send both he and Caine to Spain. No doubt diplomatic civilities would dress up this decision when, in Mexico City, it was explained to them personally; the necessity of an appearance before the Council of the Indies, in Seville, would be presented as just a civilised matter of *protocolo*. An official coach was provided for the quite rapid journey on good roads from Mexico City down to Vera Cruz, reaching there on 21st October, and in a letter written the following day to Robert Gibson, the Scot he had met at Tepic, Muir remained optimistic, though accepting that Spain would probably now be his destination.

> I have at last arrived here, treated with every kind of distinction and civility. In a few days I sail for Europe. I will write you everything addressed to Manilla. I will always esteem and honour your memory. May God grant that when these alarms subside, we may yet spend some days together of repose and happiness. The impression of your kindness in Tepic will never be blotted from my mind.

Muir knew that Don José Tovar had been arrested for having allowed him to leave the vessel at San Blas and move inland to Tepic, and in a letter to Branciforte he entered a plea. 'He erred from human-ity. Permit me to supplicate that this error may be pardoned'. Tovar, of course, could not be pardonned for exercising humanity; at the end of the court martial he was deprived of his command. After the relaxed and rule-bending treatment he had enjoyed at the fringes of Spanish rule, Muir was now back in the hands of a corrupt *Authority* not greatly different to the one he had opposed in Britain.

Prime Minister Godoy – *Duke of El Alcudia* and *Prince of the Peace*

– compounded corruption with considerable lack of intellect, but he was the Queen of Spain's lover and so his edicts were obeyed to the letter. Viceroy Branciforte's orders to the Governor of Vera Cruz had been that Muir must be despatched either to Cadiz or Coruna by the first ship available, and it is likely he was the person who wrote advising the Captain General of Cuba that a man of Muir's principles should not be allowed to roam at large. To make matters worse, before Muir arrived in Cuba, the Spanish government had aligned itself with France and declared war on Britain. The Captain General interpreted all this to mean that Muir was now one of the enemy.

> *Edinburgh Advertiser* March 17th, 1797
> In addition to what was mentioned in our last, respecting the escape of Mr Muir from Botany Bay, a letter from Charlestown states that after being a few days at the Havannah, he was committed to a prison on the north side of Cuba, called La Principia, where he is to remain until a proper conveyance offers to carry him to Spain. His confinement is not rigorous, and every indulgence is shown to him that is not incompatible with his situation. The gentleman who writes the letter containing this account, conversed with Mr Muir, who was much disappointed at not meeting an American agent there; as he had hoped, through his intercession, to be released, and be permitted to sail for that continent.

This report was based on information printed in American newspapers in January of that year, information almost certainly relayed verbally by more than one sea-traveller and sufficiently garbled in other details as to be at root of the later myths about Muir's *odyssey* on the west coast of America. It is unlikely that Joseph Caine's movements in Havannah would have been curtailed as were Muir's, and those first reports via Charlestown may well have arisen out of the Irishman's efforts to recruit American assistance. Muir's situation soon became known to the agent for the French Directory in the Windward Islands, who wrote in protest to the Viceroy in Mexico City. The Captain General quickly replied to the Viceroy's demand for an explanation.

> While investigations were made about Muir he was put in a cell reserved for distinguished persons; but this was only for a few days in which his addiction to alcohol was observed, which was excessive to the point of committing acts of indecency. Later I ordered that he be put in a fortress where he had such liberty and space as his cell permitted. As he was slightly ill, he was moved to the military hospital where he was taken good care of . . . the fear that he might spread his political maxims which might upset the laws of New Spain was

more than sufficient reason for . . . not treating him in another manner.

This report may be quite accurate or it may be another minor example of history being recorded by those who require to excuse their own conduct; everywhere else in Nueva España Muir had enjoyed consideration, respect and the development of what seems like genuinely warm friendships. He later recorded his own version of events in Cuba.

> There the scene changed. The Governor, without deigning to give any explanation, treated me forthwith as a prisoner. I remained four months shut-up in one of the forts, during which time I suffered every kind of harsh treatment.

Though the intercession of the French agent might have carried sufficient weight for Muir to choose his own route out of Cuba, that protest from the Windward Islands did not reach Havannah until shortly after Muir had been consigned towards Cadiz and a new danger that had been signalled in the same edition of the *Edinburgh Advertiser* that first reported his imprisonment.

> Expecting Spanish ships homeward bound with treasure, the British fleet is cruising to intercept. The value of the treasure is estimated at ten million pounds sterling. One ship alone is said to have twelve million dollars.

The Spanish frigate *Ninfa,* in which Muir was eventually to leave Cuba, was armed with 34 guns and carried a fighting crew of over 300 men. The frigate *Santa Elena,* similarly armed and manned, was provided as escort because *Ninfa* was carrying a very large cargo of treasure. The two vessels left Havannah eight days after the newspaper report.

Admiral Duncan, victorious against the Dutch fleet at the Battle of Kamperduin

CHAPTER 11
Old Europe

T
he two Spanish frigates bound for Cadiz cleared Havannah on 25th March, 1797, and given reasonable weather could have expected to be off the southwest tip of Spain before the end of April. Three-and-a-half years earlier, just after his 28th birthday, Muir had delivered that eloquent and erudite defence of reform politics in the High Court of Edinburgh and now, at the age of thirty-one, he was completing a global circumnavigation. In the intervening period he had spent eight months in some of the worst prisons of the time, survived fourteen months in a primitive penal colony and for more than a year-and-a-half had experienced the best and worst of life at sea. It is a pity we do not have his unguarded thoughts as he set off on this last leg of his voyage back to Europe. The detailed diaries he is known to have kept throughout this odyssey were known to have been in the hands of sympathisers in London thirty-five years later, but as yet there is no further knowledge of them.

The assertion has been made that, after exile, Muir was completely out of touch with subsequent political developments in Europe, the conclusion being that he must have been sadly lacking in judgement or overburdened with ego to think he still could have a role to fulfill there in 1797. It is true that news from Britain could take six months and more to reach Sydney Cove but the very fact that it *was* a distant penal settlement meant that much of the information there available was exactly what he sought. Transport vessels arriving from mid-1795 onwards carried an increasing number of Irish political convicts from whom he would learn of developments in their country, and radically-inclined seamen, particularly those press-ganged into His Majesty's service, would carry vital information on the developing mutinous trends in the navy.

Through such unrecorded and uncensored communications, Muir would seldom have been more than six months behind the political times, and after *Otter* had crossed the Pacific that delay would have diminished by the day. Towards the end of the eighteenth century, as the historian E.J. Hobsbawm remarked in *The Age of Revolution*, 'to be within reach of a port was to be within reach of the world'. The exchange of news and views between crews ashore has always been a

189

form of internet and on busy trade routes the use of speaking-trumpets – even inter-ship visits when becalmed – could result in surprisingly rapid transmission of information between points not directly or politically connected. This was a time when the flag under which a vessel sailed was no guarantee of the nationality or political allegience of anyone on board, master included, and the evidence confirms that even when confined in the Cuban fortress, Muir was able to have his situation communicated to sympathisers in the Caribbean and on to America. At the time he left Havannah, it is doubtful if he would be more than a month or so behind most of the political developments in Spain, France, Great Britain and Ireland and what he would learn of these can only have strengthened the conviction he was returning not at all too late to play his part in the birth of that ever more necessary New Millennium.

At his trial in Edinburgh, Muir had presented an un-foppish but not inexpensive appearance of some elegance. Style was clearly of importance, and the well-rounded fleshiness of contemporary portraits suggest that wine and good cuisine filled the breaks between lengthy periods with his beloved books. The man now standing on *Ninfa's* deck to watch the island of Cuba vanish on the horizon would probably have gone unrecognised by most previous acquaintances. The auburn hair would be the same, still tied with a ribbon at the nape of the neck, but the effects of sun, weather and the development of some muscularity must have been cause of a very marked alteration. In the hand-me-down clothes he had been forced to adopt, the former douce Scots advocate would not now look greatly different from any other able-bodied *marinero* in the service of the King of Spain. But though himself now in every way a greatly changed man, the Europe he was returning to was largely the same as before, only more so.

The continual wars that governments waged against each other in the name of trade, empire or honour had left most national treasuries on the verge of bankruptcy, while civic turmoil, caused by repression and food shortages, was everywhere verging towards insurrection.

> I see there will be new matter springing in our nation of great magnitude, which will produce events more momentous to the nation at large, until at last they produce a Revolution as compleat, though I hope not so sanguinary, as that in France, the wonder and admiration of all nations on Earth.

Such were the thoughts expressed by John Sword, a wealthy

Glasgow merchant, when writing to a friend in America at the end of 1795. Friends of Muir since school days, John Sword and his brother Benjamin had become so pessimistic over the way their country was regressing they now contemplated removing their entire manufactories to France, though it is likely their recurring visits to Europe were also being used to maintain radical connections. The Lord Advocate certainly thought so and strove to have their movements monitored and correspondence intercepted.

> Our newspapers which you no doubt frequently see will have shewn you into what a state of Sin and Misery this blessed war has brought us. . . . This very last week a Bill has passed making it felony to complain of any part of the Minister's conduct . . . It is far from improbable a civil war may soon be the baleful consequence. Were the few lines I have now wrote on this subject exhibited to our gracious, upright, and infallible Mr Pitt, I would have reason to congratulate myself if I came off as easy as Mr Muir or Mr Palmer by a 14 years' mission to Botany Bay.

Dealing with the bribes and pensions doled out from the public purse to placemen, another John Sword letter, written in January 1796, depicts a bad situation becoming worse.

> Here one person gets £60,000 or £70,000 per annum, another £30,000 or £40,000, many £20,000 and £25,000. Great numbers from £5,000 to £15,000 and these of less consequence are innumerable. The Government of our country is now so *outré* that extortion and imposition cannot be checked. . . . [It] requires such immense treasure to preserve the despotism, to bribe the numberless dependant tribes, that our industry is swallowed up, and it must very soon pass to destruction . . . Already the wages of every branch of manufacture is very much enhanced and yet the poor artificer can scarcely live.[1]

These letters, written not by any *sans-culotte* firebrand but by a successful and wealthy entrepreneur in Glasgow, point-up the conflict of interests that seemed to lead inexorably towards a resolution that now had little hope of being entirely bloodless. Sword's poor artificer who could scarcely feed his family was, to the privileged minority, no more than a creature put into the world by God to labour for and if necessary die for the maintenance of that privilege. Not only was this so, the creatures were assured from the pulpit by every government-appointed cleric, but entirely meet that it should be so.

---

1. Meikle *Two Glasgow Merchants in the French Revolution*

At the time he reached the north-west coast of America, Muir's pressing desire to rejoin exiled friends on the east coast made obvious sense. In Boston, New York or Philadelphia he would have had information on recent developments in Scotland and Ireland, time to consider his own future actions, and the choice of quick access to either country, or to France, as circumstance dictated. From the outset, he had recognised that effective co-operation between Ireland and Scotland offered Britain the surest and quickest release from despotism, but a precondition was radical unity within Ireland, and the word reaching him now would be that the Belfast United Irish leaders, with whom he had worked most closely, had lost ground to a growing north-south divide. Sectarianism had grown to the extent that the mutually dispossessed now fought pitched battles against each other.

Something of the fate of that first and inadequate French invasion fleet that had sailed for Ireland would also be known to Muir by now; a combination of bad timing, bad weather, bad luck and bad judgement having resulted in heavy French losses and no landing at all. Worst of all, perhaps, would be reports that the French had found Ireland far from ready to play its expected part.

> The danger to which the success of revolutions is most
> exposed is in attempting them before the principles on which
> they proceed, and the advantages to result from them, are
> sufficiently seen and understood.

Concern that disregard of Paine's dictum might have ruined years of hard-won gains would be offset, however, by other reports and rumours now circulating. For many months it had been known that an increasing number of crewmen in the British Navy had been agitating about conditions under which they were forced to serve and doubts were now being expressed that a near bankrupt Government would ever be able to pay their accumulated arrears of wages. The Navy Board, under Treasurer Henry Dundas, was as corrupt as the contractors it licensed, and as shipboard conditions continued to deteriorate, radicals seized this opportunity to educate and recruit. For some time past the London Corresponding Society had been distributing reform literature in ports and dockyards, whilst aboard ship members of the English, Irish and Scots United movements recruited and organised towards a complete political overthrow so successfully that, despite the capital punishment threatened on any involved in such acts, a mutiny of the whole of His Majesty's Home Fleet had begun to look not only possible, but increasingly likely.

Better still for that world-revolution concept of Paine's, there were now rumours that the Spanish Fleet based at Cadiz was itself on the verge of hoisting the Red Flag of revolt, and even in revolutionary France, that marvel of popular armed forces, previously patriotic matelots were now becoming restive over oft-promised but still unpaid arrears of pay. The old order had everywhere bankrupted itself and by its intransigence was threatening to take the new order down with it. If ever there was a moment when that *handful of rogues* could be made to go it was now. Such was probably the train of Muir's thoughts as the two Spanish frigates approached Cadiz Harbour at the end of their month-long voyage back across the Atlantic.

Edinburgh Advertiser. May 30-Fri 2 June. 1797.

Death of Mr Muir.

Extract from a letter from an Officer on board his Majesty's ship Irresistible, to his friends in Glasgow, dated at Anchor off Cadiz Harbour, April 28.

'On the 26th inst., lying off here, saw two strange ships standing for the harbour; made sail after them with the *Emerald* frigate in company and, after a chase of eight hours, they got to an anchor in one of their own ports in Conille Bay. We brought them to action at two in the afternoon; we anchored abreast of them, one mile from the shore, and continued a glorious action till four, when the Spanish colours were struck on board and on shore, and under their own towns and harbours. Our opponents two of the finest frigates in the Spanish service, and two of the richest ships taken this war. A Viceroy and his suite, and a number of General Officers were on board of one of them. I am sorry to say that, after they struck, the finest frigate ran on shore. We however got her off at twelve at night; but, from the shot she received she sunk at three in the morning with all her riches, which was a sore sight to me, more especially as I had been on board of her.

We arrived here this afternoon with the other prize and are landing our prisoners; Mr Thomson of Hamilton is on board her as Captain. Among the sufferers on the Spanish side, is Mr Thomas Muir, who made so wonderful an escape from Botany Bay to the Havannah; he was one of five killed on board the *Nymph*, the last shot fired by us. The officer at whose side he fell is now at my hand, and says that he behaved with courage to the last.'

The officer who wrote the above letter was a school-fellow of Mr Muir's.

A slightly different version of events was filed by the Commander of *Ninfa*. He reported that after arriving off Cadiz at night, they were warned by local fishermen of the presence of a very large British blockading fleet under Admiral Jervis, and the treasure brought from Nueva España was then transferred to some of the fishing boats and carried safely by them into Cadiz Harbour. By the time this work was complete, dawn was breaking and they had been sighted by two British ships, one of which considerably outgunned them. The Spanish ships ran southeast towards Conil Bay, near Cape Trafalgar, hoping the larger British ship would be prevented by the reefs across the entrance from following. It wasn't, and all four ships prepared for battle. At that moment, Muir asked if he might, as a civilian, be put ashore from the now anchored *Ninfa*. The Commander replied that he could not comply with this request, though whether this was because of the immediate situation or because he did not want to be accused, like Captain Tovar, of ignoring orders and allowing foreigners loose on Spanish soil is not clear.

Muir was still technically a prisoner of the Spanish and it is likely he faced being locked-up below decks in the midst of the sea-battle about to commence. On the basis that he was entitled to claim French citizenship, he opted to remain on deck to help defend both the Spanish ship and his own liberty. The larger British vessel, *Irresistible*, had 74 guns and the smaller *Emerald* had 36. They opened fire at two-thirty in the afternoon and by four o'clock the battle was over. British losses were one killed and one wounded, while the Spanish had 18 dead and 30 wounded, but contrary to that first report Muir was not among the slain.

> *Edinburgh Advertiser*. June 9-13th 1797.
> From a letter dated May 5 from Officer on *Irresistible* off Cadiz to a friend.
>
> By a vessel just now come out of Cadiz we understand Mr Muir is not dead, but badly wounded in the face. He came here a State prisoner, being taken up at the Havannah for an English spy. He says he made his escape from the frigate after we boarded her, where he saw some of his own townsmen and countrymen.

Later there were the usual embellishments such incidents attract, such as that Muir's body was about to be dumped over the side with the other dead when a bible slipped from his grasp and was picked up by an officer who happened to have been a schoolfriend in Glasgow. The officer is said to have recognised Muir by the inscription in the bible, then found his old chum was not dead after all. Frequently, though, there is an element of truth at the source of such tales. Muir's closest friend, the Edinburgh lawyer William Moffat, recorded what he believed to be true in a letter to *The Scotsman*, 10th December, 1842.

> The body of Mr Muir was found upon the deck by the surgeon of the English vessel, who was a young man from Glasgow and a school companion of Muir.

In the same way that there were Scots clerics like the Revd James Lapslie eager to spy on radicals for financial reward, and others like the Revd William Dunn serving three months in Edinburgh's Tolbooth for supporting reform, so there were political divisions within the officer class of the armed forces. Muir himself says he recognised some of his own townsmen and if one of them did help save his life he is unlikely to have put the man's name on record for the benefit of British prosecuting authorities. Dressed as he was in blood-soaked sailor's cottons, minus an eye and with part of his cheek-bone shot away, Muir was easily passed as a Spanish seaman and put ashore at Cadiz with the rest of the wounded. In a letter to the Directory in Paris, dictated the following month, Muir recorded what he knew of events.

> I remained six days in the hands of the English who had been informed that I was to sail from Havana on this Spanish ship. I was, in consequence, the first person they asked for. They were told that I had been killed in the fight. Disfigured, covered with blood, and almost in the throes of death, they utterly failed to recognise me. They sent me ashore with the rest of the prisoners and I was taken to a hospital.

Joseph Caine may or may not have been in that sea-battle at Conil Bay. The former 2nd Pilote of *Sutil* was not under the same political surveillance as Muir and might have slipped out of Havannah with some America-bound skipper, so it may not have been he who drew attention to Muir's situation.

> A good citizen of the Republic learned by chance of my arrival, his name is Tournée. Knowing who I was, a deep and sincere feeling of humanity brought him to my bedside the next day. Convinced of my identity he sent news to the Consul at once.[2]

The French Consul in Cadiz, *citoyen* Roquesante, sent his report on these events to the *Ministère des Affaires Étrangères* in Paris, outlining the action he was taking. He had arranged for Muir to be

---

2. French Archives. Quoted Insh Ms.

moved into a private room at the Royal Hospital and as soon as he was well enough would receive him into his own home. After this, when sufficiently recovered, Muir would be sent into the care of the French Ambassador at Madrid with a view to arrangements being made to convey him to Paris. The minister for Foreign Affairs in Paris, Delacroix, wasted no time in putting this proposal before the Directory, adding his own recommendations.

> I need hardly recall here the motives which should influence the French government to offer a refuge to all those men, distinguished for their courage and their genius, who have dared to maintain the Lamp of Liberty amid the enemies of France, at a time when Europe was leagued against her. The Directory knows how greatly this kind of national gratitude honours the Republic and multiplies the number of its friends.

The Directory unanimously approved the actions taken to provide for Muir's needs but recommended 'economy necessitated by the state of our finances'.[3] The financial costs of the struggle to free France from feudal tyranny had evidently been about as great as those attempts to prevent such emancipation from spreading over Europe.

> *Then let us pray that come it may*
> *(As come it will for a' that)*
> *That Sense and Worth o'er a' the earth,*
> *Shall bear the gree and a' that.*
> *For a' that, and a' that.*
> *It's comin yet for a' that,*
> *That Man to Man, the world o'er,*
> *Shall brothers be for a' that.*

Burns had sent this international anthem to his editor, Thomson, at the beginning of 1795, a time when ever more repressive measures in Great Britain had made open radicalism impossible. There was an accompanying note from the poet.

> A great critic on songs says that Love and Wine are the exclusive themes for song-writing. The following is on neither subject, and consequently is no song; but will be allowed, I think, to be two or three pretty good *prose* thoughts inverted into rhyme.

Two years later, despite the worsening repressions, a growing

---

3. Ibid.

number of radicals in Great Britain and Ireland were preparing to put their lives at stake in the attempt to turn such pretty good thoughts into the kind of reality that would be possible following the dawn of that long-awaited New Millennium. Ironically, the man whose writings had most inspired that vision had by now become so discouraged at events over the past couple of years that he had decided to have nothing further to do with it.

Almost at the same time Muir set sail for Europe, Thomas Paine arrived at Le Havre looking for a ship to take him forever out of it. The Englishman delayed his departure when he learned that commanders of the British Channel Fleet knew of his plans and were, in an endeavour to take him on that charge of High Treason, intercepting vessels bound for America. When he later learned that a large part of this same Fleet was virtually paralysed by a general mutiny, he returned to Paris and with increased urgency resumed his work on invasion plans.

Mutiny on the scale now developing was unknown in the British Navy and the organised and orderly manner of its progression left the Admiralty floundering. There had been warnings of its imminence for months, yet its outbreak seems to have taken government and senior officers by surprise. Perhaps the only real surprise was that it should have taken so long to commence. It is difficult to estimate how few of the hundred thousand and more seamen in the British Navy of the time were actually serving from choice, but some indication may be had from the known desertion figures. At the height of the Napoleonic Wars, up to 600 crewmen deserted every month, despite hanging being the likely punishment for anyone caught in the attempt. Because a very large proportion of the seamen had been forced into service by the activities of the hated Press-gangs, and the new Quota Act which demanded from local authorities throughout Britain a regular supply of cannon-fodder, the Royal Navy was losing many more men to desertion than ever were killed in battle or died of sickness and disease. This was a time when men with no knowledge of the sea could be snatched from their families in rural towns and villages, while others were taken when within sight of their homeland on return from long voyages on merchant vessels, and once on board Navy ships discipline was enforced by ducking to the point of near-drowning and flogging to the limits of human survival.[4] As in Paris in 1789, little left to lose is everything to gain; now that the brute quality of sea-going life in the British Navy was comparable to any threatened

---

4. Dugan *The Great Mutiny*; Laffin *Jack Tar*

punishment, radical leaders in ports and dockyards were finding ready recruits to revolution.

When the 78th Seaforth Highlanders mutinied in Edinburgh, half of the regiment, some 600 men, marched up on to Arthur's Seat leaving about the same number behind in barracks. Something similar was now happening among the seamen, where about fifty per cent of the serving crews, including marines, were in mutiny. It cannot be assumed, though, that the remaining non-mutineers were all King George's men – in such circumstances there are always many who would act but hesitate, fearful of the consequences of failure. As it was, the mutiny that started at Spithead quickly spread to paralyse the fleet at Plymouth, then did the same to the North Sea Fleet at *The Nore* and at its base at Yarmouth.

> *Come, cheer up, my lads, 'tis to glory we steer,*
> *To add something more to this wonderful year;*
> *To honour we call you, not press you like slaves,*
> *For who are so free as the sons of the waves.*

Written for theatrical performance in the 1770s by the well-heeled English actor David Garrick, the heroic words were now little more than the sycophantic chant of an officer-class avaricious for prize-money and pension. They may be contrasted with an advert in the *Glasgow Mercury* some twenty years later.

> REWARD of 40/- for anyone discovering an AB [able-bodied seaman] who may be secreted.
>
> REWARD of 20/- for anyone discovering an OS [ordinary seaman] who may be secreted.
>
> It is hoped that seamen are at last fired with the desire to serve and will cease lurking and absconding. It is hoped that JP's will assist to deliver lurking seamen to impress service.

The reality of the situation was that by 1797 a very large proportion – possibly nearing half – of the British Navy's *Hearts of Oak* were disaffected Irish and Scots with another proportion drawn from all the races of the world. Given the blind eye of all governments to high seas plunder and seizures of men, it was now not exceptional for a seafarer to find himself, at one time or another, forced to fight to the death under a variety of different national ensigns. In this climate, advertisements were used in an attempt to assure the populace that loyalty remained the prevailing mood in the armed forces,[5] and there

---

5. *Edinburgh Avertiser* 30th May – 2nd June 1797

were offers of financial rewards, graded according to rank, for any serving soldier who would provide information on those circulating 'incendiary handbills'.

Though such adverts provide a measure of how seriously concerned the government had become over the worsening situation, neither the tone nor the detail of their content can be relied upon, as another John Sword letter illustrates.

> ... every creature of Government is obliged to subscribe largely and they are indefatiguable in forcing others to subscribe, threatening them with ruining their business, their trade, and interest, if they do not, and many who have persevered in refusing to subscribe have actually been ruined by the malice of Pitt's vermin. ... The soldiers and sailors are likewise *compelled* to put down their names to this famous gift, and thousands of names appear in the newspapers as Patriotic contributors to this gift who curse the Ministry {the authors of it} curse the purposes to which it is applied, and would give twice the amount of their subscriptions to bring the heads of the Minister's to the block.

The apparent paradox that enlistment in the many Volunteer Corps remained brisk at a time when small-town populations in Ireland and Scotland could turn out to rout Press-gangs has been taken by some to indicate the strength of loyalist patriotism. Others have pointed out that wearing a volunteer uniform was regarded by many as essential to ensure continued employment, while others regarded it as useful access to arms and military training. In every issue of newspapers of the period the official alarms and fears continued to grow in scale and volume. Riots and killings were reported in County Donegal and skirmishes involving the United Irishmen were reported in Derry and Down. When the execution of Militiamen at Cork was reported in the *Edinburgh Advertiser* [June 2 to 6, 1797] it is detailed that the accused men were forced to kneel in their own coffins before being shot. They had been executed because they refused to give the names of their comrade United men.

As some kind of counterbalance to all this, there is the report that when the Government announced an increase in pay for soldiers, the news was greeted with loud cheers from the ranks and a call for God to Save The King. The King, advised by Henry Dundas, chose this as a good moment to authorise introduction of the Militia Act in North Britain, the immediate effect of which was greatly increased public disorder. This was the situation when Muir, after just over a month in the Royal Hospital at Cadiz, had sufficiently recovered from his wounds to be able to dictate that letter of 30th May to the Directory in Paris.

> As soon as my strength permits I shall make haste to return to the bosom of liberty and to salute with delight the soil on which it flourishes. I shall make my way to Paris to present to you the homage of my heart; and ready to prove my patriotism I shall hasten to such post of danger or of difficulty to which you may detail me; happy if I mingle my blood with that of my brethern already shed, or yet to be poured out to strengthen the columns of that superb edifice which you have raised for the support, the consolation and the happiness of the human race.

Though the signature to this letter is feeble and sprawling, the sentiments expressed could scarcely be more resolute. That sea-battle, and the knowledge British *Authority* remained determined on his re-capture, had proved decisive. Four years earlier the Lord Advocate's spy, Robert Watt, had reported that some then expected Muir to return to Britain 'like Coriolanus, with an army of the enemy at his back!' There was now no other way he might ever return.

Throughout May 1797, the British naval mutineers were to all intents and purposes in overall control. A President of the Floating Republic had been elected, Prime Minister Pitt's effigy hung from yard-arms and Royal Standards were everywhere replaced with the Red Flag. The mutineers blockaded traffic on the Thames Estuary and on over 100 vessels elected officers replaced those who had been deposed and sent ashore. Captain Bligh, at least not this time for entirely personal reasons, was once again bundled into a small-boat by his crew and told to shove off. For many, the mutiny could have been ended had the Government responded to petitions for better conditions, payment of pay-arrears, and higher wages, but for others the situation was being utilised to paralyse *Authority* prior to introducing a radical change in how the country was governed.

The Dutch fleet – more properly, since 1795, the Fleet of the Batavian Republic – was assembled at the mouth of the Zuider Zee, behind Texel, with a large invasion force already embarked. It was planned that the other French fleet at Brest would follow if this initial attempt proved successful and there is no reason to suppose that it could not have succeded. The situation, however, was complex and politically far from clear cut. The royalist faction which remained in the French government had recently made considerable gains and were inclined to seek a peace treaty with Westminster, a treaty that would have left Irish and Scots radicals totally exposed and vulnerable to even greater repressions. Ulster, already in insurrection, seemed willing to settle for limited French assistance if that meant immediate action, while in the south other United men, smarting from the earlier abortive attempt at Bantry Bay, insisted on a massive operation from the outset. In midst of this confused and confusing situation, while delegates from the various sections of the United movement hurried about Europe pressing individual priorities and seeking clarifications and guarantees, the French invasion's leader, General Hoche, was called away on more immediately urgent national business; his troops were required in Paris to suppress a growing royalist backlash there. Yet, despite all these many and largely unforeseen problems, there was still no real naval opposition to a fleet making the two-to-three day passage across the North Sea from Texel, and had the Dutch fleet sailed, a successful outcome remained within the grasp of the radicals. In the event, the Dutch fleet did not sail, and the moment was lost.

If the outcome of great events can ever be attributed to the abilities or actions of any one individual, it was the resolute, some would say foolhardy actions of just one Scot that saved the Pitt-Dundas government and its satellite despotisms in Ireland and Scotland from almost certain extinction. Adam Duncan, a Dundonian married to the sister of Lord Advocate Robert Dundas, had for some years been a somewhat overlooked senior officer in the navy, but two years earlier Robert's Uncle Henry had promoted him to Admiral of the North Sea Fleet. Now aged sixty-six and still a great, bluff, hearty man standing several inches over six feet tall, he had a reputation with his people for fair and honest dealing. It has been suggested he was a Whig, not a Tory, but 'blood ties were stronger than politics'. Whatever the case, he seems to have been genuinely horrified by a mutiny which drew from him a very emotional speech.

> To be deserted by my fleet, in the face of an enemy, is a disgrace which I believe never before happened to a British admiral, nor could I have supposed it possible. My greatest comfort, under God, is that I have been supported by the officers and seamen of this ship, for which, with a heart overflowing with gratitude, I request you to accept my sincere thanks.

That Duncan was more a man of action than a political thinker is clear from his subsequent references to a British navy that was 'ever the support of that liberty which has been handed down to us by our ancestors' and which he hoped would continue to be 'not only the bulwark of Britain but the terror of the world'. This desirable state of affairs, he pointed out, could only be effected by 'a spirit of adherence to our duty, and obedience'. There is probably good reason to question the historian's further statement that at the end of all this Duncan's *people*, to a man, broke down in tears and declared their resolution to continue faithful to their duty.[6] Shipboard life operates in a severely delimited world, one in which, for good or ill, individual personalities and abilities are thrown into unusually sharp focus. A commander of Duncan's type usually ends up being referred to as *The Old Man, Father*, or sometimes just *Daddy* and in the close confines and dangers of seafaring life of the time that trusting relationship could over-ride much. Duncan managed to persuade the crew of one other ship to abandon the mutiny and follow him, but though he went aboard unarmed to talk to the men, they weren't *his* people and this time words were not quite sufficient. That crew were not able to perceive their true, dutiful course till a small ringleader had been dangled over the side at arms length. Thereafter, alone of all His Majesty's vessels involved in the mutiny, Duncan's ship *Venerable* and its escort *Adamant* were able to put to sea. With orders to contain the Dutch fleet in harbour at all costs, Duncan complied by standing *Venerable* close in to land and sending orders to *Adamant*, which orders were duly relayed over the horizon to a non-existent North Sea Fleet.

Manouvering the two ships and changing their appearance over the following week, Duncan left the Dutch Admiral, DeWinter, too uncertain about the odds he faced to make a break for sea; by which time another Scot, Admiral Keith, was busy using his vessels in harbour to cut out the mutineers' ships one by one. With a record of previous radical activity in Scotland, a seaman named Richard Parker was judged to be the principal organiser at *The Nore* and along with several others was quickly hanged. More widespread punishments followed and for a time the flames of revolt were quenched. Admiral Duncan's bold handling of a crisis that was largely the creation of the family he was married into had dissipated a unique opportunity for England, Ireland and Scotland to essay a relatively bloodless transition towards early social justice and national democracy.

Throughout that summer of 1797, Consul Roquesante had pressed for Muir's right, as an honorary French citizen, to leave Cadiz for Paris. Despite this, Muir remained under armed guard at the hospital and on instructions from the Government at Madrid was closely questioned about his activities. It may be this was a method of keeping him out of action, the result of a feudal wink-and-a-nod between authorities in London and Madrid at a time when the prospects of

6. Duncan *The Scottish Nation*

peace were being discussed, but the Spanish authorities may genuinely have feared they were harbouring a global terrorist. With reference to Muir's sojourn in Nueva España, the *Prince of the Peace* penned a note in the margin of Muir's file – 'This person has behaved badly in America and I have not the details. See if it is known what this devil was doing'. The reason for official paranoia would not be unconnected to developments in the Spanish navy, later reported in the *Edinburgh Advertiser* of 18th-22nd August, 1797.

> Their ships have followed the example of the rascally part of the British Navy and eight red flags are now flying in sight of us and insist on receiving their pay before they come out. They are said to be four years in arrears and no money in their treasury to pay them.

Given that he had been put ashore for dead little more than three months previously, Muir's letter at this time to Tom Paine, firm of writing and signature, indicates that he was making a remarkably rapid recovery and looking forward to rejoining the struggle.

> Sir, I greatly rejoiced when I heard you were still in Paris. I flatter myself to be there in the course of this winter & to have an opportunity of cultivating that friendship which I value so highly. Since that evening I parted with you, in the Palais Royal, my life has been composed of many agitated & some uncommon scenes. These I will have the happiness of relating to you, in a few months.
>
> Contrary to every hope [sic], I have almost recovered from my wounds. The Directory has manifested to me the most flattering attention. The Spaniards detain me as prisoner because I am a Scotchman, but I have no doubt the interposition of the Directory will soon obtain my freedom. Remember me in the most affectionate manner to all your friends, who are the friends of liberty & of human happiness.

> I am truly & sincerely yours. Thomas Muir. Cadiz. 14 Aug 1797.[7]

Despite rabid anti-French propaganda from the government, the new Militia Act in Scotland was at this time being fiercely resisted. Parish schoolmasters had been instructed to use their registers of births to draw up lists of all able-bodied young men liable to be considered for compulsory armed service, but in many instances enraged local populations did not even give the dominies a chance to commence the task. At Carstairs, in Lanarkshire, the blazing school-

---

7. Original letter in National Library of Scotland. MS1003, f37

house was allowed to be saved only after the parish registers had been handed over to the villagers. Such protests took place nationwide, from Berwickshire in the south to Aberdeenshire in the north, east to Fife and west to Ayrshire.

The Revd James Lapslie, still striving to make himself indispensable to the Lord Advocate, tried to put the Act into practice in his parish at Campsie and returned home one evening to find all his outbuildings burned to the ground and the manse well ablaze. Angus Cameron was issuing arms and drilling men by night so effectively that the Duke of Athole – placarded as 'Black Jock, who sold the Highlanders' – was convinced all Perthshire was in revolt and signed the people's demand that he take no action on the Act till the sentiments of the whole country be known. Armed dragoons were everywhere a necessary escort for the Lord Advocate's county lieutenants, and in East Lothian a bloody riot ensued when that population assembled to retrieve the parish registers and present a petition. A wild charge by troops of the Pembrokeshire Cavalry then resulted in eleven deaths and more wounded.

> It is clear that in all places where resistance has been made or is expected, they should not proceed till they are seconded by such overpowering force as will ensure success.

That was Henry Dundas instructing his nephew on how Scotland's yeomanry corps should behave, and he had also authorised two regiments of English militia to be added to other troops crossing the border into Scotland. Attempts by Edinburgh lawyers, colleagues of Muir, to have some of the troops at Tranent prosecuted for murder were objected to by Robert Dundas and later in the role of Lord Advocate he refused to issue an indictment against any of the military.

> We still have swarms from Ireland, but have sent back as many, indeed more, persons than in strict law we are authorised to do. But we must not stick at trifles.

There was good reason for the Lord Advocate's further disregard for law when it came to the thousands of Irishmen arriving at Portpatrick during 1797. The United movement in the west of Scotland had adopted a similar structure to the Irish one, and towards the end of 1797 it had rapidly spread east up through Perth and Fife into Forfar. The brothers John and Benjamin Sword sailed from Leith at this time, bound for Hamburg, eventually France. Ostensibly theirs was a trade mission but they lost little time in making contact with both Tom Paine and Tom Muir, though in writing they took care to describe such meetings as 'accidental'. Daendels, the young Dutch radical general, was waiting for Admiral DeWinter to make his proposed new attack on Duncan's North Sea Fleet, subsequent to which he would land his 15,000 men near Leith, traverse the Union Canal and be in Ireland within days.

Initial delays were caused by the increased possibility of that peace agreement between France and England, after which a series of setbacks followed one after the other. First the weather held the Dutch fleet in harbour at Texel; then by a combination of food-shortage, ill-health and disease Daendel's forces were decimated; then the man in overall command, General Hoche, was suddenly taken ill and died within days, he was only 29 and some suspected poison; finally, in Paris, a *coup d'état* against the royalists saw a much more cynical Directory assume control, one which seemed not to have much interest in or time for those old internationalist ideals of 1793. Unwisely, and more as a reaction to political criticism, DeWinter was ordered on 7th October to sail his Fleet westward out of Texel. Admiral Duncan met him with his fleet of ex-mutineers and only 13 of the 27 Dutch vessels returned to their home port. Duncan may be permitted a little self-satisfaction.

> *Venerable*, getting up to Sheerness. Sunday, October the 15th 1797.
>
> My Dear Advocate,
>
> As I am sure no friend will rejoice more at any good fortune that attends me than you will, I write you these two lines to say I hope the action I had with the Dutch, who fought with their usual gallantry, is not exceeded by any this war. We have suffered much. The returns I have had, and have not had, exceed 191 killed and 565 wounded; from only two Dutch ships, 250 killed and 300 wounded. We were obliged, from being so near the land, to be rather rash in our attack, by which we suffered more. . . . After all my fatigue, I am in perfect health and my usual spirits.
>
> Believe me, most faithfully yours,
>
> Adam Duncan.

Within a week of that sea-battle at Kamperduin the Dundas Duo arranged for Admiral Duncan to be created Viscount, and with the sincere thanks of Parliament he was awarded a pension of £2000 per annum, payable to himself and his next two heirs. London granted him the freedom of the city, with gift of a sword worth 200 guineas. Gold medals were struck and presented to the admirals and captains of the fleet, but there is no mention if the dependants of the 191 killed and 563 wounded received any pension at all, let alone those two years' arrears of pay.

In fairness, it should be noted that one historian has insisted the only reward Adam Duncan requested for his great victory was that the 180 British naval mutineers still in prison be pardoned.[8]

Admiral Duncan's HMS *Venerable* at the Battle of Kamperduin
[Philip James de Loutherbourg, Courtesy Tate Picture Library]

8. *Scottish Pageant 1707-1802* p389

Chapter 12

Le Célèbre Thomas Muir!

C onsul Roquesante in Cadiz continued his efforts to have Muir released, and in a series of letters extending into autumn of 1797 the French Ambassador in Madrid added his protestations that Spain must regard Muir as a friend of Liberty. Prime Minister Godoy would have none of it till Charles Maurice de Talleyrand-Périgord, now heading the French Foreign Office, added his weight. Talleyrand wrote informing Muir of his efforts.

24 Fructidor, an v. [10th September, 1797.]

Homme estimable, I have just learned with as much astonishment as annoyance that you have been detained as prisoner at Cadiz, where you hoped to find hospitality. I am writing immediately to the Ambassador of the Republic at Madrid, instructing him to demand that you be set at liberty. Rest assured that your adopted country will certainly not abandon you to new persecutions. It is my pleasure to be at this moment the spokesman of the Directory to testify how much interest it takes in you. Be pleased to rely on my personal attachment.[1]

After this influential insistence that Muir must be regarded as a citizen of France, Godoy finally agreed to release his 'devil' into French custody on condition he never again set foot in any of the territories of the King of Spain. Roquesante judged his protégé fit to start the journey by the middle of October, the same week Admiral Duncan was coasting up Thames Estuary and writing that slightly exuberant letter to his brother-in-law, and on the first day of November Muir was warmly welcomed into Madrid. Three days later he and his new secretary, a young ex-soldier provided by the French ambassador, set off on the route over the Pyrénées to Bayonne, but at the onset of winter this proved a long, slow journey and it was not until past the middle of the month that the pair eventually arrived in Bordeaux.

Here, however, everything changed dramatically for Muir, Fronting the cheering crowds waiting to welcome him as he stepped down from the coach were the deferential members of the Bordeaux Academy,

---

1. Insh Papers. NLS. Dep 344

and later, on a balcony of the illuminated frontage of *Le Société de la Grande Quille*, he acknowledged the resounding cheers from the crowd gathered in the *Grande Place* below.

The brave Scottish Advocate of Liberty,
now the adopted Citizen of France!
Long live the defenders and martyrs of Liberty!

It was a moment that had demanded much of Muir, one in which he could take justifiable pride, but it may also have been a moment of ironic reflection at the tricks fate could still play. During that brief stay in Madrid, a letter had reached him, written by a Scots-American who had arrived in Cadiz Harbour just 48 hours after his coach had left the town.

Cadiz, 20th Oct 1797. Mr Muir. Respected Sir,

Having heard from Captain Joseph Kein who lately landed in New York that you were in Cadiz in a situation which your known conduct and patriotism does not deserve, I have used the liberty of chartering a vessel for purpose of landing you in America, if you have no objection of returning to Cadiz & going there, it would give me infinite pleasure & your friends the utmost satisfaction that you were there. Not [only ?] the personal knowledge I have had of you has induced me to act as I have done – injunctions from your absent friends have added to my desire. With respect to myself you may be satisfied by writing to the French or American Consul here – rest assured my motives are true, just and honourable – what your ideas on [this?] business may be, be kind enough to advise me care of the American Consul.

When I heard you had set out for Paris just two days previous to my landing here, it gave me utmost pain, but when I reflect on your past conduct, I could reconcile my mind to the idea of your having acted agreeable to the principles of a Republican Mind. Wherever you go, I wish you success – but rather wish you would write me from Madrid & advise of your return. If this be not the case all the expenses which I have incurred shall be added to the Credit side Liberty Account.

I have the honour to be, Sir, with highest Esteem & Regard, Your most obt. Serv't Charles Stewart. Brother in law to Mr Geo. Meliss, Merch't Perth.

NB I sincerely hope you will answer me in course – I left New York the 3rd Sept last – your relations at that time in Scotland were well. C.S.[2]

---

2. Insh Papers. NLS. Dep 344

The Captain Kein referred to in this letter is almost certainly Muir's *interpreter* from Mexico to Spain, the man known to Péron as 2nd Pilote Caine. The mutual friend, George Meliss, was a young man of considerable wealth and influence in Scotland, as Muir's note in the margin of this letter explained to officials in Paris when it was forwarded to them.

Known as 'the Scots boy' in the House of Commons through Burgh Reform campaigning, Meliss, like many others on the Scottish east coast, was actively interested in European politics. Perth was then a busy port, with a number of merchants from the Netherlands and Baltic countries resident in the town, and through such trade connections he had been a fund-raiser to assist Poles struggling to free themselves from the various feudal powers intent on partitioning their nation out of existence. Not surprisingly, Mellis was one of the men later named to be a member of the provisional government for Scotland. But even if Charles Stewart had arrived at Cadiz timeously, it is by no means certain his offer of immediate passage to America would then have been accepted. Muir had suffered much for a cause now as dear to him as life itself, and despite the lost opportunity in the middle of the year, all the news reaching him since then would indicate that the British Navy's mutinous spirit had only been suppressed, not extinguished. Addressing the 500-guests at the Bordeaux banquet in their own language, Muir told them he felt both great joy to be among them and great melancholy when comparing his own situation with his brethren and countrymen still in dungeons or in exile. He had no doubts, however, of the eventual outcome.

> The Liberty of the universe is not yet lost. The patriots of
> England, Scotland and Ireland will soon break their chains . . .
> the same spirit which animates you, animates them also.[3]

By now the leather half-mask that covered the side of his face where the eye and cheekbone had been shot away was a permanent feature and this portrait, together with a poem and brief biography – *Le Célèbre Thomas Muir!* – was on sale in the windows of all the principal shops when he left the city two or three days later. His progress towards the French capital was then marked by a series of similar civic welcomes and an article in *Moniteur Universel*, 2nd December, 1797 alerted Paris to his arrival there the following day.

---

3. *Edinburgh Advertiser* 15 Dec. 1797

Let this apostle of philanthropy come among us, let him find
in his new fatherland friends and brothers, and may our
victorious cohorts call him back to the country which gave
him birth, there to establish liberty.

Two days after reaching the French capital, Muir dictated a letter
to the Directory.

15th frimaire, 6th yr of Republic. Citizen Directors,

I arrived two days ago at Paris, in a very weak and sickly
state. Permit me to express to you the extreme devotion and
gratitude of my heart. To you I owe my liberty – to you I owe
my life. But there are other considerations of infinitely
superior importance and which ought to make a more forcible
impression on my mind.

Your energetic conduct has saved the Liberty, not only of
France, but also of my Country, and of every other Nation in
the world at present groaning under oppression.

It is unnecessary for me to make protestations of my love
and veneration for the Republic. To my last breath I will
remain faithful to my adopted Country.

I shall esteem, Citizen Directors, the day on which I shall
have the honour to be admitted to your presence the most
precious of my life; and, if I have passed through dangers and
misfortunes, that moment will for ever efface their
remembrance and amply compensate.

Another grand banquet was organised in his honour and discreet
official enquiries were made as to how he might now be given some
much-needed financial assistance.

I am greatly touched, Citoyen, with the delicate manner
in which you have communicated to me the intentions of
the Minister of Foreign Affairs. I do not lack, and I shall
not lack, money of my own country; you know my
character and you know my resources. There is, however,
a law which has been passed in England which makes it
high treason to send money into France. I have been the
first victim of the government. I can say without vanity
that I am perhaps the one whom the government of
England dreads most. I cannot correspond with my
father and my mother; I fear to compromise them by
writing to them. It is then necessary for me to have
French money. I shall not receive this money as an act of
charity. I shall not receive it as a loan. But I shall receive it
only in the name of the Scottish nation and if the
Government is sincere, as I believe it is, in projecting a

landing in Scotland, all that is furnished to me will be
paid in Scotland with interest and with enthusiasm.

In this letter Muir can be accused of little more than having a
reasonably justified 'guid conceit' of his own standing. Though his
return to France as something of an international hero was, in part,
being used by the French government for their own purposes, Muir
had more genuinely popular support in Scotland than any other man
of his time, had great rapport and a shared vision with the Belfast
founders of the United Irish movement, and was a highly-respected
figure in grass-roots English Reform. Tom Paine was, of course, a much
larger figure on the world stage than Muir, but both Ireland and
Scotland were now in a state verging on open insurrection, perhaps
lacking only unification of action under effective political leaders.
Despite his wounds, Muir still saw such a role for himself so far as
Scotland was concerned. In response to that previous, indirect query
regarding his financial position, he suggested a sum of 8000 livres to
meet his immediate needs, itemising his proposed way of living.

> 1. My wounds, the feeble state of my health, the loss of one eye
> and the impaired vision of the one that remains, oblige me to
> have a carriage.
>
> 2. For the reasons I have just indicated, it is necessary for me
> to have a secretary to write what I dictate. My secretary is that
> fine young fellow Molet, whom you have seen, who has fought
> for four years in the armies of the Republic. It is only fitting
> that Molet should receive honourable treatment, not because
> he has left the army with the consent of his commanding
> officer and that of the French consul at Cadiz, in order to be of
> service to me on my journey, but as continuing in the service
> of the Republic.
>
> 3. My table is not elaborate. It consists only of a soup and a
> dish of meat, in the company of one or two friends. I have no
> personal expenses, as those who know me can attest, but in
> my position I require a lodging not unworthy of my former
> status and which is not capable of inviting the wretched
> criticism that patriots have no standing in France.
>
> I have, Citizen, laid everything before you. I am anxious that
> the government should let me know without delay what it
> intends to do. Other nations have offered me shelter and
> frigates have been despatched to look for me, as the Minister
> of Foreign Relations knows well. But my heart is wholly
> French. I have sacrificed everything for the sacred cause of the
> Republic. I have very little blood remaining in my veins, but
> the little that does remain will flow another time.

It would seem from this that Muir was totally committed to the invasion project and wished to establish beyond doubt that the present French government was equally sincere. Almost exactly five years had elapsed since that international throng had gathered in Paris to share a vision of world revolution. He would be aware that all the assumptions made in those early days now required to be re-tested, and some, perhaps, abandoned. The Bordeaux reception proved that many in France still had belief in that original and, at least in part, genuinely altruistic concept of aiding an overthrow of all feudal tyrannies, but at government level much had changed. France now had a five-man Directory, four of whom are generally considered to have been honest and hardworking, but dull, while the fifth, Barras, is usually judged to have been misusing his power in truly decadent tradition. Jacobinism was still the majority political force in the capital but another royalist backlash had produced a situation requiring a second use of troops. This threatened insurrection proved not so severe as the one two years earlier, when vigorous action by a young major of artillery named Napoleon Buonaparte was required to settle the matter with, in Carlyle's memorable phrase, 'a whiff of grapeshot'. After his successful Italian campaign, the erstwhile major had returned to Paris acclaimed the most successful military leader of them all, and some trace of those acrid artillery fumes now hung over every political meeting in the French capital. Though ready access to the Minister for Foreign Affairs must have been encouraging, in the final analysis, Napoleon Buonaparte was increasingly the man with whom all now had to deal.

In Paris, Muir immediately resumed alliance with Tom Paine, and though there was also opportunity for important contact with new Scots and Irish delegates arriving there from the United movements, there was now one important gap in the circle. Tom Christie, the brilliant young scholar who had worked so closely with the early revolutionary movement, had sailed for Surinam and died there. His departure from Paris may indeed have been for reasons of trade, but it may also have had some connection to developments at that time by which many of his Girondin friends suffered the scything guillotine. How the radicals now regarded that period and those involved can be no more than conjecture, but judgements must be made in context and in the knowledge the emotive word still used to describe it obscures important truths.

Thomas Carlyle, whilst fully acknowledging the horrors of it all, was among the first to point out that the number who died in that *Terror* was about a two-hundredth part of those forced to die in the

Seven Year War, only one of the many bloody conflicts waged that century for no other reason than feudal greed and ambition, and other historians have pointed out that many, if not most of those guillotined were profiteers, racketeers, speculators or conspirators guilty of crimes against the state in time of war. Feudal Europe had used the previous execution of Louis Capet and his wife to fan the flames of anti-revolution, but the citizens of Paris, convinced their own royal family had plotted to import foreign cavalry to ride them down, had simply insisted they receive a sentence appropriate to the offence.

It is difficult at this remove to fully comprehend the strength of popular feeling but a letter written by Burns to Mrs Dunlop, December 1794, conveys some idea of how most of the so-called royalty and aristocracy of France were being seen. Referring to *Journal During a Residence in France*, written by Dr John Moore [father of General Sir John Moore, later of Corunna fame] Burns was critical of Moore's attitude.

> *Entre nous*, you know my Politics; and I cannot approve of the honest Doctor's whining over the deserved fate of a certain pair of Personages. What is there in the delivering over a perjured Blockhead, and an unprincipled Prostitute to the hands of the hangman, that it should arrest for a moment, attention, in an eventful hour?

Strong stuff from a man of fine sensibilities, certainly, but it should be remembered that the guillotine was invented to make executions more humane. For the same offence, or alleged offence in Great Britain and Ireland, the sentence was still the one *Authority* pronounced on Robert Watt – half hanging, followed by disembowelment, being made to watch the bowels burn, then beheading and quartering, followed by a geographical distribution of the various body parts. As Carlyle pointed out, the people had endured generations of masters from whom to learn such barbarities, the only surprise being that when they finally seized power, they generally eschewed their most foul aspects. He also drew attention to the fact that, from a long historical point of view, there was no previous period in which 'the general twenty-five millions of France suffered *less* than in this period which they name Reign of Terror!' The situation, as Robespierre saw it, had been perfectly clear.

> If the basis of popular government in time of peace is virtue, the basis of popular government in time of revolution is both virtue and terror; virtue, without which terror is murderous; terror, without which virtue is powerless.

Developments shortly after so many had fallen victim to distortions of that *modus operandi* are once again depicted in memorable
terms by Carlyle.

> Aristocracy of Feudal Parchment has passed away with a
> mighty rushing; and now, by a natural course, we arrive at
> Aristocracy of the Moneybag.
>
> Apparently a still baser sort of Aristocracy?
>
> An infinitely baser; the basest yet known.

As result of the cynical post-Jacobite manipulations, Ireland and
Scotland now had bitter experience of some such aristocracy of the
moneybag, the largely *arriviste* handfuls of rogues having assumed
the worst of feudal attitudes and powers so effectively that in both
countries revolution, not reformation, had become the only option.
Le Célèbre Écossais now had business with *Le Célèbre Corse*.

* * *

The Year of '98

Following the Peace of Campo Formio, signed in October the previous
year, Austria was no longer at war with France and England was left
sole combatant against the nation that had dared to challenge the
old feudalistic order. A month after appropriating credit for that Italian
treaty, Napoleon Buonaparte, as Commander-designate of the *Armée
d'Angleterre*, the invasion force that might finally force a peace on his
country's last opponent, made his triumphal return to Paris and
almost immediately opened discussions with Tom Paine and other
Irish, Scots and English representatives of the United movement. He
took ample time, though, to make a careful assessment of the
situation. Only the previous year he had been worried about Royalist
activities within the French government, describing the opposition
in general as a collection of 'cowardly lawyers and miserable chatter-
boxes', while the Speaker in the Council of 500 was 'inspired by an
émigré and in the pay of England'. The most capable and increasingly
most successful army commander in France still felt his position, even
his life threatened by such plotters and dropped hints he could use
his 80,000 men to save the Constitution from them.

The year 1798 was going to be a pivotal one for all concerned and
all concerned seem to have been intensely aware of the fact. It was

into this nervous and in every sense intriguing situation that Muir had made his re-entrance, and if he did not know in advance he must very rapidly have learned that his much-heralded return was not universally welcomed.

After the 1796-97 abortive attempts at a *descente* on Ireland, Wolfe Tone had striven mightily and successfully to remain the principal man with whom the French government had to deal. But now, for a number of reasons, his influence was in decline and Muir's dramatic re-appearance was about the last thing he could either have wished or expected. To make matters worse, Napoleon now offered Tom Paine position as political advisor to the overall project, and both Paine and Muir were insistent invasion plans needed to involve all three nations.

Before any firm decisions could be made, however, all parties involved required clarifications on a number of serious concerns. For the radicals, there was evidence the *liberation* aspect of French military successes had in recent years been seriously eroded, to the extent that many now regarded French intentions as colonial rather then fraternal. There was also the fear that Napoleon might make a successful occupation of Ireland and/or Scotland, then quickly sign a peace treaty with England, leaving radicals in one or both other countries at the mercy of a vengeful Westminster government. For his part, having missed the golden opportunity of the previous year's mutiny, Napoleon now needed accurate information on present British Naval strength. After listening carefully and often in utter silence to the various arguments put forward over the weeks by such as Tone, Paine, and Muir, the little Corsican set out from Paris to make his own assessments of all the naval harbours and dockyards on the French coast, from Britanny, through Normandy, right up to Pas de Calais.

About this same time, Grenville, the English Foreign Secretary, was himself much occupied with evaluating the strength of a spy memorandum recently received, a document which listed the names of proposed leaders for the three separate governments being planned. Those for the proposed English Directory included Paine and Horne Tooke; Hamilton Rowan, Napper Tandy and Lord Edward Fitzgerald were named for Ireland; Muir, Sinclair, Cameron, Sempill, Lauderdale, Ferguson, Macleod and Campbell were the names for Scotland. This report has been dismissed as no more than a spy's jottings of much hot-air being exchanged between frustrated *émigré* groups in Parisien cafés, but if these groups were deceiving themselves, they had also succeeded in deceiving France's first soldier. Napoleon Buonaparte, on his fact-finding mission to the Channel coast, was at this moment taking the invasion project very seriously indeed.

Of the names that can be identified with some certainty in the proposed Directory for Scotland, all are men of proven ability and commitment. Angus Cameron, a Lochaber man, drew militant support in Perthshire and from adjacent areas in Strathmore, Athole and Badenoch. Lord Sempill, from an ancient Renfrewshire family and for some time Preses of the English Constitutional Society, was the cashiered officer of Foot-Guards who, in 1792, had personally guaranteed finance to provide the French 'soldiers of liberty' with one thousand pairs of shoes per week for at least six weeks. Norman Macleod is usually and quite misleadingly referred to simply as Colonel Macleod, the MP for Inverness. In fact, Norman Macleod of Macleod, 23rd Chief of his clan, had campaigned so successfully in India that he held the rank of Lieutenant-General, 2nd-in-command the Army there. Prior to that, during the American Revolution, he was for a time prisoner of George Washington, who seems to have been a considerable influence. At Westminster, as the MP for Inverness-shire, Macleod was notorious for fiery nationalist-republican speeches.

My purse, my sword, and my influence are at your service, and I will stand by you till the last drop of my blood.

So Macleod had promised a late 1792 Friends meeting in Edinburgh and the following year, after Muir's first escape to France, he was the energetic reviver of Scottish Reform in the capital. For years Macleod had been a particularly well-informed thorn in the flesh of Henry Dundas over debates on India and attempts had been made to get rid of him back into Empire service there. Now, though officially gazetted back into the rank of Major-General, the government's refusal to let such an experienced soldier raise regiments of Highland infantry 'for defence' was almost certainly based on Home Office concerns as to their actual intended purpose. Though firm evidence may yet lie unexamined in many family papers, everything suggests that the information reaching Paris at this time gave rise to genuine hope for large and militant support in Scotland behind such figures as Cameron, Johnston, Sempill and Macleod. Writers with personal knowledge of the last decade of the eighteenth century are largely in agreement that Scotland was then balanced on a political knife-edge.

The novelist, James Galt, provides a 1790s landscape of artisans in every town and village clubbing their finances to buy the most politically informative newspapers available to them and in Lord

Cockburn's judgement the revolution in France had become the sole focus of all concerned. Walter Scott is another evidence. In letters written in 1794 he tells how Loyalists like himself were now organised in district troops, each under a Captain, ready to respond in less than five-minutes to the official signal from the bells of St Giles, while new regiments being raised were displaying 'a dangerous spirit of mutiny'. A very worried Lord Provost Elder wrote Henry Dundas at this time informing him that some such troops had been arrested after it became known they were in direct contact with Radical groups in Paisley. George Penny, referring to Perth about the time of the 1798 Rebellion in Ireland, wrote 'vast numbers were sworn into the United Scotsmen, including at least one town officer' and this radical recruitment, extending into the army, presented 'a formidable attitude'. He described the entire county of Perth as divided into 'Democrats and Aristocrats' and, with the possible exception of the remoter areas, this seems typical of Scotland as a whole. Recent research provides evidence that pikes were being manufactured in the Perthshire villages of Dunning and Auchterarder about this time and in quantities that required the staging of mock funerals for their transport.[4] A mock funeral seems all but impossible without something close to village unity on the project but even if it were possible to prove that the radical share of Penny's division fell well short of fifty per cent, that would still suggest a much greater percentage demanding immediate change than most of history's successful revolutions have been able to recruit at their commencements.

Sir James Gibson-Craig, chairing the gathering to lay the foundation stone of the Calton Hill monument to the radicals and speaking from his own personal involvements in those events fifty years earlier, depicts something very close to the civil war.

> Society was in a great degree dissolved, the dearest friendships severed, the nearest relations separated, the most bitter hostility prevailed, and everyone acted as if those who entertained opposite opinions were his deadliest enemies.[5]

Macleod's counterpart in Ireland was Edward Fitzgerald, who though not a Gaidheal had recognised the need to learn something of the language and culture of his country. Fitzgerald did not have Macleod's extensive military experience but he had likewise served in America against the rebels. After the last battle in the War of

---

4. McFarland. Op cit.

5. Gibson-Craig Appendix D

Independence, a runaway slave found the young British lieutenant who was Lord Edward Fitzgerald still alive but unconscious among the many corpses scattered around Eutaw Creek, and in return for the ex-slave saving his life and nourishing him back to good health, Fitzgerald offered the man security of lifetime employment. When the war ended, Fitzgerald set out with his rescuer to explore Canada, the pair living at first off the land then later as guests of native Indians, one tribe of whom appointed the Irishman an honorary chief. William Cobbett, the English political scribe who had been Sergeant-Major to Fitzgerald, described him as 'the only really honest officer I ever knew in the army' – doubtless a factor in Major Fitzgerald later being cashiered for expressing political opinions. Now steeped in the writings of Rousseau and Paine, Citizen Eddy had been using his home at Kildare for unobtrusive meetings and military training exercises. Ostensibly, he was recruiting for the Government Militia; in reality, he was training United Irishmen.

> A combination of Irish revolution and French invasion, particularly in 1797-8 when Britain was temporarily the only belligerent left in the field against France, might well have forced Britain to make peace. But the technical problems of invasion across so wide a stretch of sea were difficult, the French efforts to do so hesitant and ill-conceived, and the Irish rising of 1798, though enjoying massive popular support, poorly organised and easily suppressed. To speculate about the theoretical possibilities of Franco-Irish operations is therefore idle.

Whilst accepting Hobsbawm's conclusion, there may still be profit in speculating on that joint Scots-Irish co-operation with the French that came so close to fruition.

If the inevitability of events up till the time of Muir's escape from Botany Bay be granted, the outcome thereafter could have been very different. There was nothing inevitable about the war that then broke out between Britain and Spain and in any case, had the ship taking him from Havanah to Cadiz managed to evade the blockading British fleet, as it almost did, Muir would have arrived uninjured and able to accept immediate diplomatic assistance from the French consul. Apart from being influential in Paris, his status within the Scots, Irish and English United movements would probably have resulted in more accurate intelligence on the true state of Admiral Duncan's North Sea Fleet than was then available to the somewhat isolated Wolfe Tone. A *descente* at that time under General Daendels, the young Dutch radical, with Paine as English political advisor, Tone as Irish equivalent and Muir for Scotland might still have failed, but such failure must have been very far from inevitable. Foregone conclusions seldom have existence prior to hindsight.

Historians of the North British Tendency have been utterly dismissive of the suggestion Angus Cameron could gather 15,000 men in Perthshire, or that 50,000 Highlanders in total would come forward to join an equal number of their Lowland countrymen. Such dismissals, drawing comparison with the much lower numbers who took part in the last Jacobite rising, are not comparing like with like. Accept that the radical estimates refer to militant support, rather than a gathered army, and the figures begin to look almost modest. The radical campaign in Scotland is acknowledged to have enjoyed truly nationwide support and a successful outcome would have been of immediate and much-needed benefit to some 90% of the population.

The role of figures such as Major-General Norman Macleod of Macleod is still difficult to estimate with accuracy but as a successful commander in wars of Empire and the highly regarded commandant of regiments based in Inverness and Perth, it would certainly have been considerable. As one of the few clan chiefs still striving to maintain something of the old Celtic traditions, Macleod's influence extended out to the western isles, from whence many of the soldiers who served with him in India were recruited and it was some of Macleod's soldiers who were suspected at that time of spreading sedition on their return to Scotland.

In Ireland, despite the disastrously increasing sectarian bloodshed, Lord Edward Fitzgerald estimated that 45,000 in the Dublin area would rise to the occasion with another 110,000 expected to act in Ulster, and given Hobsbawm's 'massive popular support' those figures do not seem wildly optimistic.

The radical leaders were intelligent men, well versed in history, and none would have expected the figures quoted to be assembled armed and ready for the fray; but at a time when half a regiment of determined infantry could hold most towns to ransom, they had every reason to believe effective bridgeheads could be established. Thereafter, the supply of arms and ammunition carried over would be available to those expected to step forward when convinced success was achievable, and though documentation remains scanty, it seems likely their ranks would have included a large number of professional, military and naval personnel, some of very senior rank.

Those in the latter category would have included George Mellis, the international banker based in Perth; John Clerk, later Lord Eldin; James Gibson, later Sir James Gibson-Craig; Lord Sempill; Adam

Gillies, later Lord Gillies and Robert Cutlar Fergusson, later Attorney-General in Calcutta before becoming Judge-Advocate-General and Privy Councillor at home. Many other leading figures who jeopardised their livelihoods by remaining openly pro-French and who could be expected to have responded positively include Alexander Nasmyth, the artist; Professor Dugald Stewart, Moral Philosophy, Edinburgh University; Professor George Jardine, Logic, Glasgow University; Professor *Cockie* Millar, Civil Law, Glasgow University; Professor Young, Greek, Glasgow University; Dr James Brown, St Andrews University; Andrew Fletcher, Lord Lauderdale, Lord Maitland and Alexander Adam, the highly influential Rector of Edinburgh High School.

That long overdue research into this period should show that this list, far from being that of a small and unrepresentative minority, can be added to by the names of noteworthy men and women of all professions and from every shire in the country. If time can allow leading American Republican's now to boast that radical – even Red Indian – blood is to be found in their veins, we may expect that those changes noted in Scottish historical orthodoxy will soon allow much that is thought-provoking to surface from family papers that were perhaps thought best kept out of view during an extended and intense period of North British prejudice.

From 1797 onwards there had been increasing government concerns over the re-forming and growing distribution of the United movement throughout the kingdom. George Mealmaker, of Dundee, had been implicated in the 1793 accusations against the Revd Fyshe Palmer and now, early in January 1798, was sentenced to fourteen years transportation for sedition and administering unlawful oaths. Then in February three members of the United Irishmen, Arthur O'Connor, Father James O'Coigley and John Binns were arrested at Margate while on their way to France. Two men who essayed their rescue, the Earl of Thanet and Robert Cutlar Fergusson [son of Alexander Fergusson, JP in Dumfries and close friend of Robert Burns] were arrested at Maidstone. Both Fergusson and the Earl of Thanet were found guilty as charged and sentenced to twelve months imprisonment; his Lordship in the Tower of London, Cutlar Fergusson in the King's Bench prison. Binns was aquitted on the treason charge, O'Connor was held pending further investigations, and Father O'Coigley was executed.

Nothing but terror will keep them in order. [6]

6. Tillyard p224

Under Castlereagh, this had been General Lake's pronouncement on Ulster, where recruiting for the United movement was punished by hanging, followed by decapitation and the head stuck on a pole. Many otherwise good servants of government were appalled by what was then happening in Ireland and in early 1798 the new Commander-in-Chief of the army there, Lt General Sir Ralph Abercromby, was one. Almost immediately after arriving in the country, his report amounted to an accusation that the British army in Ireland was guilty of committing atrocities, the forces he was to command being in such a state of licentiousness that their conduct 'had but too much tended to increase the spirit of insubordination and discontent that prevailed'.

Abercromby issued a proclamation that promised to punish 'with exemplary severity' any future outrages and made no secret of the fact he blamed the largely Anglo-Irish gentry for most of these problems, considering them ignorant men and oppressive landlords. It seems the General knew what he was talking about. Though he had been a successful and popular army officer for over 40 years, tribute to him as a laird in Clackmannanshire is recorded.

> As a country gentleman, ever attentive to all within his circle of movement, he stands high in the estimation of his neighbours and dependants; and when his military glory shall have fallen into oblivion, it will be gratefully remembered that he was the friend of the destitute poor, the patron of useful knowledge, and the promoter of education among the meanest of his cottagers.[7]

Such behaviour, of course, brought him into the category described by Cockburn.

> ... a country gentleman with any public principle except devotion to Henry Dundas was viewed as a wonder, in fact a monster.[8]

Abercomby made clear he was willing to reshape the army into an effective force against French invasion but was not prepared for military matters in Ireland to continue as before. Such a stance generated vicious political reaction from some of the criticised gentry in the Irish Parliament and had him labelled a 'Scotch beast'.[9] After a number of senior army officers threatened resignation if he was

7. *Biographical Dictionary of Eminent Scotsmen*

8. *Memorials* p67

9. McFarland Ireland & Scotland in the Age of Revolution.

dismissed, the General, elder brother to the Lord Abercromby who had fulminated at Muir's trial, resigned a command that had become 'disagreeable for many reasons' and returned home. After that, General Lake's terror – which included house burnings, floggings, pitch-cappings, mutilations, half-hangings and rape – was resumed, if not increased. This was the situation about the time Napoleon returned from his tour of the Channel coast and filed his report to the Directory.

> Whatever efforts we make, we shall not for some years gain the
> naval supremacy. To invade England without that supremacy
> is the most daring and difficult task ever undertaken. If, having
> regard to the present organisation of our navy, it seems
> impossible to gain the necessary promptness of execution,
> then we must really give up the expedition against England, be
> satisfied with keeping up the pretence of it, and concentrate
> all our attention and resources on the Rhine, in order to
> deprive England of Hanover and Hamburg; . . . or else
> undertake an eastern expedition which would menace her
> trade with the Indies.

Napoleon had liked Paine's initial proposal, which was to build a minimum of 1000 small boats, one cannon mounted at the bow, which might set out from the extensive French and Dutch coastline to make widespread landings in Britain. In Paine's view, the general enthusiasm in France for forcing England to peace talks was such that new taxes would not be needed for the project, the necessary naval constructions, he calculated, might be funded entirely by patriotic contributions. These would be voluntary, but on a recommended scale according to ability to pay, and he himself advanced more than the maximum that would have been expected of anyone. Now that Napoleon had expressed such pessimism over the time element of Paine's plan, the five-man Directory manoeuvred to keep the advocates of *descente* onside while they considered their country's other options, but this was a delay that allowed the problems within the Irish radical groups to reach disastrous proportions.

Irish spies in the pay of Westminster had now infiltrated the movement so successfully that some of them, like Robert Watt in Edinburgh four years earlier, were on the organising committees and at least one was named to be on the Provisional Directory for Ireland. It was in this situation that the conflict between Wolfe Tone and Thomas Muir came to a head, the Irishman and some of his supporters visiting the Scot at his apartments to demand that he cease writing articles for *Le Bien Informé* that claimed to speak for both Ireland and Scotland.

Of all the vain, obstinate blockheads that ever I met, I never saw his equal. Muir told us roundly that he knew as much of our country as we did . . . that he had seldom acted without due reflection, and when he had once taken his party, it was impossible to change him; and that he had the sanction of the most respectable individual of the United Irishmen whose authority he considered as justifying every syllable he advanced. . . . The fact is, Muir and Tandy are puffing one another here for their private advantage . . . issuing accommodation bills of reputation.

This much-quoted pronouncement on Muir, recorded for posterity after a heated and obviously frustrating three hour debate, requires some examination. Tom Paine, in Tone's recorded opinion, was also a man of intolerable conceit and vanity. Recent Irish research has been taking a more critical look at Tone himself and his very personal version of events. When the United Irishmen first formed in Belfast, Tone's continued employment by the Catholic Reform leaders in Dublin raised concern that the United movement was being used to force concessions out of London for a middle-class Catholicism that would, thereafter, behave no better towards the great mass of the population than present Protestant landowners. Given Tone's reputedly somewhat snobbish attitude towards the Irish *Gaidhealtachd*, it is possible that Muir, well aware of the historical Ulster-Scots connection,[10] did indeed understand the Irish situation at least as well as the other man, and the fact that he and Paine had both taken the United Irish oath before Tone cannot have improved matters.

But there were probably more immediate though unrecorded causes for dissent and division. For years, Tone had pressed the French government to concentrate on Ireland alone, expressing doubts over Scotland's readiness to revolt and utterly dismissing England. Now, when it had become the only option open to him, Tone was advocating invasion of Ireland via the Forth Estuary and the Union Canal, a militarily secured route across Central Scotland being seen as the way to a free Ireland. Whether this might prove successful or not, it involved a rather cavalier attitude towards Scotland's eventual fate and must have seemed to many Scots radicals like a proposal simply to use their country in a way likely to give rise to that civil war they had long striven to avoid. In these circumstances, the east-west split between Tone and Muir seems as inevitable as the north-south split among the Irish themselves.

---

10. Gaelic was still used by some Ulster Presbyterian congregations. [McFarland, p25, n7]

The promised support of the French Directory still not appearing, many in Ireland now talked of acting, if need be, without assistance. Some estimated that if arms were made available, over 100,000 men would come out in Ulster, with the Dublin area increasing that number by half again. In all Ireland they might count on over a quarter of a million insurgents. The thing could be done, a supply of weapons being all that was now required of the French. This development was, of course, well known to the British military and apparently not entirely unwelcome.

> I shall not lament the attempt at insurrection. It will enable
> us to act with effect.
>
> In a letter from Lord Lieutenant Camden (Ulster)
> to Home Office London [11]

The story of what then happened in Ireland is well known, but in any conflict that has human emancipation at its heart the people's songs retain their own truth.

> *Oh, ye men in name have ye no shame*
> *To see this beauteous land.*
> *Turned into one vast wilderness*
> *By a cursèd grazier band?*
> *This land so kind was ne'er designed*
> *By Providence on high,*
> *To keep John Bull with mutton full*
> *While natives starve and die.*

As had been planned in Scotland four years earlier, the non-arrival of mail coaches from principal cities was to be the signal for the country to rise. Despite the arrest of many leaders in the week prior to May 23rd, the chosen date, the mail coaches did not run and the work was begun with a will.

> *Oh then tell me, Sean O'Farrell, tell me why you hurry so?*
> *Hush,* a bhuachaill, *hush and listen, and his cheeks were all aglow.*
> *I bear orders from the Captain, get you ready quick and soon,*
> *For the pikes must be assembled at the rising of the moon!*

The pikes did come together, and for a time to such effect that County Antrim was soon almost entirely in the control of United Ulstermen, who had marched out singing *The Marsellaise* and the

---

11. Tillyard p263

ironic *Swinish Multitude*. In the south, too, there were gains.

> *Enniscorthy's in flames and old Wexford is won,*
> *And tomorrow the Barrow we cross.*
> *On a hill o'er the town we have planted a gun*
> *That will batter the gateway to Ross!*
> *All the Forth men and Bargy men will march o'er the heath,*
> *With brave Harvey to lead in the van;*
> *But the foremost of all in that grim gap of death*
> *Will be Kelly, the Boy from Killane!*

United Irishmen. The Presbyterian Henry Joy McCracken leading his forces to that early success in the north, while Father Murphy played a similar role in the south. It was an endeavour deserving of success.

> *But the gold dawn of freedom grew darkened at Ross,*
> *And it set by the Slaney's red waves;*
> *And poor Wexford, stript naked, hung high on a cross,*
> *With her heart pierced by traitors and slaves!*
> *But Glory O! Glory O! to the brave sons who died*
> *For the cause of long down-trodden man,*
> *And Glory O! to Mount Leinster's own darling and pride-*
> *Sean Kelly, the Boy from Killane!*

Incomplete unity had allowed the spies, the informers, the faint-hearted, the imported foreign troops and those 'ignorant and oppressive landlords' to triumph. If General Abercromby was sickened by what he saw in the Spring of that year, one wonders what he made of that Summer of Blood. In the space of a few weeks 'thirty-thousand people, men, women and children were cut down, shot or blown like chaff by cannons' according to Thomas Pakenham and other historians have put the figure at nearer double. United men were hung or flogged to death before ending up in mass graves called 'Croppy holes', and this was followed by trials of the leaders, followed by hangings, followed by a display of the heads of some of the best men of their generation stuck high on the spikes surrounding Belfast Court House.

> *It was on the Belfast mountains I heard a maid complain,*
> *And she vexed the sweet June evening with her heart-broken strain,*
> *Saying – Woe is me, life's anguish, is more than I can dree,*
> *Since Henry Joy McCracken died on the gallows tree.*

If there exists a song in praise of Robert Stewart, then Lord Castle-reagh and later Marquess of Londonderry, I never yet heard it sung.

* * *

Whether Talleyrand and the French Directory had been deliberately deceitful over promised invasion support or were, in midst of great political and financial problems, intent on keeping London guessing, is still cause for debate. The indisputable fact is that when Napoleon set sail for his Egyptian campaign, just days before the conflict began in Ireland, he left behind an irretrievably shattered United movement. Within weeks, Ireland had lost some of its most able leaders, among them Edward Fitzgerald, who died of wounds after betrayal and capture. Scotland had lost all possibility of that original concept of a coordinated rising; and England, its radical voice drowning under a torrent of cheap but long-fostered xenophobic patriotism, was a lost cause entirely. Wolfe Tone's initial reaction to this seemingly final disaster was to offer to serve France by following Napoleon to the east.

From the outset, Scots radicals had insisted on education, inform-ation and preparation as the means by which that handful of rogues might be isolated, rendered powerless, and bloody confrontation between people and military prevented. William Penny recorded that the date of the proposed Irish rising was known among Perthshire's United Scotsmen weeks before it happened and the crucial role that leaders such as Cameron and Macleod might have been expected to play still has to be properly assessed.

When the readiness for revolution in America was questioned at the Second Continental Congress, East Lothian's Dr John Witherspoon thundered, 'Not ripe, Sir? In my judgement we are not only ripe, but rotting!' Conditions in the doctor's native land had degenerated to that same unhappy condition, the important difference being that Scotland was now trapped in the grip of a lawless but quite official corruption that Westminster, for its own reasons, allowed to continue and lent its power to protect.

After nearly two centuries of neglect, or largely dismissive comment, there has only recently commenced that long overdue research into this vital period in Scottish history and future findings are certain to paint a much more positive picture of radical strength and potential than has hitherto been the case. It simply is not credible that Scots radicals of that time, led by some of the most able of their generation, were as gullible, misguided or ill-judging as North British historians of the past two centuries would have us believe.

Despite those earlier failures in Ireland, Scots radicals believed a successful *descente* was still possible, and the strong support expected from the *Gaidhealtachd* would arise from the fact that those 1792-93 distributions of radical literature, translated into *Gàidhlig*, would have offered most of the dispossessed there a United way out of post-Jacobite despair. In a memorandum to the Directory, May 1798, Muir estimated that a total of 50,000 Highlanders would come out in support of a properly organised invasion, with the expectation that these would be joined by about the same number of militant Lowlanders. He drew attention to English newspaper reports that Highland regiments had recently refused to fire on United Irishmen, but stressed the absolute need for further preparatory work. To counter the effects of continual anti-French propaganda, a proclamation was needed prior to *descente* that made clear the people's right to choose their own religious leaders for their own form of worship, and French troops should be cautioned to conduct themselves as allies, not occupiers, under a Provisional Government charged with establishing an independent republic.

The new French Directory's response to this and to urgent pressures from the divided Irish groups was to authorise some support for a further attempt on Ireland alone, which then went on to prove itself a particularly tragic case of far too little, far too late. General Humbert, massively outnumbered and dismayed over the quality and level of Irish support, surrendered early in September near Ballinamuck, the military reinforcements intended for him, with Tone a leader, having been delayed from leaving Brest by bad weather. Napper Tandy's force did get through the naval blockade to land a large supply of arms in Donegal, but after learning of Humbert's defeat, Tandy had a drunken night and was carried back on board his ship, now bound for Bergen.

Tone did not know of the disaster that had ended with his brother Matthew and others being tried and hung, it being well into October before his small fleet of nine ships reached Lough Swilly where, caught and outgunned by the blockading men-o-war, all but two of the French ships were taken, along with 2500 troops. Delayed by further gales, it was November before Tone, in chains, reached Dublin, where he was found guilty of treason and refused a firing squad. He is believed to have cut his own throat as he waited to be hanged. He took a week to die.

Who fears to speak of Ninety-Eight? Who blushes at the name?
When cowards mock the patriot's fate, Who hangs his head for shame?
He's all a knave or half a slave Who slights his country thus;
But true men, like you men, Will fill your glass with us.

Concurrently with these events, the Irish Parliament, capitulating totally to Westminster control, was preparing to vote itself out of existence. As in Scotland a century earlier, even corrupt self-government was being bartered beyond reach by another handful of rogues.

* * *

Le Célèbre Inconnu

After news of the September defeats in Ireland had reached Paris, but before the final outcome and fate of the leaders was known, Muir again wrote Talleyrand enclosing a detailed and revised proposal concerning a descente on Scotland. He warned that though this was not action that could unduly be delayed, the Scots would not be provoked into a premature or partial rising and nothing should be attempted until the preparatory work was complete. It is possible this memorandum of 18th October was a joint effort, largely the work of Muir and Robert Watson, but probably with input from others. John Sword is one who continued to provide information on the political situation at home, as his letter from Emden, August 1798, addressed to citizen Graham in Paris, shows.

> The fate of Britain is wearing nearer and nearer its crisis . . .
> Citizens John McKenzie, John Pattison, John Monteith, and a
> hundred more in Glasgow would give all the cloaths on them
> to be as clear of the country as you and I are . . . The
> manufactures are much in the decline, and if the French
> Republic should stop them from Hamburgh, and the American
> and West Indian markets, they might soon make what sort of
> peace they pleased . . . The whole nation would be in arms,
> and indeed nothing prevents this just now but unabated
> efforts of the Ministers bribing the landed Gentlemen to act
> against their own interest.

John Sword also wrote at this time to Muir outlining his own recent experience at the hands of the Lord Advocate. Just at the commencement of the Irish Rising he had been arrested when on his way to board a Danish ship lying at Leith Roads, and despite bail being offered by

three Edinburgh magistrates – £1000 sterling each – Lord Advocate
Dundas had Sword imprisoned without access to legal aid.

> I have endured a part of the persecution you so unjustly
> suffered. I have occupied the same appartments in Edinburgh
> jail which you have done before me . . .

From the interrogation at that time it seems he and his brother
were also suspected of involvement in that American attempt to
rescue Muir from Spain, in Spring 1797 [Appendix D] but the Lord
Advocate's men were unable to make any charge stick and John Sword
was released on a six-month bail, in the sum of 4000 merks.

> The only thing they can prove against me is my having been in
> France contrary to law, but my intentions, or any conversation
> I had with my work people about going there, I trust will not
> be discovered; so that if no action is commenced against me
> by the 29th of November, my bail bond is then discharged, and
> I fly to the glorious land of liberty, justly the admiration of
> Europe and of the whole world.

Though much of the co-operating Three Nations route to emancipation had by now perforce been abandoned, something of the
concept remained. The Scots memorandum to Talleyrand recommended that continuing unrest and resentments in the British Navy
should be used to support diversionary tactics by the United Englishmen, in the London area, while a main force landed in Scotland.
Success there, aided by a further outbreak in Ireland, would so weaken
government power in general that Westminster would be forced to
peace negotiations with France and reform would be back on the
agenda. Over-optimistic as this might seem after recent events, the
proposal recognised that rebellion in Ireland, brutally crushed as it
had been, was in no way eliminated. Lord Castlereagh might have
reduced every town and village to shocked and silent obedience but
the silence was a sullen one, a hatred-filled silence that would say
nothing of bands of armed men still maintaining a freedom in the
hills.

Both Ireland and Scotland had long-standing military links with
France but it was the cultural and educational exchanges that had
more recently come to predominate. Many of Muir's associates at this
time had completed their adult education in Paris. William Duckett,
who is known to have been close to Muir and often at his lodgings,
was one ex-student of the Irish College deeply involved in Paris-Dublin
communications and Nicholas Madgett, though his student days at

the same College were long in the past, was employed at the French Foreign Office and reported by a spy to be 'in strictest intimacy' with Muir.

The Scot who was Muir's closest collaborator in this crucial period was the Elgin-born Dr Robert Watson, who as a young man had attended the Scots College in Paris before going on to fight on the republican side during the American War of Independence. Watson had eventually become Preses of Hardy's London Corresponding Society, for which radical activities he had recently spent more then two years in Newgate prison, after which he seems to have acted as principal contact in Paris for emissaries arriving at the Channel ports.

In his memorandum, Muir had advised Talleyrand to rely on Thomas Hardy and another Scot, a printer named Ross, for advice about the situation in London; in Scotland, George Meliss, the Perth banker, and the Edinburgh advocate, John Clerk could be relied upon. He warned, though, that previous leaders such as the Earl of Lauderdale and Lord Sempill were now so closely watched they must be considered for the moment to have done all they could.[12] Among the very practical suggestions of this report is one recommending that British Naval crews be assured they could keep the whole value of any ships surrendered into French ports, thus offering seamen the means to recover long-standing arrears of wages at the same time as reducing the opposing fleet. The Carron Iron Works near Falkirk, as ever, is seen as the source of necessary artillery and Edinburgh Castle, without which the capital was all but defenceless, could be taken via a known underground tunnel. All that was now needed to further these proposals was a suitably trusted envoy from France to Britain, and that Muir was giving full weight to the seriousness of the project is exemplified by his not recommending any of those around him for this key role.

> . . . I must confess that I know not one of my countrymen in Paris whom I could propose. I know the purity of their principles. I have scrutinised their conduct with a watchful eye. They have not the prudence, that secrecy and that fortitude indispensably requisite for so delicate and so dangerous a trust. The superior wisdom of the Government no doubt will discover a person properly qualified . . .

The clarity of perception and absence of any egocentric assumptions of omniscience in this final political memorandum refute

---

12. Recent research confirms the accuracy of Muir's information at this time. McFarland, p177. n50.

allegations that have been made on Muir's mental state at this time. In an earlier letter to the Directory, requesting a loan sufficient to purchase a house in France, Muir had been equally perceptive and frank about his own situation.

> I eat your bread without being of any use to the Republic. If my physical strength had matched my inclinations I would have asked for the honour of fighting your enemies, but alas that is impossible. Only one means remains by which I shall no longer be a charge on the Republic. My property in Scotland is small, but sufficient for me to live anywhere I wish in honourable independence. As much as possible of that must be obtained quickly for, in the event of the death of my father and mother, who are already advanced in years, and who weep for me night and day, it will be taken from me, not perhaps by the British Government, but by heartless, avaricious relations who, to achieve this end, pretend to be its devoted partisans.

The threat to his inheritance may have arisen from the activities of his brother-in-law, David Blair, the ex-naval officer of dubious integrity who had been cited as a prosecution witness at the 1793 trial. Come the worst, though, Muir intended to pay his way in France.

> I have notes of my exile and travels which only need editing. They will form a two-volume quarto work. This is awaited with the greatest eagerness in England. I should get at least £3000 from the London booksellers. All that needs to be done is to send the MSS to any agent you choose at Hamburg and the bookseller's agent will pay up at once.

There is no record of any official reply to this letter. There may have been a verbal response, or no response at all from a Directory intent on trying to salvage something from the disaster in Ireland. All that remains is a note penned in the margin of this letter by some unknown French official.

Since then Muir has died.

Sometime towards the end of the year Muir had moved thirty miles north of the French capital to the small lace-making town of Chantilly, where he lived in a rented room. His need to be out of Paris had been expressed in that memorandum to Talleyrand. An inconspicuous habitation, suitable for unobserved rendezvous with delegates arriving in France, was what he sought. Among those he was anxious to contact were Angus Cameron, thought to be in hiding from Scots law in London at the time, and James Kennedy, formerly assistant Secretary to William Skirving in Edinburgh, probably at that moment trying to make his way to Paris.[13]

Apart from what may be implied from his communications to the Directory, and to Talleyrand, there is as yet no other explanation for Muir having moved to Chantilly nor any exact date for his change of location. Throughout his stay in Paris he had remained politically active and in constant touch with various French departments, sometimes on behalf of new Scots, Irish or English arrivals, once on behalf of some Irishmen taken prisoner by the French Navy, and always in promotion of plans to liberate his country from political and cultural despotism. It had been stressed to the French government that, while many Scots would oppose a foreign invasion, sufficient of them were so disaffected with Westminster rule that a revolution originating with their own countrymen would now be widely welcomed. In most *coups d'état* it is a minority who take the lead, ultimate success being dependent on that minority having correctly read the trend of public opinion.

The record shows that, to an exceptional degree, Muir had understood that trend in Scotland six years earlier when he became the most unswerving and therefore most influential and trusted voice of the people. His desire to be away now from the ever more complex intrigues of the French capital at this crucial period is understandable. There were spies of every persuasion in Paris and often to be found in very unexpected corners. One of the official ushers to the French Constituent Assembly, for example, a Scot named Rose, was suspected by the Sword brothers of supplying information to a relative in London's Treasury.[14] But though such factors would influence a decision to leave the capital, there was probably also a realistic acknowledgement that his own driving energy was largely expended, and what little remained was diminishing by the day.

Although staying in Chantilly long enough for regular postal communications to be established, Muir remained very much a stranger to the inhabitants. Citizen Lepauve, the postman, knew the stranger's name to be Thomas Muir only because the newspapers arrived so-addressed. But of the stranger's nationality, birthplace and age, Lepauve said he knew nothing. In the spirit of the times, it is possible Muir ensured that all important communications after his

13. Kennedy Appendix D

14. Rose Appendix D

arrival at Chantilly were carried out *viva voce*, or perhaps those wrapped newspapers arriving from Paris contained, at times, something more than just printed matter.

However that may be, on the morning of 26th January, 1799, postman Lepauve arrived at Muir's lodgings to find only widow La Bussine's twelve year old son there, and it was this boy who told him the stranger lodging with them had died at six o'clock that morning. After completing his deliveries, Lepauve made his report to the *Mairie*, and a small deputation then set off to verify matters officially.

That low ebb of the year as January wears into February had this time proved too much even for one of whom it had been said 'his constitution is of iron'. Muir had died on the morning following the date poet Burns had been born. It seems the seasonal 'blast o Januar wind' that blew hansel in on Robin brought Tam nothing but the gift of eternal rest.

Muir had retained to within months, if not hours of his death, a clear and focussed aim for the rebirth of his native land. That had been the driving purpose throughout his whole adult life. It is to be hoped that in his final lonely moments he was able to hear again an echo of that thunderous applause ringing up through the hammer-beams of Scotland's Old Parliament Hall, that enthusiastic response to his final words there.

> My mind tells me that I have acted agreeably to my conscience; and that I have engaged in a good, a just, and a glorious cause. A cause which, sooner or later, must and will prevail, and by timely reform save this country from destruction.

Kay's depiction of Prime Minsiter Pitt (left) at the time of the 1798 Rising in Ireland. He is seen lamenting to Henry Dundas the popular conception of him as a murderer of his fellow men

CHAPTER 13

Unfinished Business

I n the year after Muir died, and by much the same process that had applied in Scotland a century earlier, Ireland too lost its Parliament. A 1799 proposal it be dissolved had been rejected by just one vote but after Lord Castlereagh had placed suitable money in suitable hands there were, the following year, 45 more in favour of dissolution. With both nations now directly under Westminster control they were to endure, for a generation and more, increased and unremitting repression.

There was just a glisk of hope for reform in 1805 when the Tory majority, reducing with Pitt's declining health, could not prevent he and *King Harry* Dundas being investigated over large sums of missing public money. Pitt blocked investigation into how £100,000 of Navy Fund money could have been paid to anonymous figures for 'secret services', while Henry Dundas insisted his own silence on the matter resulted from a sense of 'public duty' and 'private honour'. Of two sums, £20,000 to himself and £40,000 to Pitt, though he knew what they had been used for he insisted nothing would compel him to disclose that information. He did admit that Navy Funds had been used to make investments for private profit but insisted the money so borrowed was always repaid. No civil action against the two was possible because vouchers for monies actually removed had officially and expressly been ruled, beforehand, to be inadmissable in any subsequent prosecution. Pitt died in the first month of 1806, his 'self-deifying' life's work to maintain Europe's feudal states a failure and his legacy to Britain a hugely increased National Debt. He was, of course, buried in Westminster Abbey to a brass-band playing. For reasons of 'shattered health and broken reputation' Henry Dundas never again held public office but the statue his beneficiaries erected to his memory in Edinburgh's St Andrew Square is mounted on the highest column in the capital. As continues to be evidenced in our own time, the height of a monument frequently gauges nothing but the depth of deception supporting it.

British radicalism had been opposed to the war with France, nowhere more strongly than in Scotland, and the coalition government formed after the collapse of the Dundas regime sent Lord

Lauderdale – he of the Jacobin costume in the House of Lords – to attempt peace negotiations in Paris. By then, of course, feudal Europe had sent Napoleon Buonaparte off astride his own messianic charger and the peace bids failed. Had the change of government at Westminster occurred a decade earlier, as leading radicals at the time believed possible, peace negotiations between Britain and France would almost certainly have been successful. Measuring achievement is relatively simple, it is more difficult but potentially much more important to attempt an evaluation of what might have been possible.

After that brief coalition government had failed, Henry Dundas's only son, Robert, assumed the role of Scotland's Manager though he held no official position in the country. He continued his father's work from London and, according to Meikle, 'only his inferior abilities, political and social, were to prevent him from exercising as complete a sway as his predecessor'. This less competent despotism went on to make John Sword's gloomy 1798 prediction the stark reality of 1812 when, according to Peter Mackenzie, 'starvation, lean and gaunt' was to be seen on the faces of Glasgow's weavers and cotton-spinners. On the advice of Whig lawyers, these artisans petitioned for fair work rates to be fixed by the city's Justices of the Peace, but the manufacturers refused to pay the rates so determined and 40,000 men came out on a strike described by Cockburn as 'the most extensive and peacable combination of workmen that had ever appeared in this part of the kingdom'.

With the Lord Advocate's connivance, strike leaders' homes were entered illegally in search of evidence and at the subsequent trials eighteen-month sentences were handed down. Shortly afterwards, the legal right of artisans to request Justices of the Peace to fix fair wages was abolished.

When dealing with wealthier opponents, however, official incompetence was more evident. After news of Napoleon's escape from Elba reached Glasgow, the Professor of Moral Philosophy, John Mylne, delivered a sermon to students that was judged by some beagle to be seditiously or even treasonously in support of the French leader. Word of the University Chaplain's crime was despatched *post haste* to Lord Advocate Archibald Colquhoun in Edinburgh, who sent a Sheriff to Glasgow to create evidence for a prosecution. Many leading Glaswegians, including Sir John Maxwell of Pollok, offered bail to any amount demanded should the Professor be arrested, and faced with such united opposition the Lord Advocate abandoned the case but sheltered behind his office in refusing either to identify the accusers, apologise, or retract the charges. Students from the University, led by their Preses, the young Lord Glenorchy, then held a meeting from which Mylne was presented with an address which began:

HONOURABLE AND REVD. SIR,

Our minds have been roused to indignation by the cowardly and malicious attack which has been made upon you by certain concealed enemies. These are the men who are the real traitors to their country – men who, for their own selfish and crooked ends, imprint a stain upon the fair fame of our venerable laws.

MacKenzie records that the Reverend Professor continued thereafter to be one of the 'small but choice band which led every popular movement in Glasgow' and among such popular movements would be the at times violent protests against Corn Laws that continued to deprive the majority of basic sustenance. A Department of Moral Philosophy must surely have understood those who rejected the despised charity of Soup Kitchens and simply took food where they found it.

Despite public awareness of his increasingly gross and insulting extravagances, there were still some who thought the Prince Regent might yet respond to a petition for redress of grievances, but when a public meeting for that purpose was planned in Glasgow, in 1816, its proposers were threatened with military intervention if they attempted to use the Green for the purpose. They were then debarred from the Trades Hall in Glassford Street and cries of 'sedition and treason' frightened-off the proprietor of the Eagle Inn when he, as a last resort, offered use of his stableyard. The well-known Glasgow street character, Jamie Blue, would have had eager buyers for radical satires like those of Sandy Rodger.

> *Vile 'sooty rabble', what d'ye mean*
> *by raising a' this dreadfu' din?*
> *Do ye no ken what horrid sin*
> *ye are committing*
> *By haudin up your chafts sae thin*
> *for sic a meeting?*
>
> *Vile Black-nebs! doomed through life to drudge*
> *And howk amang your native sludge,*
> *Wha is't gies ye the right to judge*
> *O siccan matters,*
> *That ye maun grumble, grunt an' grudge*
> *At us, your betters?*

*We've walth o' sodgers in the toun
To keep sic ragamuffins doun;
And gin ye dinna settle soon,
By a' that's guid!
We'll gar the common sewers rin
Wi' your base bluid!*

James Turner, a shopkeeper specialising in tobacco and snuff, then came to the rescue by offering the organising committee use of a field he owned, and despite infantry and dragoons standing by for the magistrates' signal an estimated 40,000 attended. MacKenzie records that this Thrushgrove meeting attracted national attention, sparked off similar meetings all over Britain, while James Turner's shop became 'the most frequented of any of its kind in Glasgow'. Turner, himself imprisoned a time on a possible High Treason charge, later became a much-respected Magistrate in the city.

As 1816 drew to a close, Home Office agitation over such radical actions increased with the increased number of reports linking them directly to the earlier developments forged in the Muir era.

> Several of them who were particularly active in the seditious transactions of 1793 have been the first to step forward on this occasion.
>
> A spark was kindled at the French Revolution which the enemies of freedom think they have extinguished, but it still burns, and every fresh occurrence fans the flames.

The Hampden Clubs, under the leadership of Sir Francis Burdett, William Cobbett, Major Cartwright, Admiral Cochrane [10th Earl of Dundonald] and Henry Hunt were recruiting throughout Britain but there was still insufficient unity of action to counter Westminster's increasing use of *agents provocateur* in local situations. Those arch-reactionaries, Lord Sidmouth at Home Office and Lord Castlereagh at Foreign Office, were virtually dictating policy for a sick Prime Minister and the trials resulting from this situation led, in the north of England, to hangings and transportations.

In February of 1817, an agent employed by the Lord Provost of Glasgow caused the arrest of a number of Calton weavers on a charge of taking Treasonable Oaths and two of them, Andrew MacKinlay and John Campbell, were held incommunicado at Edinburgh Castle. The defence, organised without fee by lawyers who had been colleagues of Tom Muir, received unexpected assistance when John Campbell smuggled word to MacKinlay [a Presbyterian Ulsterman recently arrived in Scotland] that he had been offered the bribe of a government post abroad, guaranteed by Lord Sidmouth, if he would turn King's evidence. Campbell vowed he would not turn and MacKinlay's lawyer, the later Lord Jeffrey, gambled on him remaining true to that promise. Campbell did more than hold true. In court, he publicly identified the Advocate-Depute as the man who had offered him the bribe and when he went on to name the Sheriff of Edinburgh as his witness to this felony the Crown case collapsed 'midst the most ignominious confusion' of its 'right trusty' Lord Advocate. The agent provocateur involved in these charges, Robert Richmond, later recorded that had the Lord Advocate succeeded against MacKinlay, it was intended that several other indicted Glasgow weavers were to die with him on scaffolds erected on Edinburgh's Royal Mile.

Sandy Rodger,[1] born in the Lothian village of Mid Calder but now himself a Calton weaver, reached again for his quill to record the latest *Wailings of Corruption.*

> *She curses the fate of her Spies and Informers,*
> *She wails o'er their efforts so fruitlessly made,*
> *When they prowled thro' the land for the blood of Reformers*
> *Seduced the unwary – then basely betrayed.*

The last verse expresses the nobility of concept that had all along driven the radical movement.

> *For Truth must prevail over Falsehood and Error,*
> *In spite of the devil, Corruption and Spies,*
> *Who down to their dens shall be driven in terror,*
> *While Man to his scale in creation shall rise.*

That the 'swine, rabble and wretches' could have any scale at all in creation was a concept so beyond the handful of rogues that Rodger's terror, unfortunately, does seem the key word.

There were moments, though, when *Authority's* incompetence must have been cause of much popular amusement. Shortly after being forced to release Campbell and MacKinlay, the Lord Advocate ordered the Revd Neil Douglas to be arrested. Douglas had been using the pulpit all his life to deliver radical sentiments and he had never been afraid to name names. In his sermons, King George III always featured as more seriously insane than Nebuchadnezzar with his Prince Regent son a Prodigal abuser of Concubines, but now that the current activities of Castlereagh and Sidmouth were featuring in the

---

1. Rodger Appendix D

seventy-year-old cleric's deliveries, enough was enough and the Glasgow Magistrates ordered three legal functionaries to church. Identifying these unfortunates sitting below his pulpit, notebooks at the ready, Douglas addressed the more virulent morsels of his sermon straight down at them. They were, he fumed, 'infernal scamps, or spies, sent by Beelzebub the Devil from the Council Chambers to entrap him'. The Reverend Douglas did end up in that much-abused dock of the High Court in Edinburgh but Beelzebub's beagles went on to disagree so profoundly over interpretation of the sermon they had been made to suffer that the Solicitor General, 'with some degree of mortification on his lips' was forced to abandon the case. The suspicion is raised that this radical cleric was saved from jail by a tongue-in-cheek manipulation of legal procedures such as was seldom available to accused less well connected.

Throughout his reign, George III had opposed any review of laws that sent juveniles to Botany Bay for nothing more than appropriating a necessary loaf of bread and by which he authorised death-warrants for men and women guilty of nothing worse than minor theft. As far back as 1792 the *Glasgow Herald* reported the case of a woman confined for 35 years over a £20 debt – 'the horrors of the Bastille could not be more terrible than this' – but the King's son, now Prince Regent, still saw no need for change when Tom Muir's former agent [now *Sir* James MacKintosh, and back from serving as Bombay's Chief Judge] had his 1819 law-review proposals thrown out of the House of Commons. No one can be surprised that about this time women began to form Sister Reform Associations to co-operate with their menfolk and 'instil into the minds of their children a hatred of tyrannical rulers.'

The trio of Prince Regent, Lord Sidmouth and Lord Castlereagh answered such protest by promoting new bills to prevent meetings, expedite punishments and reduce the power of the English press towards the level long enforced in Ireland and Scotland. The prodigious Prince also sent word of his 'high approbation' of official action when, on 16th August, a cavalry charge against a radical meeting at St Peter's Field, Manchester, went on to make the name Peterloo as well-known in English history as that of Waterloo. No doubt he was equally well-satisfied, early the following year, when the Government-manipulated Cato Street Conspiracy ended in five very public hangings.

While Cato Street was being hatched at Westminster, *Authority* in Scotland was plotting an equally important project, one it was hoped would finally deliver an enduringly servile North Britain. Lord Advocate Sir William Rae, Robert Dundas [the 2nd Lord Melville] and

Lord President Charles Hope were in control of the country when a network of agents engineered a premature outbreak of the rising for which radicals all over Scotland had been recruiting and training. In the subsequent confusion a great many escaped to America and Canada but of those put on trial, three were hanged and beheaded and twenty-two transported for life. In a subsequent protest at Greenock, eight unarmed civilians – four of them men, three still boys and one a child – were shot and died, a greater number of both sexes being more or less seriously wounded. After devoting more than a dozen pages to Manchester's Peterloo, Cassell's *Illustrated History of England*, which did cover Scotland's 1820 rising, did so briefly and inaccurately in one paragraph.

> Other arrests were made in different parts of Scotland, and they were tried in the following July and August; but, so little interest was felt in this attempt, or in the details of what was called 'The Battle of Bonnymuir', that three only were punished, and the rest discharged.

North British history, of course, scarcely mentioned this event at all and it was from a basis of folk-history that Berresford Ellis and Mac a' Ghobhainn went on, 150 years later, to research and for the first time reveal something of the true scale and nature of the event in their important work *The Scottish Insurrection of 1820*.

George III's death, in that year of insurrection, ended a reign in which it is estimated some one-million citizens of Great Britain and Ireland lost their lives in war, with at least the same number again lost to the nations opposed. Because of this history, the ideals born of Bastille Day continued to have popular currency, so much so that Westminster now had resort to a cynical 'hearts and minds' strategy. The year after George IV's coronation, a grand Royal Visit was organised in which the new monarch was presented in Dublin as a benign, be-shamrocked and, be jocular, *King Paddy the First*, and the following year he was given lead-role in the bitter farce stage-managed in Edinburgh by Sir Walter Scott.

It is difficult to imagine a more fitting symbol of the utterly *ersatz* identity now proposed for Scotland than this prodigiously-tartanised descendant of 'Butcher' Cumberland posturing as King of the Scots at the head of the people's equally tartanised betrayers. This time, though, the Tories had overplayed their hand. Not even in England was the behaviour of this dysfunctional son of a dysfunctional family any longer acceptable. Choosing his moment badly, the new Prime Minister, the Duke of Wellington, set his firm features ever more firmly against renewed and stronger demands for reform and as result met his own political Waterloo. After more than a generation of bitter struggle Tory rule was ended, George IV died and the 1832 Reform Bill was passed by the new embryo Liberal Party.

> *See Glasgow under Earl Grey*
> *Frae Glasgow under Castlereagh –*
> *Ha! ha! the differ o't.*

Once again the direct connection to earlier struggles featured in the subsequent celebrations. In Perth, one elderly radical, James Craigendallie, carried a copy of the Scotch Reform Bill stitched to the indictment for Sedition that had been served on him at the end of the previous century,[2] and at the Edinburgh Trades Council parade, from Bruntsfield Links, a banner proclaimed Lafayette's dictum – 'For a nation to be free it is sufficient that it wills it'. But the black-draped empty chair borne aloft in memory of the historic and noble leadership given by Muir was symbolic in a way that probably wasn't intended. The final result of this Great Whig Reform Bill was that Edinburgh had two MP's instead of one, Glasgow had two instead of a quarter of one, and nearly ninety per cent of Scotland's population was still denied the right to vote. The struggle for democratic government remained, as it ever must continue, a matter of unfinished business.

In the decade immediately following these great changes the distinction between the two main political parties gradually became meaningless; Carlyle's *Moneybags Aristocracy* now being in overall control, dehumanising wage-slavery was replacing the less profitable feudal-serfdom, and from being the disdainful Tory's *Swinish Multitude* the mass of the population had gone on to become the amused Whig-Liberal's *Great Unwashed*, a class of people causing much coarse merriment in Parliament with their demand that women, too, must have the vote. Within a few years the working class in Scotland marked a renewal of the struggle by first acknowledging their debt to the past; in 1846 a memorial to James Wilson, the executed weaver's leader was erected at Strathaven and a monument on Edinburgh's Calton Hill was erected to commemorate the stand taken by Muir, Skirving, Palmer, Gerrard and Margarot; the following year, a memorial to Baird and Hardy, the other two radicals hanged and beheaded in 1820, was completed at Glasgow's Sighthill. In the same way that many of the leaders at the time of the 1820 Insurrection had been young men active

---

2. Penny *Traditions of Perth*. See also Craigendallie Appendix D

in the 1790s Friends of the People, so there were now Union leaders and Chartists who had been active in 1820. *Plus ça change . . .* the renewed demands met with the same old responses.

> Multitudes of people would be enfranchised who have no claim or fitness whatever in the sight of God or man to exercise the rights and privileges of citizens.

This was the mid-nineteenth century attitude of the *North British Daily Mail*, the leading Liberal newspaper, which now had its colours nailed firmly to its Edinburgh masthead as the cavalry were once again ordered to draw sabres and prepare to disperse 'Unwashed' meetings.

* * *

> The century that is passing away has every chance of leaving Scotland but an English County . . . I feel my own indignation often roused. But though particular examples may justify this, it is useless and wrong to resist the general current.

Every generation of Scots, it seems, must produce its end-of-an auld-sang threnodist, but by a coincidence of two largely unforeseen factors, that mid-nineteenth century view of the gloomy Lord Cockburn[3] had now become so typical among the professional classes that this time the prophecy came very near to self-fulfilment and Scotland, as a nation, was indeed close to being left with nothing to mark all that had been but a tartanised equivalent of the cigar-store Redskin. While the North British Tendency had tightened its grip on education, continually driving for complete anglicisation, the two historical bulwarks against such previous assaults were themselves so altered as to be for a time, a dangerously long time, all but ineffectual. The population displacements initiated by enclosures and clearances in the first half of the century, subsequently accelerated by the labour needs of an expanding industrial revolution, had led to a breakdown – in some areas almost a complete eradication – of centuries-old social bonds. The inhabitants of the jerry-built hovels thrown up around coalfields and iron-foundries were more often than not strangers to each other, of different faiths and nationality, at times sharing little but a near animal-level struggle for survival. One Moneybags attitude to this is typified in a colliery-landowner's letter published in the *North British Daily Mail*, 27th October, 1863.

---

3. Cockburn *Journal* Vol2. July 10, 1853

> There must be rich and poor, there must be fortunate and
> unfortunate, for blessed purposes. For if there were no poor,
> there could be no sweet and holy charity.

At this same time the church, long a focus for national identity
despite political inroads, was itself cataclysmically Disrupted. The
demands for an end to the patronage which forced the likes of the
Reverend James Lapslie on a resentful congregation had left Presbyterianism cleft clear through the centre. This religious schism left the
nation without leadership of any kind, social, political, or religious,
at a time when the people's own sense of identity was least able to
withstand the daily undermining it suffered under a system of
compulsory North British education. George Davie's *The Democratic
Intellect* illustrates in detail just how far-reaching and sustained were
the efforts made at this period to enforce a completely anglicised
education on Scotland, a time when its history, languages, and cultural
attitudes were at best devalued and at worst derided or suppressed
by many of its own professional classes.

It was a time when many in senior office seem to have succumbed
to the same defeatist attitude with which Lord Cockburn had ended
his days and most of their underlings, probably weary of trying to
square the circles of their own confused identities, seem to have
accepted the enforced changes as some kind of necessary evil. Dating
from about this time and strengthened through the generations by
dutiful repetitions, Muir's stance has been depicted as that of an
idealistic individual but one so ill-judging as to leave himself isolated
and completely abandoned by all right-thinking men. Quite apart
from the very selective use of evidence to support this view, the
inherent contradiction in attributing the acknowledged official over-
reaction against him as arising from an unjustified governmental
panic, bordering on hysteria, merely begs the question. The effects of
such professional capitulations were, for a time, little different to those
that would have resulted had some foreign power set out to enforce a
quite ruthless programme of cultural genocide but fortunately for
future generations there were always the *seanachean*, bards, pamph-
leteers and publishers of sixpenny political booklets determined on a
renewal and refurbishment of that *auld sang* rather than just hear its
last whisper die on their lips. The debt to such people is great, for that
third quarter of the nineteenth century was a very, very low ebb in
the tide of Scotland's cultural and political fortunes.

We have suffered the misery which is perhaps inevitable to a lesser and remote country in a junction where the Governing powers are united but the Nations are not united.

The leaders of the subsequent resurgence of national spirit, taking cognisance of that judgement of the radicals in Muir's era, increasingly framed their strategies in clear awareness that the inherent power of the larger to subsume the smaller would never voluntarily be renounced. Though his new party advocated Parliamentary Reform almost identical to that of the Friends of the People, and included a list of proposed social benefits taken largely from Paine's *Rights of Man*, Keir Hardie became convinced it was in the end futile to continue sending Scots Labour MP's to Westminster; when out of office, the NB Tendency became vociferous in support of Home Rule only to fall silent on the subject once elected; independent Parliaments in Ireland and Scotland were no more on Westminster's agenda than they had been in 1790, though Keir Hardie's radical name was later misappropiated to adorn Labour's HQ in the English capital.

Another key figure, R.B. [*Don Roberto*] Cunninghame Graham, went on from being first President of that 1888 Scottish Parliamentary Labour Party to become, in 1928, first preses of the newly formed National Party for Scotland. In 1934 he was appointed Honorary President of the newly-formed Scottish National Party, whose avowed aim 'independence within the British group of Nations' echoed the concept advocated by Scots and Irish radicals a century and a half earlier. Greatly influential in this renewal was the earlier work of John MacLean, who in 1923 had founded the Scottish Workers Republican Party. As Muir 150 years earlier, MacLean recognised that close alliance and joint political action with Irish radicals was an essential counter to the process whereby ostensibly democratic methods would always hinder and might eventually end the natural development of the smaller nations. These two men, separated in history and quite unlike in most other ways, shared several noteworthy characteristics. Both were gifted orators, both had resolved to put their abilities at the service of the community from which they had arisen and both had very large popular support. Both also managed to maintain a quite remarkable personal integrity through many personal trials, a fact which left *Authority* with no alternative but to encourage the notion both were, in the end, mentally unbalanced.

> Many considerations could no doubt be advanced to explain this phenomenon but perhaps the real reason is simply that he was too dangerous a man to remember.

So wrote John Broom in his 1973 biography of John Maclean. Muir, like Maclean, had the ability to articulate clearly what the masses know instinctively to be true. That is the reason the two names survive and, despite *Authority*, continue to be an inspiration.

> *Is beò duine an déigh a shàrachaidh ach cha bheò e idir*
> *an déigh a nàrachaidh.*

A man o'erwhelmed lives on, a man disgraced does not.

Twenty-one poets and songwriters, including Sorley Maclean, Hugh MacDiarmid, Hamish Henderson, Sydney Goodsir Smith, Tom Law, Tom Scott, Edwin Morgan, Uilleam Neill and Ruaraidh Mac-Thomais contributed to the 1973 centenary publication *Homage to John Maclean*. Acknowledging the significance of this work, a second edition was published in 1979 by Edinburgh University Student Publications Board.

> *Give me the making of the songs of a nation and I care not who makes its laws.*

That thought, attributed to Andrew Fletcher of Saltoun, suggests that if we listen to the burden of a nation's bards we already know much of its history, and a great deal, perhaps, of its future. Included in that Maclean tribute was a song written by Thurso Berwick [Morris Blythman] the last two verses of which wittily top-and-tail the whole of our story, from the sixteenth to the twenty first century. Its setting to *The Wark o the Weavers* could not have been more appropriate.

> *Noo there's some wad sell their mithers for a ha'penny or a cent,*
> *There's some wad sell the Scottish folk a puppet parliament,*
> *But the rebel wheel is turnin, an we'll scotch their ill-intent,*
> *Wi Perfervidum Ingenium Scotorum.*
>
> *Wi Perfervidum Ingenium ye hear the ring o bells,*
> *Ye watch the Wheel o Fortune an see whit it foretells;*
> *We'll win oor Independence, ay, by takin it oorsels,*
> *Wi Perfervidum, Ingenium, Scotorum.*
>
> *Sae here's tae George Buchanan,[4] wis first tae gie't a name,*
> *An here's tae William Wallace, {Tammas Muir} an John MacLean,*

4. *Scotorum præfervida ingenia* – the ardent temper of the Scots. Phrase recorded by George Buchanan, 1506-1582. Reformer, historian, scholar and poet, it seems inevitable that Buchanan was another whose education embraced St Andrews and Paris.

An here's tae Bonnie Scotland – we'll see her free again,
Wi Perfervidum Ingenium Scotorum.

Given Morris's pioneering work in ballad workshops, I feel sure he would have wished Muir's name included without my parenthesis.

Over sixty years ago the essayist and journalist, William Power, expressed his belief that by the end of the eighteenth century Scotland was 'potentially the most democratic and progressive country in Europe'. Another quotation from Hobsbawm suggests this thought, not at all widely welcomed in the early 1940s, has validity.

> English education was a joke in poor taste, though its deficiencies were somewhat offset by the dour village schools and the austere, turbulent, democratic universities of Calvinist Scotland. . . Oxford and Cambridge, the only two English universities, were intellectually null . . . Even such aristocratic families as wished their sons to be educated relied on tutors or Scottish universities.

Well aware of this advantage that historical happenstance and their own *ingenium* had created, the country's most able minds set out to establish, with their counterparts in Ulster, conditions under which both might reach towards a historical peak of social and political achievements.

> Our cause is your cause. If there is to be a struggle between us let it be which nation shall be foremost in the race of mind; let this be the noble animosity kindled between us, who shall first attain that free Constitution from which both are equi-distant.

That was the Ulster-Scots vision of 1790. By 1970, the reality was that Scotland and Northern Ireland shared the worst housing and highest unemployment figures in western Europe, had inherited the dispirited outlook that necessarily arises from confused senses of identity, and continued to be destructively diminished by the bloody tragedy of three centuries of those sectarian *Troubles*.

The radicals of the United movement would have failed, of course, to achieve anything resembling the glorious millenium they envisaged and *man-to man the world o'er* would yet remain no more than a life-enhancing aim. But it must be perverse to argue that what was achieved by a venal minority, recruiting support by bribery financed from the public purse and led on by a delusional and drunken prime minister, is the best that human endeavour of that period could ever have achieved.

Speculation on developments that might reasonably have been expected in these islands had the Franco-phobic and narrow-nationalist mindset of Westminster government ended with the end of the eighteenth-century cannot now be other than instructive; particularly not when, two-centuries later, the Prime North Briton at Westminster is reported to be further diminishing Lord Cockburn's depressed vision by suggesting that government of one of the oldest nations in Europe should now require no more than the powers of an English *parish* council.

> *Dico tibi verum, libertas optima rerum,*
> *Nunquam servili sub nexo vivito, fili.*

Attributed to the Priest of Dunipace, a precept for his nephew, the young William Wallace.

> *My son, I tell thee soothfastly,*
> *No good is like to liberty.*
> *Then never live in slavery.*

It has been said that freedom is no more than the freedom to choose one's own restrictions. For a people, as for an individual, that is a vital freedom.

※※※

Engraving by Holloway from the 1794 bust of Muir by Thomas Banks

Muir's exile commenced on the morning of Friday, 15th November, 1793, when the official coach and armed escort carried him from the Tolbooth down through the wooded estates bordering Leith Walk, then along the coast to the quay at Newhaven; from there, a boat ferried him out to the revenue cutter *Royal George*, lying ready at anchor in Leith Roads. Because of an administrative error, however, six days were to elapse before the Revd T.F. Palmer was transferred on board from Perth Jail and so it was the morning of the following Friday before the government vessel set sail for the Hulks at Woolwich. From the outset, one of the other four prisoners in Royal George began to stir up trouble for the convicted radicals, a pattern of behaviour that commenced during that week off Newhaven and continued throughout the year it took them to reach Sydney Cove.

John Grant, a Dundas-appointed Sheriff-depute at Inverness before being sentenced to transportation for forgery, tried to give damaging evidence against Muir when the two duelling pistols gifted by Hamilton Rowan were confiscated, then on the passage to the Thames he started a rumour that Muir and Palmer intended to murder the captain and alter course for France. Captain Ogilvie of *Royal George* appears to have had the measure of Grant, reporting that both Muir and Palmer 'had behaved like gentlemen'; they in turn praised Ogilvie, with whom they dined, for his 'attention and civility'. According to Palmer's later accusations [published Cambridge, 1797] Grant had been acting as some kind of agent-provocateur while they were held in the Hulks at Woolwich, and after a month at sea on the voyage to Sydney Cove was responsible for reporting a planned mutiny involving Palmer, Skirving and some of the soldiers. After that appearance on the quarter-deck 'accoutred like a perfect Robinson Crusoe', Captain Campbell of *Surprize* ordered Palmer and Skirving to close-confinement below, under armed guard, while every second accused soldier was to be flogged that day, the rest on the morrow, with a pardon on promise for confession. Two confessed, and as result a number of convicts ended up chained on deck in what amounted to torture positions. Though by every account Campbell comes across as a dangerously unstable character, attempted mutinies in such transport vessels were far from uncommon.

John Grant had already been caught stealing from both Muir and Palmer when in the Hulks, so perhaps everything from Leith Roads outwards had resulted from nothing more than his desire to earn a copper or two, but it is also possible someone in Edinburgh had dropped Grant the hint of eventual leniency if the political prisoners he was shipped with could be implicated in some terminally serious offence. Suppression of mutiny on the high seas ended in hangings, and without a doubt there were some in Scotland who would have welcomed news such had been the radicals' final fate.

> Justice compels me to say that Mr Muir's behaviour was the reverse of Margarot's. At the time of my imprisonment we were not on the best of terms, but the moment he discovered the measures taken by Campbell his resentment was forgotten, he sent me word that he would join heart and hand with me in the vindication of my innocence, and in bringing my oppressors to justice. He kept a watchful eye on Campbell and collected some curious facts.

This record by Palmer is very critical of Margarot's behaviour in siding with the Captain Campbell from the outset of the trouble and possibly explains the ostracisation that followed once ashore at Sydney Cove; but though they might now be beyond investigation, there are other testimonies to suggest a possibly darker and more complex tone to the whole affair. Bewley quotes a published letter from Skirving to the Revd Jeremiah Joyce.

Morning Chronicle. 10th July, 1795.

> You must by now have heard of the deep plot against Mr Palmer and me. It was laid against Mr Muir, not me, but the design of it was blown before the plot was ripe and he escaped. The odium I incurred by aiding his escape and openly showing my sentiments of such conduct provoked putting myself in his place. I thank God, being convinced this impolitic step was a principal hindrance to the execution of the infernal plot against the life of Mr Palmer.

This suggests Muir and Palmer had remained the prime targets of Grant's ploys and Captain Campbell clearly believed serious official action would follow when he hurried ashore at Sydney Cove to lodge his accusations of mutiny. The previous behaviour of Lt Governor Grose suggests a stickler for discipline, one who would not shirk from ordering the severest of punishments, yet he appears to have let the stramash of this affair dissipate quietly with time. Perhaps the conflicting testimonies were just too numerous to permit of any resolution at all, or perhaps the Governor wrote Campbell off as someone best ignored. It is also possible that someone did not want questions on Grant's behaviour to be raised in public. All in all, the Revd Palmer's description of the transport as *'the most flatigious brothel in the Universe'* seems appropriate in more ways than one.

My Lord Viceroy

I am a native of Scotland. I am come to solicite your protection & your permission to pass through your dominions to General Washington, President of the United States, at Philadelphia. It is proper I should state to you both who I am & my situation. Concealment of any circumstance would be to you unjust & to me dishonourable.

I have exposed myself to the hatred & incurred the vengeance of those Ministers who, if not now, lately governed England. I blush not to unfold the causes. The people of Scotland have long groaned under the most hideous oppression. Their antiant rights have been ravished away from them. Their antiant Lawes have been insulted. Of their antiant Constitution at this hour they possess not even the shadow. This brave & high spirited people have made exertions to break their chains.

Upon the 11 of Dec. 1792 Deputies from most of their Cities & Provinces assembled in Edinburgh to deliberate upon the restoration of their antiant Lawes in a mode the most contitutional & the most Loyal. The Ministry of England took the alarm. The Militia of the northern counties of England were drawn out upon the frontiers of Scotland. The Regiments of England, stationed in the interior of Scotland, were held under arms, ready to proceed to execution. Of that Assembly of Deputies, so solemn & so august, I had the honour upon the first day of its convocation to be called to the chair.

The situation of the people of Ireland, if possible, was even more deplorable than ours. Three Millions of Catholics were denied the rights of our common nature, were excluded from all the priviledges of the social state, their properties exposed to sanctioned robberies & their persons to insult & persecution. With the Presbyterians, who were equally oppressed they had formed an union. They turned their eyes to Scotland, to the assembly of its delegates. From mutual co-operation they rationally expected an exertion more strenuous & an effect more successful. They transmitted a solemn & pathetic[1] address to the Assembly then sitting in Edinburgh.

---

1. Ignoring the now obsolete sense of the word – impassioned – this sentence has recently been quoted in isolation, attributing to Muir a somewhat overweening attitude towards Ireland.

This address came officially into my hands. I read & published it in the Assembly & with all the energy of my abilities defended its principles. The Assembly of Delegates framed and concluded their resolutions in the course of three days. These Resolutions, loyal to the King & faithful to the Country, appalled a guilty Ministry who were the enemies of both. Recovered from their consternation, they attempted by every device of art & of intimidation to terrify & to disunite us.

In Ireland, to the Catholics, they held out some paltry, unavailing priviledges, intended to skin the surface of the wound but not to effectuate its cure. In Scotland, defenceless & unarmed, they directed the storm in its most envenomed fury. The First in action, it is my glory likewise to have been the first in suffering. Disdaining every form of Law, I was exiled to New Holland with certification of Death if in the course of fourteen years I should return to Britain.

The Country trembled with horror & with rage. The emotion extended to England & we who, in Ireland & in Scotland, had lately in consequence of the artifices of the ministers been considered by that people in a state of Rebellion, were now regarded as the champions & as the Martyrs of our country. With invincible eloquence my cause was pleaded & defended in both houses of the English Parliament. I count in the number of my Advocates & Freinds [sic] the illustrious names of Sherridan & of Fox, of the Earles of Stanhope & of Lauderdale. The Ministry would have triumphed if I had stooped to solicit their favour. Exile was out of the question. I reverenced my country & I reverenced my name. I was conveyed to New Holland. Ministry had expressly admitted in Parliament my Right of departing from thence to any country but Britain. In that distant & dismal prison I was completely in their power. I was then to vindicate my right of Departure by my owen exertions & by the Providence of God.

After remaining in that tomb of Existence thirteen months[2] I went on board the first neutral ship which arrived belonging to the United States. I proceeded to Nootka. I there found a vessel belonging to his most Catholic Majesty. Eighteen months must have been consumed before I could have reached any Port in the United States. In China & in India I again exposed myself, if they are still in office, to the power of the enemies, both of my country & of myself. This inconvenience & this danger I avoided by passing into his Majesty's ship. I committed myself to the faith & to the protection of a Great, a faithful & Magnanimous Nation. The Hospitality which I have received will be eternally impressed upon my remembrance.

---

2. In fact, over fourteen months.

My Lord Viceroy, I have told you all. I have concealed nothing – I know and I feel that I am not unworthy of your protection. To have defended the antiant lawes & constitution of my country – To have contended for the instant & immediate Emancipation of Three Millions of the Professors of the Catholic Religion – These are No Crimes. I come into your country with no improper intentions & from no slight causes. I wish to pass through it without delay to an Allied State & to the Chief of that state, who with open arms will receive me as a freind & as a son. May I therefore for this purpose presume to solicit your permission.

The Gratitude, not merely of the Individual who presumes to address you, but of Millions interested in his fortunes will be forever called forth.

My Lord Viceroy, I have the honour to be with the most profound respect your Lordships Most Obt & Most humble servant.

[*signed*] Thomas Muir. Monterrey, 17 July, 1796.

The letter, sent to the French Foreign Office, is undated. Some official hand subsequently added a date – *27 Vendémaire, an 9* [18th October 1800] – though the year of writing certainly was 1798. Both letter and memorandum are in Muir's handwriting and signed by him.

> Au Citoyen Chas. Maur. Talleyrand, Ministre des Relations Exterieures.
>
> Citizen Ministre
>
> I have the honour of transmitting to you the enclosed memorial. It is ill-transcribed, as upon account of the importance & delicacy of its contents, I was obligd to transcribe it myself.
>
> It relates to three important objects.
>
> 1st. Insurrection in Scotland. 2d. Insurrection in London & 3d Insurrection aboard the English fleet.
>
> With little expence & little danger these objects might be accomplished. The Republick might strike a rapid & decisive blow.
>
> If I had the means by a safe & confidential messenger, who furnished with no written instructions, could invite one or two persons from Britain to meet me not in Paris but in some other place less suspicious, I could give instructions & arrange the plan of operation. I earnestly entreat your attention to the sentiments of the English sailors. In their highest irritation, if attacked by a foreign force they will fight well & desperately. No hopes, founded upon their discontentment will be realised on the day of battle. The Republick must avail herself of their discontentment while they are in a state of inaction brooding over their wrongs & meditating revenge.
>
> Believe me, Citizen Ministre, to be impressed with every sentiment of personal consideration.
>
> Thomas Muir. Rue Pelletier, No 1.

The enclosed memorandum appears to record conclusions reached in Paris between political émigrés and more recent arrivals from Great Britain – an updated version of memoranda submitted earlier in the year.

> I have had already the honour of stating my reasons for believing that the present political situation of Scotland demands the most serious attention of the French Government. I will now proceed to point out the means by which a revolution can be soon & effectually accomplished.

> All will depend upon prudence & secrecy. The Scots will not rashly compromise themselves. With sorrow when I think of Ireland, with pride when I speak of Scotland, I can with confidence assert few in that nation will be found who will represent the ridiculous & fatal comedy of O'Quoigley & O'Connor.

This is perhaps an insensitive comment on events leading to the Treason trials of these two United Irishmen earlier that year [page 128] but it does confirm Muir's grasp of the situation.

> ... It is of high importance to send a confidential Agent to Scotland. He will survey and calculate the force of the patriots. He will arrange the preparatifs & fix the moment of action. I know the great difficulty of finding a person qualified for this important mission. I must confess I know not one of my countrymen in Paris whom I could propose. I honour the purity of their principles. I have scrutinised their conduct with a watchful eye. They have not that prudence, that secrecy & that fortitude which indispensably is requisite for so delicate & for so dangerous a trust. The superior wisdom & information of the Government no doubt will discover a person properly qualified.

One trusted activist, James Kennedy,[1] was expected to arrive in Paris at any moment but Muir expressed certainty that it would be impossible for Kennedy to return again to Scotland. The transcript goes on to deal with the requirements of the 'not compleatly armed' patriots at home, a section for which James Smith, the ex-Glasgow gunsmith, may have provided some information.

> ... There are arms to be purchased in the country. Let France transmit for that purpose money. Individuals will arm themselves without observation. When least expected & most to be dreaded, Scotland will once more again start up an armed Nation. Provided, as they already are, the sum of 20,000 £ Sterling may be sufficient for this purpose. Pouder is what they mostly want & this must be conveyed to them. The Bays and Creeks which indent the mainland are almost innumerable. They are greatly resorted to by smugglers & any

---

1. Appendix D

quantity of pouder might be conveyed without suspicion as
contreband liquors. To avoid discovery neutral vessels should
be employed, from the ports most engaged in that species of
clandestine trade. The Patriots have no Artillery. Yet if the
insurrection is well combined they will be amply supplied in a
few hours almost without effort & without blood. Regard for an
instant the map of Scotland. You will perceive that the Atlantic
is separated from what is commonly called the Northern sea
by a narrow neck of land of 15 leagues stretching from
Edinburgh the capital to Glasgow the great commercial city.
The Adjacent country is the very centre of Republicanism. To
unite the two seas a canal has lately been compleated. Upon
its banks & halfway between the two cities are the celebrated
works of Carron, which have supplied the North of Europe
with arms. In its vicinity are other manufactures, highly
important but less extensive. Within a league of Glasgow are
the great Clyde works. In one hour well organising the
movements, the Patriots might become masters of those
immense repositeries of Artillery.

You know the topographical plan of Scotland. Her
mountains, her lakes, her hazardous & narrow passes might be
so fortified by an invisible foe as no army could either march
or act. If they dared to advance, death in every form would
await them. Indeed the smallest portion of sagacity would
induce the military commanders to retire before the English
troops to seduce them gradually into the interior incessantly
to harrass their progress & before the exterminating blow to
watch assiduously the consuming havock of fatigue, of disease
& of famine. The Royal force would melt away among the
mountains of Scotland. There are no fortified places which to
the skill of the French Engineers could oppose any long or
formidable resistance.

These suggested military tactics possibly owe much to the
previous planning of Angus [Neil] Cameron[2] but Muir went on to
indicate a very personal contribution.

A singular accident led me to the knowledge of a
subterraneous passage by which the castle of Edinburgh could
be easily surprised. This important discovery, a few years ago,
was, even to the Government, the effect[?] effeir [?] of Hasard.
It is needless to mention, every precaution was instantly used
to prevent its being knowen. It can however be easily found. I
question if one of the patriots, excepting myself, suspects its
existence. And I had too powerful reasons ever to divulge it
untill the moment when it could be useful.

---

2. Appendix D

Though he may have had unique knowledge of the *location* of the tunnel into Edinburgh Castle, its possible existence was revealed at the treason trial of Robert Watt four year's earlier. The next section echoes Norman Macleod's experiences when prisoner of George Washington during the American revolution.

> . . . The Real Scotch soldiers are deeply tinctured with revolutionary principles. In combating liberty in America they caught its spirit. They have reared [raised?] their children in its principles & the tyranny of England now forces them to wage war against France. They only want the moment when Insurrection may present a rational hope of success.

That need for a rational hope of success is best understood by the fact that there were many men and women still alive who could tell of the butchery of Culloden and the widespread savagery in the aftermath of that battle. With another insistence that Scotland never would be precipitated into premature and ill-combined insurrection, the current situation in the British Navy is then detailed with considerable accuracy.

> . . . I have had the means of knowing the sentiments of the sailors in the British Navy & I entreat your attention, Citizen Ministre to an observation which I deem of importance. You know the discontentment among the sailors. In their highest discontentment they will still fight bravely against an enemy who attacks them. Their late victories furnish no proof of their attachment to the Government.
>
> France should not permit this discontentment to exist without drawing from it important advantages.
>
> In the Affair of Parker [3] one circumstance alone prevented the British Navy from being deposited in the harbour of Brest. The insurgents conceived the idea that the French Government would treat them as prisoners, would as such exchange them & that they were destined to perish ignominiously.
>
> Let then the Government hold out to the discontented not merely the hope of protection but the assurance of reward. Let them be promised superior pay, their inferior officers equal if not superior rank but above all let it be guaranteed to the Sailors that they shall receive the full value of every vessel they may conduct safely into the ports of France.

---

3. Leader the previous year of the naval mutiny and first to be hanged.

More than two-thirds of those employed in the Marine service are Scotchmen & Irishmen.

I need not devellop this idea farther. Carried into execution its effects will be rapid and decisive.

The Republick has it in her power to annihilate the English Navy, by the Navy itself.

Muir then painted a Hogarthian picture of the general populace in London, the misery of whose debauched situation left bribery the sole means of rousing them to militant action.

... The sum of 20, or 30,000 £Stg prudently employed & distributed would be sufficient to accomplish that effect, once produced.

This was probably the attitude of Thomas Paine, effigies of whom were burned by paid mobs all over England at the time Muir was addressing popular political meetings in Scotland. It was reported in the English Press that the same hired mobs would as enthusiastically burn an effigy of Paine's political opponents if offered additional remuneration.[4] It was assumed that once this financially-driven insurrection was under way, men of talents & of pure principles would appear to give it orgamisation & consistency. Muir, however, was not particularly sanguine over the likely number of such leaders.

... Consider the three classes who composed the London Corresponding Society. The 1st. are men slightly tinctured with letters who were too idle or too conceited to follow the humbler occupations of life & who neither possessed talents nor science sufficient to raise themselves to the higher classes of literature. Necessity oblidged them to adopt Politics as a means of gaining a subsistance.

There is a reference to the likes of Robert Watt in the next.

The 2nd. Class is composed of men who had what is called a learned profession but whose habits of dissipation were too great to permit them to prosecute it. They beheld in a revolution & in the transient disorder occasioned by its progress the surest means of gratifying all their passions, of rising to a guilty distinction & of indulging a criminal luxury.

It is evident, Citizen Ministre that the Government can place no confidence in these two classes. Depositaries of an

---

4. Aldridge p182

important secret, they would hasten to betray it, to receive the mercenary reward of their profligacy.

There were, however, another two classes in whom confidence could be reposed.

The 1st. is composed of men of distinguished talents & of distinguished name in the world of letters. In England, many of them have the honour to rank you in the list of their personal friends. I will mention some of their names.

Dr Hamilton The Revd Mr Lyndsay   Mr Shields

Revd Dr Parr Dr Priestley in America   Mr Barbauld

Mr Hall, Cambridge Mr Freind, Cambridge
Mr Flower, Cambridge

Mr Brand Hollis   Dr Dysney   Mr George Dyer

I could add many more but deem it not necessary. These respectable men however are not fit persons to put a revolution in motion. There still & sequestered habits of life have rendered them almost entire strangers to the people. With all their Eloquence they could not win their assent. With all their Virtues, they could not gain their confidence.

Though stressing that such men's abilities 'to prevent the horrors of anarchy' would be vital once insurrection was under way, others 'whose habits of life have led them to associate with the people' and who possessed 'the proper degree of courage & of Moral Honesty' would be essential from the outset.

In England, it would be extremely difficult to find a sufficient number. In that country, there exists hardly a middle class. Information is also entirely confined to the higher ranks of life & of literatture.

Yet in London some of the order which I have described may be found. I can but mention a few names & they too are mostly Scotchmen. Thomas Hardie, Geo. Ross, Printer of the *Courier,* William Ross

It is sufficient for me to have mentioned these persons as they can easily furnish any agent of the French Government with the surest & most satisfactory information.

In Scotland there is not the same difficulty. The lower orders in general are the best informed.

I shall mention the names of a few persons whose influence

extends to every corner of the country & who merit entire confidence.

John Buchanan, Edinburgh   George Paton, Edinburgh

John Clerk, Edinburgh

John Brock, Glasgow   William Riddell do
Geo. Mellis, Perth

Muir records no high regard for the behaviour of the men who stood trial for Treason in 1794 and who were saved in the London Court by use of the defence he had formulated at his own trial.

> You will be surprised Citizen Ministre why I have Assigned to neither class the names of John H. Took, Thelwall & etc. The reason is a very plain one. I contemn their past conduct & I suspect the purity of their principles. I regard their inglorious conduct at their trials & I blush for their meaness.

He goes on to name others he is proud to claim as friends and who can be relied upon – Lord Lauderdale, Lord Stanhope, Mr Frances, MP; Lord Orford and Lord Semple – and again he is aware of their immediate situation.

> These persons cannot act in the commencement. Any Motion of theirs would be fatal to them & hurtful to the cause. They are narrowly & keenly watched. Their exertions have been most meritorious & they can do no more.

Muir did not include in this choice company the name of Charles James Fox, one of the leading Whig politicians at Westminster and cousin of Lord Edward Fitzgerald who had lost his life in the Dublin rising a few months earlier. He restricted himself to an ambivalent 'with regard to him I submit to your superior judgement' and in so doing was displaying considerable prescience; strongly pro-French at the time of the Revolution, Fox acquiesced in the war against France when serving as Foreign Secretary in the 1806 coalition government. The memorandum then gives the reason Cameron and Kennedy were so eagerly awaited in Paris.

> The first has organised the Highlanders {les Montagnards} of Scotland & the second is equally well informed of the state of the low country of Scotland & of England.

> Cameron has been outlawed & is now concealing himself in London. He could easily be found. Kennedy I sincerely hope is upon the road to Paris.

In a recapitualtion, Scotland was depicted as 'compleately disposed & compleately organised' awaiting 'the moment only when she can act with safety & with effect'. As to the cost of such a well-organised *descente*, the memo is confident it could be achieved with very little bloodshed and at quite modest financial expenditure. 'The sum expended upon a first rate ship of war might be sufficient to Republicanise the Kingdoms of Britain'. There remained, however, one serious difficulty to be overcome.

> ... there is a very momentous class of the people, highly discontented, who wish a revolution but who tinctured with deep rooted prejudices declare that they never will accept of liberty if it is not entirely of their own manufacture. In proportion to the strength of their prejudices they would oppose an invasion. The scene to them would be changed if they perceived the revolution originating among their countrymen.

So far as the premature and now doomed insurrection in Ireland was concerned, since the situation could not now be reversed, it should be utilised.

> Let me then earnestly entreat the french Government to attack the tyranny of the English government in its interior. The attention of that Government is now drawn to Ireland. Let it be fixed there.
>
> I would likewise observe, the Government should impose silence upon the journals with regard to the affairs of Scotland & of England. These countries should not seem to occupy the least porport [?] of attention. Ireland has now committed herself. With regard to other portions of the empire, the English Government would be lulled into security.
>
> Thomas Muir.

However uncomfortable the content may prove to some, this memorandum, composed a little over three months before Muir's death, contains little evidence to support those nineteenth century 'diseased in body and mind' dismisals. Even a modest endeavour towards that much acclaimed 'historical objectivity' would have exposed such phrases and the variations they continue to spawn a century later as expressions of little more than a very subjective political prejudice.

ABERCROMBY, General Sir Ralph [1734 – 1801]
After resigning from that 'distasteful' service in Ireland, he was for a time C-in-C armed forces in Scotland, before being sent to war against General Daendels in Holland. After 45 years in the army, still leading successful campaigns against Napoleon's troops in his 68th year, he died of wounds received in battle at Alexandria, Egypt.

ANDERSON, Professor John FRS [1726-1796]
In his will, Anderson left his entire estate to fund the setting-up of the very influential Andersonian College, which from the outset had about 1000 students of both sexes for its courses in Natural Philosophy and Chemistry. His will stipulated that 'drones, triflers and drunkards' need not apply for tutorial posts; no doubt a comment on some of his colleagues at Glasgow College. Anderson's College went to become the very influential Royal Technical College of Glasgow, which itself later evolved into the present Strathclyde University.

BLAIR, David
Naval officer who married Muir's sister after falsely reporting her fiancé's death abroad. Became merchant in Glasgow. His two sons, one a lawyer, the other a captain in the East India Company, went on to honour their uncle's memory.

BRAXFIELD, Lord [1721-1799]
Robert MacQueen. His father a Sheriff-substitute in Lanark, a grandfather gardener to the Earl of Selkirk. 'A coarse and illiterate man, with a keen and vigourous understanding, a hard head both for drinking and thinking, and a tyrannical will', according to Cockburn. 'Strong built and dark, with rough eyebrows, powerful eyes, threatening lips, and a low growling voice, he was like a formidable blacksmith. His accent and dialect were exagerated Scotch, his language, like his thoughts, short, strong and conclusive'. In 1783 Braxfield sold some riverside acres of his estate to the cotton-spinning partnership of David Dale and Richard Arkwright. Dale then established New Lanark as a model mill-village which his son-in-law, Robert Owen, subsequently made internationally-famous. 'They consist o millions o the maist profligate monsters that ever disgraced humanity!' was Braxfield's opinion of the French in 1794. One wonders what comment might have resulted had he lived to see the constant stream of foreigners trecking through his estate to observe and learn from the world's then most advanced experiment in social engineering.

CAINE, Joseph
Whether Caine, Quinn, Kein and Kendruic are in every case one

and the same person is still to be resolved; some of the confusion over the names, added to by many transcribers, probably arising from K and Qu having similar pronunciation in Spanish. A young Captain Caine returned to Boston and married in 1799, and that same year a Captain John Kendrick was at Monterey seeking permision to winter there. In 1804, in partnership with Russians, Captain Caine inaugurated on that coast a factory-ship method of collecting otterskins hunted for them by the Indians. The Spanish records state that Caine/Kendruic was a skilled carpenter as well as pilot and it is known that after Kendrick senior had sailed for China in the early 1790s, his teenage son, left on the Vancouver coast, was able to build a sizeable trading vessel out of local materials. This is the son stated to have been 'lost' to the Indians.

CAMERON, Angus
According to Penny, Cameron was arrested in Perth but escaped to Edinburgh and Glasgow, on part of this journey travelling unrecognised in the same coach as George Williamson, the King's Messenger who had arrested Muir. Nothing more is known of him after he reached London. His leadership ability suggests a possible military background. If so, it would be interesting to know if this was connected in any way to Norman Macleod's regiment.

CASTLEREAGH, Lord
Finally of completely unsound mind, accusing members of the Royal Court of spreading rumours of his homosexuality, he killed himself by cutting the carotid artery in his neck with a penknife just as Sir Walter Scott welcomed George IV ashore at Leith.

CLERK, John, later Lord Eldin [1757-1832]
A noted connoisseur in the Arts and son of the man who, in 1779, devised revolutionary naval tactics said to have been used successfully by Duncan at Camperdown and Nelson at Trafalgar. MacKenzie [Old Reminiscenes, Vol 2, pp60-113] got the Braxfield story from Clerk's writer, later the solicitor Aeneas Morrison, who was present at the confrontation. The Edinburgh publisher, William Creech, was on the jury of that trial but for fear of offending the Bench, it was said, did not include the event in his later published account. Clerk, renowned for clear perception, powers of resoning and 'a quaint, sarcastic humour', objected when the testimony of a convicted felon turned King's evidence was accepted in one of his cases. On being told the man had just received His Majesty's free pardon, Clerk's reply was – 'Gentlemen o the Jury, I ask ye, on yir oaths, can His Majesty mak a tainted scoondrel intae an HONEST man?' MacKenzie records the wide belief that this quote influenced Burns when he wrote the fourth verse of 'For a' that and a' that'.

COCHRANE, Thomas. 10th Earl of Dundonald [1775-1860]
Entered Parliament after notably successful career in Royal Navy. Attacks on Navy Department abuses led enemies to implicate him in 1814 Stock Exchange fraud. Expelled from Parliament, fined

£1000, spent year in jail. Thereafter involved in radical Hampden Clubs in England. In 1818 took command of Chilean Navy and became a national hero of that country's independence struggles, as in those of Peru and Brazil. After Reform Act of 1832 was restored to his rank in British Navy, eventually becoming an admiral.

COCKBURN, Henry Thomas, Lord [1779-1854]
Born into a Tory family and too young to have been involved in 1793 events, he sided with the reactionaries who opposed the Calton Hill monument to Muir, Palmer, Skirving, Gerrald and Margarot in the 1840s. Henry Dundas was Cockburn's uncle by marriage.

COLLINS, David
Despite legal duties, this Secretary to the colony was not a man of the law; formerly a Captain of Marines, he had come out to Botany Bay seven years previously with the first fleet. His diaries are an important record of the early days of Sydney Cove.

CRAIG[EN]DALLIE, James
According to Penny [*Traditions of Perth*] he was on the 'extreme left' of radicals and was the first target of authority. Forewarned by a supporter within officialdom, he burned documents that might have incriminated himself and others, then was moved from one safe house to another before escaping to join Manchester radicals. Later – 'as better cover' – he enlisted in Clan Alpine

Fencibles. The 1797 William Scott report to Robert Dundas on a United Scotsman called Craigendallie almost certainly refers to this same person. [McFarland, p150, n73] Other Perth names associated with him such as John Burgess, James Wylie, Dr Bisset, David Johnston, Andrew McLeish and George Meliss should repay further research. Penny, not totally sympathetic to left-wingers, also lists Robert Sands and Walter Miller as two radicals who succumbed to official pressure, possibly for financial gain.

DAENDELS, General Herman
Young Dutch radical patriot, exiled a time in France. Understood concerns of Ireland and Scotland over French assistance. In his own country, many were becoming concerned at later development of increasingly harsh terms of 'liberation'.

DUNN, Revd William
Minister to whom Muir served as elder. At a Kirkintilloch Friends of the People meeting it was minuted 'that the public and private conduct of the Revd William Dunn, parish minister, has long raised him high in the affections of his people; and particularly that by his noble, manly and eloquent vindication of the cause of Reform and Freedom in his Sermon at the opening of the last Provincial synod of Glasgow and Ayr, he deserves well of his country'. When *Authority* arrived in Kirkintilloch seeking evidence of this treason, the weavers refused to hand over the

minute-book. The minister himself was then confronted, but before surrendering the minutes he ripped out the incriminating page and threw it in the fire, the offence for which he received that sentence to lie three months in Edinburgh's Tolbooth with all those other things that are 'vicious, base and criminal'.

ERSKINE, Henry [1746-1817]
Attempts to appease Robert Dundas by removal of Muir from the Faculty in 1793 proved unsuccessful, shortly afterwards was himself deposed as Dean. Became Lord Advocate when Tories briefy out of power, 1806, but thereafter completely sidelined. With a small mansion and grounds at Almondell, West Lothian, he finally opted, in his own humorous phrase, for 'otium cum diggin-a-tautie'.

ERSKINE, Thomas [1750-1823]
Younger brother of Henry Erskine. MP for Portsmouth. Great display of altruism in 1792 when he unsuccessfully defended Paine's *Rights of Man*. Benefitting from some English outrage after the Scottish travesties of justice, and making full use of Muir's defence arguments, he successfully defended Horne Took, Thomas Hardy and others against their treason charges in London. Five years later, he conducted a successful prosecution of one of the publishers of *Rights of Man*, who got 12 months in jail.

FERGUSSON, Robert Cutlar [1768-1838]
Descended from the Fergussons of Craigdarroch 'a line that have struggled for freedom with Bruce' as Burns had it, and the Cutlars of Kirkcudbrightshire, some of whom had been among the first to sign and fight for the Covenant. The repressions of 1794 probably drove him to England, where in 1797 he was called to the bar. After that spell in King's Bench prison for assisting United Irishmen, he spent the next twenty-three years practising his profession in India. On return, was elected MP for Kirkcudbright, and in 1834 the new Whig administration appointed him Judge-Advocate-General and Privy Councillor. Married to a Frenchwoman, Mlle De Beauchamp.

FISHER, Anne
Her usefulness having ended after Muir's conviction, she seems to have been abandoned by *Authority*. Mackenzie records that her subsequent life, as a prostitute, was brief and squalid.

FLETCHER, Archibald [1745-1828]
Born in Glenlyon. Worked in law but not Advocate until 1790. The 'Father of Burgh Reform' in Scotland, Secretary 1784, and delegate to London 1787. Acted without fee in defence of Gerrald and others. Continued for many years to celebrate the French Revolution. 'One of the most upright men that ever adorned the profession, and a man of such stern and resolute firmness in public principles as is very rarely found united with the amiable character which endeared him to private society'. His wife Eliza was a close friend of Mrs Mellis, sister of the Captain Stewart who attempted Muir's rescue at Cadiz. At height of loyalist frenzy in Edinburgh, the rumour was

circulated that Eliza had a model guillotine in the backyard, on which she decapitated chickens as practice for larger fowl. Ostriches?

GERRALD, Joseph
Born in West Indies where father, of Irish descent, had a plantation. Educated and brought up in England. After marriage, practised at the Bar in Pennsylvania before returning to England to become active in Reform. Greatly admired for his conduct while on trial in Edinburgh, but his appeal to historical precedent 'our Lord, Jesus Christ, he too was a reformer' made no impression. The ugly humour of Braxfield's clincher was typical. 'Ay, and muckle He made o that! He wis hingit, wis he no?'

GIBSON, [later GIBSON-CRAIG] James, Sir [1765-1850]
Son of Edinburgh merchant. Supported Reform 'with purse, pen and influence' when others hung back for fear of consequences. A tall, commanding figure, always called upon as 'the man for action when it was time to replace speculation'. [*Scottish Nation*] Chaired meeting to lay foundation stone for Calton Hill Monument, 21st August, 1844.

GRAHAM, Dugald [d. 1779]
Chambers Biographical Dictionary of Eminent Scotsmen, volume 2, provides an intriguing glimpse of Glasgow's Bellman. In the preface to the 8th edition of his rhyming history of the Jacobite Rebellion, Graham wrote – 'If I have done well, it is what I should like, and if I have failed, it is what mankind are liable to. Therefore let cavilers rather write a better one, than

pester themselves and the public with their criticisms of my faults', a sentiment with which this writer happily associates. Graham's style of writing, chosen to suit his abilities, proved popular at the time and for that reason the content of his other works might still provide some historical insights.

GROSE, Major Daniel
In charge of the penal colony when Muir arrived there. According to John Kay [*Portraits*] his father was Captain Francis Grose, author of *Antiquities of Scotland*, the man of whom Burns wrote 'a chield's amang ye takin notes, and faith he'll prent it!'

HARDY, Thomas [1752-1832]
Born near Larbert, Stirlingshire; self-employed shoemaker in London from 1774. Formed London Corresponding Society with a few friends, 1792, 'as a means of informing the people of the violence that had been committed on their most sacred rights, and of uniting them in an endeavour to recover their rights'. Writing to Francis Place, 1824 – 'I was on board the Surprise at the time and saw the late Mr Banks of Newman St., an eminent statuary, take a cast from Muir's face from which he afterwards made a bust, and from which the present engraving is taken by Thomas Holloway. It is a correct likeness. I send this print for your acceptance. At the same time you will receive a copy of The Declaration of the Rights of Men and Citizens; adopted by the National Convention of France, 23rd June, 1793, translated into

Gaelic by the Revd Dr Shan, and printed at my expense. Some copies have lain by me for many years, it has now become a great curiosity'.

HONYMAN, William [1756-1825]
Faculty of Advocates 1777, married eldest daughter of Lord Braxfield the same year. Sheriff-depute for Lanarkshire in 1786. Promoted to Bench in 1797 as Lord Armadale. Created baronet in 1804. The large castellated mansion he had built, near Lanark, would be financed in large measure from the rewards for his actions against the development of democracy. Smyllum House, still standing, was recently made just a shade more democratic by conversion to luxury flats.

INGLIS, Captain John, of Auchindinny
Sometime after Muir's trial, Inglis was restored to command of a ship-of-the-line, said to have been with Duncan's North Sea Fleet at the crucial Battle of Camperdown. Another example of the Dundas skill in utilising opponents' qualities while placing them in perilous situations.

KENNEDY, James
Manufacturer and merchant in Edinburgh, notably involved in Friends of the People alongside William Skirving. Cited to appear at Watt's trial, May 1794, he 'eloped' and a reward was offered for his capture. Arrested on North Bridge, July-August 1795 and committed to prison. [*Scots Magazine*, August 1795, p539] Nothing more is known of him,

except Muir's expectation of his arrival in Paris, 1798.

LAMBERT, Jane [or Joan]
The woman convict who escaped in *Otter* at same time as Muir. Earnshaw speculates she may have been one of Muir's two servants, perhaps more than a servant. He records all that was then known of her fate. She was with other ex-convicts Captain Dorr later put ashore at Monterey, allegedly at pistol-point, though that may have been a yarn to excuse illegal immigration.

LAPSLIE, Revd James [1754-1824(?)]
Adopted aristocratic manner and extreme Tory principles but reduced himself to tearful, hair-tugging sobs when sermonising from the pulpit. 'He can turn oan the greet fair wonderfu,' his brother-in-law is recorded as saying. 'Just an awfu character awthegither for greetin. Man, he would greet readin an almanac!' Reputed to have won fist-fight with a radical and credited with providing a good account of his parish for Sinclair's new Statistical Account. Local tradition has it that he failed to thrive after the sedition trials, though the £50 per annum reward for preaching one sermon per year to the Blue Gown beggars at Stirling continued, after his death, to be paid to his family.

LAUDERDALE, Lord, 8th Earl Lauderdale [1759-1839]
Education started in Edinburgh, continued in Glasgow under Cockie Millar, and completed in Paris. Faculty of Advocates 1780. From 1790 a representative peer

for Scotland, notorious for appearing in Lords dressed in *sans-culotte* costume and for haranguing the mob in Paris '*pour la Liberté*'. Fought Muir's case vigorously in the Lords. In the brief coalition government of 1806, was principally involved in the much too late and unsuccessful Peace negotiatons with Napoleon and Talleyrand.

MACKINTOSH, James, Sir [1765-1832]
Son of the Laird at Aldourie, on shores of Loch Ness. Studied mathematics, Greek and moral philosophy at the University of Aberdeen, then qualified in medicine at Edinburgh University. Settled in London after tour of the Continent, enrolled Lincoln's Inn. His *Vindiciæ Gallicæ* established him. Called to bar 1795 but mainly a lecturer till into the 1800s. Knighted 1803, accepted post of Chief Judge in Bombay, credited with dispensing justice there with 'discriminate lenity'. Later an MP and rector of Glasgow University. Despite an accusation of having behaved improperly with a small fund intended for some of the political prisoners sent to Botany Bay, he appears to have enjoyed esteem as a moderate reformer till the end of his days.

MacKENZIE, Peter
Sometime editor of *Reformer's Gazette* in Glasgow, and very active in keeping Muir's memory alive. Informative on 1820 Rising but has to be cross-checked for accuracy. Said he had been told on good authority that had trials against Thomas Hardy and Horne Tooke succeeded in 1794, there were 1500 other warrants ready to be enforced against leading English reformers. If so, English democracy in general owes something to Muir's stand in Edinburgh.

MACLEOD, Norman, Major-General [1754-1801]
23rd Macleod of Macleod. Campaign successes in India led to rank of Lt General in command of British forces against Tipu Sultan [commonly Tipoo Sahib] with whom he banquetted and whose pistol-shot, in the course of peace negotiations, nearly ended his life. Ceased to be MP 1796. Appears to have made genuine attempts to save communities on Clan lands but in *The Chiefs of Clan Macleod* Morrison points out that the prize money he earned in India, had it not been expended on the nabob's life, was a fortune that would have worked wonders in Skye, Harris and St Kilda. Failures of French descentes probably led to disillusion, and it is possible that in his final years Tormod-the-General was aware that fate had only narrowly cheated him of a historic role in his nation's re-birth. Another indicator of the complexities of Scots politics of that period is provided by Tormod's grandfather, the 22nd chief of the clan, who was also for a time MP at Westminster despite possibly having played an ambivalent role in the '45 Rebellion. The grandfather remained on terms of close friendship with Rob Roy and chose to be garbed in MacGriogair tartan for his portrait by Raeburn.

MAITLAND, Hon Major Thomas
With his brother, the 8th Earl of
Lauderdale, a founding member
of early Reform societies and an
enthusiastic participant in
meetings with Macleod and Muir
in Glasgow, Edinburgh and
London. Visited Muir in Newgate
Prison. In 1805, as Lt-General
Maitland during the Whig
coalition, he accepted
appointment as Governor and
Commander-in-Chief armed
forces, Ceylon.

MARGAROT, Maurice [1750-1815]
Educated Geneva, resident a time
in revolutionary France, later
joined London Corresponding
Society. The only one of
thenMartyrs who returned home
from Sydney Cove. Re-appeared
briefly in Glasgow area when the
40,000 Cotton-spinners were on
strike.

MEALMAKER, George
On trial with Fyshe Palmer in
1794, then in 1798 found guilty of
being main organiser in Perth,
Dundee and Forfar areas for the
United Scotsmen. Sentenced to 14
years in Botany Bay.

MELISS, George
Penny refers to his father, Andrew
Meliss, as one of the wealthiest
men in Perth, long established in
thread manufacture, bleaching,
printing, cotton-spinning and
with shares in other concerns.
George Meliss took over the
businesses after his father's death
and became involved in reform
activities, eventually named on
Muir's memorandum as a member
of the proposed provisional
government of Scotland. Anthony

Cooke refers to a George Mellis,
almost certainly the same man,
who in that fateful year of
'seventeen and ninety-eight', was
refused business credit and had to
close his cotton mill at
Cromwellpark, on the River
Almond, making hundreds of his
employees redundant. Meliss then
moved with his family to
Manchester.

MILLAR, Professor John [1735-1801]
Minister's son, born Shotts,
Lanarkshire, brought up Blantyre.
Throughout last three decades of
eighteenth century he had
remarkable influence on many
who went on to make their mark
at home and abroad. 'Millar is a
jolly little dog and the sharpest
fellow I ever saw' was the
judgement of one of his students,
Lord Melbourne, the future Prime
Minister. Another, who went on to
become Lord Advocate when the
Tories finally fell and who later sat
on the bench as Lord Jeffrey,
described Millar's free discussions
with his students as 'the most
exciting and instructive in which
they ever took part'. Though his
politics attracted constant and
damaging hostility, his abilities
were such that even English Tory
families sent their sons to him for
education. Among his many
students were James MacKintosh,
William Adam, Lord Lauderdale
and his brother Thomas Maitland.
Like many other academics of the
time, he took a keen interest in
necessary improvements of
agriculture, having himself a small
farm at Whitemoss, near East
Kilbride.

MUIR, William
Official correspondence, May 1794, refers to his arrest as master of the schooner *Alert*, suspected of spying in Firth of Forth. He was American and known to have been at Le Havre for a lengthy period the previous winter; on release from captivity, he set sail again for Hamburg. It may be this was the cousin, merchant at Hamburg, Tom Muir hoped to meet in 1798; the same man, perhaps, that Muir's father referred to in a 1793 letter to the master of the ship *Hope* at Belfast. [The letter said this cousin, previously of Leith, had his own vessel at Philadelphia] [*State Trials*]. If so, he may have been involved in the French navy's rescue attempt in 1794.

NASMYTH, Alexander [1758-1840]
A thriving career as society portrait painter being abandoned rather than his radical politics, he then left the nation a legacy of fine landscapes. Draughtsman to Miller the steamboat pioneer, consultant in design of Edinburgh's New Town and designer of the Dean Bridge, he is also credited with inventing the bow-and-string girder principle on which many famous bridges were later built; a prime example of the latter being Sydney Harbour Bridge, whose northern pylon Earnshaw judged to rest on the probable location of Muir's farm.

OSWALD, John
Member of the Jacobin Club in Paris before going off to the Vendée War. Numerous writings translated into French in 1792. There were rumours that, as an obnoxious commander, he and his sons were murdered by his own soldiers, [*Scottish Nation*, vol. 3] though this may be another example of anti-radical propaganda.

PAINE, Thomas [1737-1809]
Paine finally left France for America in 1802. Lodging in Greenwich Village in the year before he died, he was visited by Alexander Wilson, the Paisley poet, and took out a subscription to Wilson's *American Ornithology*, then just about to be published. Wilson recorded an impression of the man he much admired – 'the penetration and intelligence of his eye bespeak the man of genius and of the world'. Paine died the following year but his final resting place, like that of Muir, is unknown. William Cobbett, the English political writer who from being vehemently opposed to Paine had gone on to become his disciple, arrived in America, 1819, to exhume the remains and ship them back to England. His intention to provide a monument in England ran into prolonged opposition, and after Cobbett's own death, sixteen years later, Paine's bones went from one hand to another before finally disappearing, somewhere, in the land of his birth.

PALMER, Revd T.F. [1747-1802]
Palmer's eight year transportation sentence expired in 1801, when he left Sydney Cove with the plan of trading his way back to England. The vessel proving unseaworthy, he put into Guam, where he and the others were arrested by

Spanish authorities. Palmer became ill during confinement and died 18 months later.

PÉRON, Capitaine Pierre François [1769-post1830]
Retired from sea at 35, apparently wealthy, with a mansion in his native Finisterre region and was Mayor of the Commune for about 20 years. When finally persuaded to record his *Mémoires* many years later, his recall of names was less than certain; for example, he gives the Captain of *Sutil* as Cuba, not Tobar and he may also at times have conflated personal experience with information later absorbed from other sources. In general, though, where verification is possible, he proves reliably accurate. Days after Muir transferred to the Spanish vessel, some of Péron's seamen were attacked by Indians with whom they had been trading. One matelot was killed, another badly wounded and a third had his hand blown off when his gun backfired. Péron also recorded that a slab of wood intended to mark a seafarer's grave was now being used as a seat in an Indian canoe. The engraving on it, in large block letters, might answer some long outstanding query.

IN MEMORY OF CAPTAIN N
ELIAS NEUBURY

WHO DEPARTED HIS LIFE IN
THE YEAR 1795, JULY THE 10TH,
35 YEARS OF ADGE.

Péron had difficulty getting all the money due from Captain Dorr but the matter was finally settled in his favour in a Boston court. In a subsequent voyage, 1800-1801, Péron returned to Amsterdam Island to collect a large number of skins he had hidden away in caves. The cautious Frenchman had never mentioned these to anyone but when he landed again on Amsterdam Island he found his erstwhile assistant, Gaudin, busily gathering this harvest for Captain Dorr. Gaudin proved contrite, Péron retook possession, and when sold in China those skins probably facilitated that early retirement.

POWER, William
Twentieth century writer. An article by Oliver Brown – 'This Golden Age of Personality' – in the Winter 1968 edition of *Catalyst* provides an assessment. 'Must be reckoned as one of the great teachers whose articles, based upon a remarkable catholicity of interests, left a deep influence on the minds of his contemporaries'. Based on the French *Syndicats d'Initiative*, Power promoted the idea of a Scottish National Development Council, later The Scottish Council [Development & Industry]. His other work, including an important contribution to the Scottish Convention, should be of renewed interest.

RODGER, Sandy [Alexander]
Most prolific bard for radicalism in first decades of nineteenth century, he was himself imprisoned in Glasgow Tolbooth during the 1820 Rising, during which incarceration he and his comrades bawled themselves hoarse with – 'Scots Wha Hae' – though possibly not, as was said, just to annoy the screws. Two years later, he was the author of 'Sawney, noo the King's Come',

published in London to ridicule Sir Walter Scott's sycophantic 'Carle, now the King's Come', written for George IV's visit to Edinburgh. In better times, Rodger might have been known for much more light-hearted rhyme, judging by his depiction of Glasgow's founding cleric, Saint Mungo, apparently quite joco distilling *uisge-beatha* by the banks of the Molendinar, where he:-

Dranke o ye streame o ye wimplane worme,

And loote ye burne rynne bye.

ROSE, J. A.
The Scots usher at the French Assembly suspected by Sword brothers of communicating with London. It is thought he may have conspired in Paris to save titled royalist lives. [*Scottish Nation.* Vol 3]

ROWAN, Archibald Hamilton
After challenging the Lord Advocate in Edinburgh, he returned to Ireland and shortly afterwards was sentenced two years for activities there. On threat of a treason charge against him, he escaped jail, took a fishing boat to France and remained there a time with Tom Paine. Later settled in United States of America.

SANDS, Robert
Weaver in Perth, particularly active with local Friends of the People. After arrest [probably 1794] his behaviour, according to Penny, was 'not so honourable'. Unlike others arrested with him, Sands gave information on George Mealmaker and after being set free took up post as schoolmaster to

Perth's 70th Regiment. Perhaps his conscience troubled him over this; in 1806 he wrote to Charles James Fox, temporarily back in Westminster government, politely but pointedly reminding him of his duty to secure the release of George Mealmaker from Botany Bay. The original letter, Sands to Fox, is in the National Library of Scotland. [MS1003, f130].

SEMPILL, Hugh, 13th Lord [1758-??]
Of an ancient Renfrewshire family and one of Muir's proposed Directory for Scotland. Ensign 1st regiment Foot Guards 1777, Lieutenant 1781. Married daughter of Charles Mellish of Ragnal in London, 1787. [Not known if connected to Perth Mellis family]. Cashiered circa 1792. Published 'A Short Address to the Public on the Practice of Cashiering Military Officers', 1793.

SWORD, John
From Meikle's *Two Glasgow Merchants in the French Revolution* a confused account of the brothers' activity emerges. Arrested at time of 1798 Rising, Benjamin in Glasgow and John about to sail from Leith, they were questioned – individually – not only about current business but also concerning movements the previous year. John admitted leaving Greenock for Charlestown, South Carolina, in March/April 1797, but said they were captured by a French privateer, itself later taken by a British vessel, after which the brothers were put ashore in Ireland to find their own tardy way back to Glasgow. This tale, designed to place the pair all-at-sea throughout Spring and

early Summer of 1797, was later confessed by John to be 'a cock-and-bull-story'. One possible reason is that the pair, having read the mid-March newspaper report Muir was imprisoned in Cuba, [news that had reached the Scottish newspapers from Charlestown, South Carolina] had set off on a rescue attempt, and this might also have a connection to Captain Stewart's voyage to Cadiz. Once convinced the Sheriff-Depute had no real evidence on any of this, they might readily have confessed only to what *Authority* already knew, that they had left Leith for Hamburg in August of 1797, ostensibly for business reasons. Though both brothers made their subsequent Paris meetings with Muir, Paine and other political figures seem largely accidental, they gave different reasons why they had not then met the radical Helen Maria Williams. John said Muir, after a debate on theology with Paine, took them to her house but she was out, and Benjamin said that after that debate Muir was too drunk to take them anywhere at all. Which answer is the smokescreen? Both? Such ambiguity can lead to doubtful certainty, however, one historian recently being quite definite that on this evidence Muir and Paine had indulged in 'a drunken squabble over religion'.

TANDY, Napper
After Hamburg had given way to pressure from London, Tandy was taken by a British force to stand trial for his part in '98. In a Dublin court, 1799, he was found guilty of treason and sentenced to death. Napoleon interceded, Tandy was exchanged for some English

prisoners-of-war at Bordeaux, and lived a long time afterwards as a General in Napoleon's army.

TYTLER, James [1747-1805]
Son of a minister in the Forfar area. Ambition to be the first to achieve manned-flight in Britain earned him the nickname Balloon Tytler, with the reductive assessment he 'lookit at the moon but lichtit in the midden'. In fact, according to *Stories of Inventors and Discoverers* Tytler achieved a height of 350 feet, beat Lunardi by three weeks, and had his thirty-foot diameter and forty-foot high Edinburgh Fire Balloon exhibited in the British Museum. Till the last year of his life, in Salem, he edited a newspaper. One source gives his death as due to a severe cold in 1803, another says he accidentally drowned in a claypit in 1805. Whenever and whatever the case, I hope that when the end came, Jamie Tytler was comfortably fu' and still wearing that 'sky-lighted' hat at a jaunty angle.

WATT, Robert [17??-1794]
Judged to be around his mid-thirties when executed. His letter to Henry Dundas, 1792, states he had been eleven years in Edinburgh and the same length of time in Perth, where he was educated; the extra years of childhood before commencing education would thus suggest he was only in his late-twenties. If he was the Robert Watt intermittently at St Andrews University, this would account for a further 8 years, consistent with him reaching his mid-thirties. The signatures in the Matriculation Roles of the University [1780 and

1784] compare closely with those of Watt and Patrick Moir in letters later sent to Edinburgh officials, and if this is correct, Watt obtained an MA degree in 1784 and was a divinity student after that till 1788, while Moir continued divinity studies till 1790, without graduating.

WATSON, Robert M.D. [1746-1838] Native of Elgin, colonel in George Washington's army, lamed in American War and on return to Scotland graduated M.D. One-time Secretary to Lord George Gordon and later Preses of the London Corresponding Society. Arrested 1796, spent over two years in Newgate Prison. It is thought a Lady MacDonald may have aided his escape to France and some in that country referred to him as Lord Watson. Later, when English tutor to Napoleon, he was known as Chevalier Watson. He was Preses of the Scots College in Paris, c1802-08 and English tutor in Rome, 1816-19. Among his writings is a work on Fletcher of Saltoun. He died in London, by strangulation, which some thought was possibly suicide using a cord and stick. His corpse, which was found to bear the scars of nineteen old wounds, seems evidence enough that he did not choose to spend all his time with books. [*Concise Dictionary of National Biography and Dictionary of National Biography*]

WITHERSPOON, Dr John [1722-1794] Theologian, born in East Lothian. Was witness to the 1746 Battle of Falkirk and in its aftermath was for a short time made prisoner. After a period as minister in Paisley, he left in 1768 to become President of Princeton College, and as such was elected delegate for New Jersey to the Convention, and later elected to Congress. In 1785, raising money for war-damaged Princeton College, he returned to Scotland and preached again at Paisley.

The version of Muir's story I grew up with was the partly mythical account reproduced by MacKenzie and it was not until the 1960s that I became aware there might be a more factual account available. In a pamphlet, published in 1949 to commemorate the 150th anniversary of Muir's death, the historian Dr George Pratt Insh had written of having a completed biography ready for the press. From subsequent enquiries at Glasgow University, it appeared that the Grants Committee had failed to fund the project, and neither the University Library nor its Department of Scottish History had a manuscript copy.

Sir Paddy Dolan, ex-Lord Provost of Glasgow, did interest himself in the project, but after his own death the manuscript copy he had passed to others eventually becoming divided and in two separate hands. Once located and reunited, a 1969 attempt at limited-edition publication again failed, but Professor Weston of the University of Massachusetts responded at this time with the offer to publish a more complete work, one that would bring Insh's pioneering research up to date. Since there seemed to be such a new work nearing completion, I recommended Dr Insh's manuscript and papers be lodged with the National Library of Scotland and resumed my own long-term project of gathering background material for a possible historical novel. Several decades later, still no adequate biography appearing and the old distortions on Muir and his times still being circulated, I put thoughts of a novel aside for this work.

At the outset of my researches the Australian historian, John Earnshaw, took the trouble to find me a copy of his 1959 limited edition, then out of print, and Dr Margaret Insh granted extremely helpful use of her father's manuscript and a number of photostat documents he himself had used. Thereafter, I am indebted to many librarians for assistance over the years, but in particular those of the National Library of Scotland, Edinburgh Central Library, the Glasgow Room of the Mitchell Library, the Mitchell Library, Sydney and the A.K.Bell Library, Perth. The staff at Register House in Edinburgh were helpful in easing a prolonged and finally rather blear-eyed trawl through the mass of reverse-image photostats which record much of the relevant Dundas correspondence of the time and copies of Muir documents were supplied by *Association des Amis des Archives Diplomatiques*, Paris. I am grateful to Dr. Norman H. Reid, Keeper of Manuscripts at the Library of the University of St Andrews, who took the trouble to find me evidence that tends to support my conjecture that the Lord Advocate's two spies, Patrick Moir and Robert Watt, had both studied there.

John Earnshaw and George Pratt Insh collaborated by correspondence and their combined works remain a useful starting point for any researcher. Insh seems to have been the first Scots historian to undertake serious investigation into foreign archives on the subject and Earnshaw, as well as drawing attention to the important connection between Muir and Péron, was first to publish Muir's letters from *Nueva España*.

Benefitting greatly from both these earlier works, Christina Bewley's biography offers some extensions to the relevant bibliography but the content of her work, perhaps due to its provenance and period, leaves a very great deal to be desired. All three make use of the same sources in Home Office Correspondence, London and Edinburgh; Archives of the Indies, Seville, Archives General of the State of Mexico, and the French Foreign Office Archives, Paris. They do so, however, in an individually selective manner that leaves the usefulness of this source material far from exhausted, and further development of recent research into Irish archives now promises to unearth much that is quite new.

PRINCIPAL WORKS CONSULTED

CORBETT - HOWELL. *State Trials* 1809
> Apart from the one in this highly-edited series, there are also several contemporary versions of Muir's trial. William Moffat maintained that of these, Robertson's is the more accurate, but this may be with reference to preferred quotations of Muir's words. There does not appear to be any substantial difference between any of them.

On Muir

BEWLEY, Christina. *Muir of Huntershill* OUP, 1981

CLUNE, Frank. *Scottish Martyrs* 1969

EARNSHAW, John. *Thomas Muir, Scottish Martyr* 1959

INSH, Dr George P. *Life of Thomas Muir* MS in National Library of Scotland. *Thomas Muir* Booklet. Golden Eagle Press, Glasgow, 1949

MACKENZIE, Peter. *The Life of Thomas Muir* 1831

The Life & Trial of Thomas Muir [from MacKenzie] reprint by Peter Walsh, Rutherglen, 1919

Memoirs

BANNATYNE, E. *Memoirs*

COCKBURN. Henry. *Memorials of His Time* 1856
Journal

PALMER, Revd T.F. *Narrative of the Sufferings etc* 1797

HARDY, Thomas. *Memoir etc* London 1832

PÉRON, P. F. *Mémoires du Capitaine Péron sur ses Voyages* 2vols. Paris, 1824

Letters

SCOTT, Sir Walter. Vol 1. 1787-1807. Ed. H.J.C. Grierson, London, 1932

Biographical

ALDRIDGE, Alfred Owen. *Man of Reason. The Life of Thomas Paine* London, 1959

ANDERSON, William. *The Scottish Nation* Edinburgh, 1870

BROOM, John. *John Maclean* Loanhead, Midlothian, 1973

CHAMBERS, Robert. *Biographical Dictionary of Eminent Scotsmen* 4vols., Glasgow, 1835

CUTHBERTSON, D.C. *Quaint Scots of bygone days* 1939

DUNNE, Tom. *Wolfe Tone, Colonial Outsider* Cork, 1982

ELLIOT, Marianne. *Wolfe Tone* Yale, 1989

GILFILLAN, Revd George. *The National Burns* [pub Wm MacKenzie. 18??]

GRANT, J.F. *The Macleods* 1981

KAY, John. *Edinburgh Portraits* 1836. [Some portraits in National Library of Scotland Rare Books were deleted for this edition.]

LOCKHART, J.G. *The Life of Sir Walter Scott* 1871

MacKENZIE, Alexander. History of Clan Macleod [18??]

MORRISON, Alick. *The Chiefs of Clan Macleod* 1987

OMOND, G.W. *The Arniston Memoirs* 1887
Lord Advocates of Scotland 1883

TILLYARD, S.K. *Citizen Lord* 1997

TONE, W.T.W. *Life of Wolfe Tone* London, 1825

Scotland

ANDERSON, Revd Robert. *History of Kilsyth* 1901

FERGUSON, Professor deLancey. *Letters of Robert Burns* 1931

CAMERON, John. *Parish of Campsie* 1892

COOKE, Anthony. *Stanley* 2003

COUTTS, James. *History of the University of Glasgow* 1909

DAVIE, George Elder. *The Democratic Intellect* Edinburgh, 1961

EYRE TODD, George. *History of Glasgow* 1931

GARNETT, T. *Observations on a Tour in the Highlands* 1810

GROOME, Francis H. [Ed] *Ordnance Gazetteer of Scotland* 2nd edn., London, c1895

HAMILTON, H. *Economic History of Scotland in the 18th century* 1963

HAY, J. B. *Inaugural addresses by the Lord Rectors of the University of Glasgow* 1839

JOHNSTON, Thomas. *A History of the Working Classes in Scotland* Glasgow, 1929

LYNCH, Michael. *Scotland* London,1991

McFARLAND, E.W. Ireland & Scotland in the Age of Revolution EUP, 1994

MACKENZIE, Peter. *Old Reminiscences of Glasgow* 2vols.,1890

MATHIESON, W.L. *The Awakening of Scotland. [1747-1797]* 1910

MEIKLE, Henry W. *Scotland and the French Revolution* 1912
    The King's Birthday Riot in Edinburgh
    Two Glasgow Merchants in the French Revolution. [S.H.R 1911]

MITCHISON, Rosalind. *A History of Scotland* London, 1970

MURDOCH, *Recent & Living Scottish Poets* Glasgow, 1883

MURRAY, D. *Memories of the Old College of Glasgow* 1927

PENNY, G. *Traditions of Perth* Culross Reprint,1986

PREBBLE, John. *Mutiny. Highland Regiments in Revolt 1743-1804* London, 1975

RODGER, Sandy. [Alexander] *Scotch Poetry* 1821
    Poems & Songs. 1901

TAIT'S MAGAZINE. Article 'Memoirs & Trials of the Political Martyrs of Scotland' Special Supplement. Edinburgh, 1837

France

CARLYLE, Thomas. *The French Revolution* Glasgow, 1888

England

HOWITT, William. *History of England*

Ireland

CONNOLLY, James. *Labour in Irish History* Booklet, Dublin, 1973

KEE, Robert. *The Most Distressful Country* 1976

McFARLAND. Ireland and Scotland in the Age of Revolution EUP, 1994

MOODY & VAUGHAN. *A New History of Ireland* 1984

PAKENHAM, Thomas. *The Year of Liberty* 1969

Australia

COLLINS, David. *An Account of the English Colony in NSW* 1798

America

BANCROFT, H.H. *History of the Pacific States of North America* 1890

MORRISON, S.E. *The Maritime History of Massachusetts* 1923

Naval

DUGAN, James. *The Great Mutiny* 1966

LAFFIN, John. *Jack Tar* 1969

General

HOBSBAWM, E.J. *The Age of Revolution 1789-1848* 1964

MOOREHEAD, A. *The Fatal Impact* 1968

PAINE, Thomas. *Rights of Man* London, 1944

TIMBS, J. *Stories of Inventors and Discoverers* London, 1863

Pamphlets

Life and Character of Robert Watt A. Shireff. Edinburgh, 1795. [Nat. Lib. Scot. 3.855{3}]